How to get a small business loan, even with poor credit, weak collateral, and no experience

The

SBA

LOAN BOOK

Charles Green

Adams Media Corporation
Holbrook, Massachusetts

For my wonderful children,
Gordon and Meredith

―――――――――――――

Published by
Adams Media Corporation
260 Center Street, Holbrook, MA 02343

ISBN: 1-58062-202-X

Printed in the United States of America.

J I H G F E D C B

Library of Congress Cataloging-in-Publication Data
The SBA loan book / by Charles Green.
    p.   cm.
ISBN 1-58062-202-X
Includes index.
1. United States. Small Business Administration. 2. Small business—United States—Finance.
3. Loans—United States—Government guaranty. I. Title.
        HG4027.7.G74   1999
    658.15'224—dc21   99-27509
                CIP

This book is available at quantity discounts for bulk purchases.
For information, call 1-800-872-5627.

Visit our home page at http://www.businesstown.com

Contents

Acknowledgments

There are many people I wish to thank who were instrumental in the production of this book. Without their invaluable assistance, this project would have never been possible. My longtime friend Gene McKay gave me the original idea to take consulting one step further into publication and provided encouragement and many ideas to help make it happen. My dear friend Ellen Kierr Stein helped me find the words to communicate this information through countless hours of painstaking review.

Friends Victoria Denson, Andrew J. Tate, and Terry Pickren reviewed my work for accuracy in their respective fields. Tom Abernathy gave the project a tremendous boost to get launched.

And Henry Green, my Dad, taught me how to count money and the value of entrepreneurship.

Introduction

According to the 1995 White House Conference on Small Business, 99.7% of all business entities in the United States are small businesses. These businesses represent 54% of the private work force, 52% of all commercial sales, and 50% of the private-sector output.

Yet obtaining capital financing continues to be a challenge for most small businesses. With the advent of stringent banking regulations, the consolidation of major banking companies, and the prospect of interstate banking, the situation for small businesses does not promise to improve.

Many small businesses are inadequately served by lenders who do not adequately understand the dynamics involved in a small commercial enterprise. Loan officers are often required to handle too many responsibilities and should be allowed to focus solely on the attributes of the market they serve, to understand the broad range of traditional industries and the expanding list of new business entities.

Obtaining credit is an artful skill. If learned and applied, this skill will reward the borrower's efforts by maximizing the financing available to the company, regardless of past problems or future uncertainties. Borrowing money is successful when the applicant learns the dynamics of the lender's decision-making process.

Certain attributes are especially helpful in obtaining financing, but none is more important to success than perseverance. A friend of mine sought to borrow funds to construct a personal care home he intended to operate. He was experienced in mortgage banking and knew the process of borrowing money. However, he had marginal equity to invest in a start-up business and he planned to be his own general contractor. He finally overcame these obstacles and got a loan approved—from the sixtieth lender he approached. That is perseverance.

Most of the books I have reviewed on this topic were written by accountants, business consultants, and even educators. Although these

"" 99.7% of all U.S. business entities are small businesses. ""

books contain valid information about lending and the SBA, they are obviously not based on firsthand experience. My understanding is based on my experience as a bank loan officer, as an independent commercial loan originator, and also as a borrower. This book is written in order to share what I have learned in originating, underwriting, and servicing small business loans, particularly loans guaranteed by the U.S. Small Business Administration.

Crucial information about financing small businesses has to be researched in such diverse places as construction sites, factories, power plants, automotive shops, convenience stores, archeological sites, truck terminals, restaurant kitchens, day care centers, retail stores, insurance agencies, machine shops, equipment liquidation auctions, bankruptcy court, and even the courthouse steps on foreclosure day. These are the kinds of places where small business experiences unfold.

There are important lessons to be learned on both sides of the loan transaction and, unfortunately, many loan officers see it only from behind their desks. Loan officers who have not visited these different venues may have limited their capability to understand the upside potential and the downside risks of many small businesses. This perspective cannot be acquired over a lunch table.

In this book, the term "lender" is used in lieu of "bank" in recognition of the emergence of many nonbank finance companies or Small Business Lending Companies (SBLCs), which have played an important role in the delivery of SBA loans to small businesses. These nonbank companies hold a limited number of licenses to make SBA-guaranteed loans. SBLCs provide a significant portion of SBA-guaranteed loans in most of the country.

This book provides a comprehensive study of how a qualified borrower can successfully prepare for, apply for, and obtain a business loan. Because this process is very time-consuming and costly, I recommend that any business consider employing a competent consultant to assist with the solicitation of a business loan.

Throughout the text I have attempted to communicate the information in language that can be easily deciphered by the most inexperienced entrepreneur. The book incorporates general information about many disciplines in order to describe and detail the dynamics of commercial lending. In its essence, finance can sometimes be very complex and sometimes be very simple. My goal is to collaborate with readers to provide information, direction, and expectations for the loan application process.

CHAPTER 1

The SBA Loan
Guaranty Program

So, the government is here to help! Understanding the SBA program will ease some of the concerns many people have about getting assistance from the government for their business. Learn:

✦ How the SBA works
✦ The different options of SBA financing
✦ Why not to worry

What Is the SBA?

The U.S. Small Business Administration is an agency of the federal government, established in 1953 to assist small business enterprises. The most important program operated by the agency is the loan guaranty program, which provides a financial guaranty to qualified, eligible businesses to enhance their ability to obtain long-term capital financing from the private sector.

The SBA loan guaranty program has grown steadily over the years. Since 1989, with the advent of many regional bank consolidations and stricter federal banking regulations, the volume of SBA-guaranteed loans has more than tripled. In FY 1998, the agency guaranteed over $10 billion in loans to over 50,000 small businesses. In the process, the agency assisted with the creation of hundreds of thousands of jobs across the United States.

Although the SBA conducts many programs to assist small businesses, the focus of this book is on the assistance provided by the 7(a) Loan Guaranty Program. This information is also applicable to the 504

Program, which is administered through SBA-licensed, certified development companies.

The regulations governing these loan guaranty programs are subject to change from time to time. However, this book will provide the reader with a broad view of the regulatory and financial requirements necessary to determine eligibility and qualifications for the borrower. Mainly, the book will help the reader in the efficient and effective development of a commercial loan application.

The Loan Guaranty Programs

The two SBA loan guaranty programs that are currently funded by Congress for small businesses are the 7(a) Loan Guaranty Program and the 504 Program. They are governed by different regulations and are distinguished by: (1) eligibility standards, (2) restrictions on the use of loan proceeds, (3) repayment terms, and (4) the borrower's approval process. These two programs are described below in order for the borrower to understand what kind of funding can be obtained through the agency.

The 7(a) Program

This program is the primary loan guaranty program of the SBA. Eligible uses of the program are small business financing for acquisition or improvement of assets, refinancing existing debt, or working capital. Repayment terms are determined by the actual use of the loan proceeds:

   ✧ *Real estate loans* can be extended for up to a maximum of twenty-five years (twenty years for refinanced real estate loans).
   ✧ *Equipment loans* can be extended for up to a maximum of fifteen years (though usually limited to ten) or to the expected useful life of the acquired equipment, whichever is shorter.
   ✧ *Working capital loans* can be extended for up to seven years.

Lenders are guaranteed for up to 75% of the total loan amount (80% for loans under $100,000) to a maximum guaranty of $750,000. Most lenders will finance up to $1,000,000 under the 7(a) program although there is no actual limit on the size of the loan a lender may extend with a 7(a) guaranty.

Eligibility to participate in the 7(a) program is limited by a maximum level of either the borrower's revenues or the total number of employees, as defined by the SBA, according to the borrower's Standard Industrial Code (SIC) classification. A complete list of SIC classifications can be found in the Appendix with the corresponding SBA limitations.

Generally, most businesses that produce no more than $5 million in total revenues or have no more than five hundred employees are eligible for SBA assistance, although the industries that are limited by the number of employees can exceed $5 million in revenues. 7(a) loans provide for full amortization of the loan with no prepayment penalties.

There are several initiative programs under the umbrella of the 7(a) program that enable the borrower to obtain higher guarantees if the borrower qualifies. These special initiative programs are primarily intended to assist the private sector in accomplishing specific public policy objectives and involve the following borrower categories:

SBA defines a small business according to limits established of either revenues or employees, for each respective SIC code.

- ✧ *7(a) 11 Program*—This loan program is for designated areas of high unemployment or concentrations of low income individuals.
- ✧ *Veterans Loan Program*—This loan program is for Vietnam-era veterans.
- ✧ *Handicapped Assistance Loan Program*—This loan program is for business owners who have a permanent mental, physical, or emotional handicap, or for nonprofit workshops operated for the benefit of handicapped individuals.
- ✧ *Contract Loan Program*—This loan program is for short-term contract financing for entrepreneurs needing temporary financing during their growth stage.
- ✧ *Solar Energy and Conservation Loan Program*—This loan program is for businesses that design, engineer, or manufacture equipment or systems to convert alternative sources of energy, provide for cogeneration of energy, or increase energy efficiency.
- ✧ *Employee Trust Loan Program*—This loan program is for Employee Stock Ownership Plans (ESOPs) to finance employee-owned enterprises.
- ✧ *Pollution Control Loan Program*—This loan program is for businesses involved in the planning, design, or installation of pollution-control facilities.
- ✧ *International Trade Loan Program*—This loan program is for businesses that are pursuing international trade opportunities to accommodate their ability to engage in export sales and develop new markets for their products.

Borrowers involved in these preceding economic categories can contact the agency or their lender for more specific information about the benefits and qualifications of these initiative programs.

There are a few types of businesses that are ineligible to receive financing assistance from the SBA. In general these business activities include those based on a passive investment, those engaged solely in financing third parties, or those operating a purely speculative business activity.

Ineligible businesses include:

✧ nonprofit corporations
✧ gambling and illegal activities
✧ investment real property
✧ pyramid sales organizations
✧ academic schools
✧ speculation
✧ lending or investment
✧ lewd or prurient goods or services

The LowDoc Program

In 1993, the agency responded to a growing concern of many very small (called "micro") businesses, which found SBA-guaranteed financing difficult to access. The difficulty was due to most lenders' resistance to go through the laborious process of obtaining a loan guaranty for loans less than $100,000. Lenders found the process to be more difficult for smaller loans due to the fact they were dealing with less sophisticated borrowers, usually with less information available—and these small loans were much less profitable.

The SBA responded with a pilot program designed to test alternatives that would ease the documentation requirements of the lenders in processing these loans, and encourage their participation on behalf of smaller borrowers. The result was the LowDoc program, which has been a huge success, more than doubling the number of participating small businesses benefiting from the 7(a) program.

The SBA LowDoc program pilot was recently extended to September 30, 2001, and expanded to cover loans up to $150,000. The agency consolidated LowDoc processing in one central location to be able to respond to guaranty requests in thirty-six hours, thereby assuring smaller borrowers quick service. SBA relies on credit scoring tests to make quick determinations on whether to grant a guaranty for these loans.

Borrowers should understand that lenders still must approve all loan requests prior to the SBA's review, and the program's reduction-of-information requirement is designed to lower the lenders' burden—not borrowers'. Most lenders will still require enough data to fulfill their need to thoroughly evaluate a loan request against their own credit policy. However, the LowDoc program does enable the lender to move forward with a guaranty request with less documentation, reducing their time and effort in facilitating smaller loans.

Also, while the LowDoc program has been enthusiastically embraced by many lenders across the country, many have chosen to not participate. It is a matter of credit risk (small company vs. large company) and the lender's ability to effectively address their chosen marketplace (real estate loans vs. working capital loans).

« The 504 program has more layers of approval required, but offers some flexibility in the eligibility criteria. »

The 504 Program

The 504 program was authorized by Congress to foster economic development, to create or preserve jobs, and to stimulate small business expansion. The program is offered through SBA-licensed Certified Development Companies (CDC), which are either for-profit or nonprofit financial entities responsible for processing loans under this program.

CDCs facilitate 504 loans but are not the direct funding source for the loan proceeds. The CDC works in conjunction with an approved SBA senior lender, which provides at least half of the approved financing. Subordinate financing is arranged by the CDC through the issuance of SBA-guaranteed debentures.

The CDCs add another layer to the approval process for the borrower. Eligibility for the 504 program is determined by the net income and net worth of the borrower, which usually allows more flexibility than the 7(a) program eligibility.

This program is structured as two loans to provide up to 90% financing for qualified real estate and capital asset financing, although recent program changes have limited leverage to 85% for many participants. Construction or acquisition loans are permitted, but borrowers cannot refinance existing debt under this program. The borrower is required to have a minimum 10% equity contribution. Although start-up companies and single-purpose real estate improvements may lead lender to require a 15% equity contribution. The lender provides senior financing for 50% of the transaction and the CDC provides the 40% balance with funds generated from debenture sales.

These debenture funds are obtained from public security markets. Since the debentures provide a guaranteed return to investors, the debenture portion of the 504 loans carry a prepayment penalty if paid out during the first half of the loan term. The 504 program financing is available only in ten- or twenty-year terms.

Mechanics of the Program

Because the mechanics of the SBA loan guaranty program are often misunderstood, there is some criticism of the program or dissatisfaction from the businesses that do not qualify. The program is a fairly well-managed endeavor of the federal government to provide needed assistance to the small business sector seeking to secure adequate capital financing.

In light of often contradictory federal banking regulations, it is doubtful that the private sector would fulfill the demand for small business financing without assistance from the SBA. The agency provides the private sector lender with a financial enhancement to permit the extension of credit that would otherwise be unavailable.

The program essentially allows the lender to apply to the agency for a guaranty for a portion of a small business loan. The agency considers this application based on a set of eligibility standards that defines the characteristics of borrowers permitted to receive this assistance. There are also some restrictions on how the proceeds of these guaranteed loans may be used.

The lender actually provides the funding for the loan and will always have direct exposure for a constant percentage of the outstanding principal balance. The lender will be the primary contact for the borrower in servicing the loan account.

Unless the loan is not repaid as agreed, the borrower may never be aware of the presence of the SBA after the loan closing. The borrower is not involved directly with the agency unless there is a loan default. The agency may then be required to buy the guaranteed portion of the loan from the lender and initiate collection efforts directly with the borrower.

Since the agency rarely meets the borrower or visits the business, the SBA must rely on the written application of the lender in order to approve the lender's request for a guaranty. The requirements for this application include an extensive list of information designed to ensure the borrower's compliance with myriad financial, regulatory, and business qualifications which reduce the lender's exposure to default.

These guarantees are available to small business owners, regardless of age, gender, or ethnic group. When approved, the guaranty is provided under a standard SBA authorization agreement executed by the lender and the SBA, similar to the lender's loan agreement with the borrower. Borrowers utilizing the SBA program are not more susceptible to being scrutinized by or subject to attention from any other federal agency.

Any federal or state chartered bank is capable of participating in the SBA loan guaranty programs. In addition, there are a limited number of SBA-licensed nonbank lenders that have the capability to make SBA-guaranteed loans. Each lender is required to enter into a Participation Agreement (Form 750), which outlines the lender's agreement to comply with the program regulations.

These lenders have many benefits available to them through participation in the loan guaranty programs. For example, the financial guaranty permits lenders to enter into lending transactions with noncredit risks that otherwise might prevent them from being able to accommodate the borrower. These risks might involve longer loan terms, the type of industry (such as recreational facilities or convenience stores), or the type of collateral used to secure the loan (such as single-purpose real estate improvements or specialized equipment).

In addition, the SBA guaranty carries the full faith and credit of the federal government, enabling lenders to sell the guaranteed portions of these loans to investors and provide some liquidity to the lender's loan portfolio. This feature is particularly important to smaller community-sized banks, which may have limited capital with which to expand.

The SBA loan guaranty programs are administered by over sixty district offices located throughout the country and are managed by a district director. Supervision of the 7(a) program is managed by the finance chief in each district. These districts are organized into ten regions, which are headed by a politically appointed regional director, who is involved with broader policy issues involving the agency. A complete list of SBA District Offices is included in the Appendix.

The agency operates the loan guaranty programs under a common set of rules known as the Standard Operating Procedures (SOPs). In theory, lenders should be able to expect uniform implementation of the

“ Some lenders sell the guaranteed portion of SBA loans to provide portfolio liquidity. ”

SOPs throughout any region or district office in the country, but such consistency is not always the case.

Each district office has a great deal of latitude in implementing the SOP and determining policy for administering the program. Some districts are more stringent than others in the interpretation of the SOP. While these differences can lead to some frustration among lenders serving multiple markets, most borrowers are not affected beyond the restrictions of their particular district office.

Regulatory authority for the Small Business Administration and the general regulations of its business credit programs are drawn from the Code of Federal Regulations, Volume 13, Business Credit and Assistance.

There are many Web sites which have been opened over the past few years to give small business owners access to services and information offered by the Small Business Administration. Other sites offer information helpful to small businesses seeking financing. A list of some of these sites can be found in the Appendix.

CHAPTER 2

Dealing with a
Business Lender

Understanding the process of getting a loan is as important as being qualified for a loan. In this chapter, the mechanics of dealing with a lender are explored. Learn:

- ✧ How lenders approach your loan
- ✧ What to expect from the process
- ✧ The financial side of getting a loan

Putting the Process in Perspective

Borrowers are frequently frustrated with lenders who seem disinterested in considering a business loan proposal or with the lengthy amount of time required to move through the application process. Borrowers may also be indignant about the conservative approach lenders utilize to underwrite business loans. These situations are very common and they originate from a number of factors.

Primarily, lenders are averse to risks. Their job is to make loan investments in situations where risk is minimized. For the risks that lenders elect to accept, they protect themselves by having several options for liquidating their investment.

In recent years, bank lenders have been bogged down with an enormous amount of bureaucratic requirements to document loans. Lenders are responsible for providing a paper trail of all their decisions for eventual review by internal and external auditors and by government regulators.

In fact, the time and effort to pacify bank regulators and comply with federal banking rules have become a disproportionately large cost of doing business, interfering with the lender's capability to meet the needs of customers. The Comptroller of the Currency estimates that 14% of an average bank's operating costs are directly attributable to the cost of compliance with various laws and regulations.

When lenders seem too conservative, they are responding to conditions that support their position and contribute to the borrower's frustration.

First, the lender is in business, too. The lender has a responsibility to provide a financial return for its shareholders by obtaining funds from depositors or investors and then prudently lending these funds to responsible borrowers. Lenders must contend with the continually changing cost of funds and with competition from other regulated and nonregulated financial institutions. They must also produce a motivated and competent labor force to provide prudent loan investments in a rapidly changing economy. In addition, bank lenders have the burden of federal or state regulators to manage.

Second, most loan officers spend their lending careers concentrating on underwriting thousands of various business entities. They know a little about everything, but not much about anything. Because small business loan officers are usually not specialists, they will have only an outsider's limited perspective of the mechanics of the hundreds of small business industries. They will act single-mindedly to protect the interest of the institution that employs them.

There are many lenders who do an exemplary job of evaluating transaction proposals according to the guidelines that their institution has chosen. But many loan officers have had to deal with great ideas that went wrong and with individuals who tried to defraud them. All lenders have been subjected to exaggerations, ineptness, and imprudence on the part of borrowers they trusted. This experience evolves into a tangible degree of caution in every new transaction succeeding the bad ones.

Some lenders, particularly many large, regional-sized banks, simply do not accept the risks in commercial loans to small businesses. Their policy is to accommodate opportunities in the market so long as their funds have absolutely no risk concerning repayment, which is tantamount to not lending to small businesses. Small businesses seeking loans should accept that position and confine their search primarily to smaller banks or nonbank lenders with a more accommodating posture toward the small business market.

Challenges to getting credit from a lender:

◇ **Lender's tendency to avoid risks**

◇ **Requirement for multiple repayment sources**

◇ **Burden of regulatory oversight**

◇ **Documentation responsibilities**

When applying for a business loan, the borrower will be required to provide considerable information designed to educate the lender on every aspect of the business. The purpose of this requirement is to enable the lender to evaluate the business—its management, performance, products or services, and prospects for success. But, most importantly, the lender must be convinced that the borrower understands this fundamental information and is capable of using this knowledge to succeed.

The focus of preparing a loan application should be to utilize information that is currently available to the borrower as a primary function of good management. Is the business earning money? How strong is the cash flow? What are the long-term trends of the financial results?

This information protects the borrower as well as the lender, and may prevent the business from borrowing into failure. It may give the borrower notice of impending problems, providing time to change strategies and alter the business course if necessary.

The lender is an enterprise in the business of renting capital. Loans are made only in situations where the likelihood of being repaid is very high. By not being an investor, the lender avoids the risks often taken by small businesses or by venture capitalists. Lenders will always require more than one exit strategy to get the loan proceeds out of the business, usually involving collateral and personal guarantees.

The protection a lender requires for a loan provides a safeguard for the borrower as well, in the form of a second opinion of the business. While lenders are seldom experts in the borrower's industry, many will have extensive general business experience that may be helpful to the borrower's situation.

❝ The lender is an enterprise in the business of renting capital.❞

How the Lender Views a Loan Application

Lenders earn the majority of their revenue from loan interest. The lender's primary job is to make and collect good loans. However, it is easy to lose money by extending loans in a haphazard way, so lenders have developed strategies to reduce the risks associated with loans.

Most lenders use a formal loan policy to define the types of loans and the method of administering them. These policies may be based on the particular expertise the lender employs or on the prevalent industries in the lender's geographic region. Lending money to finance oil and gas wells in west Texas requires a different expertise than lending against wheat crops in Kansas. Lenders will generally operate within the confines of their familiarity to control the risk of their portfolio.

In a loan application the lender is seeking information. This information may be as trivial as the borrower's federal tax identification number or as detailed as a projection of how fast the inventory will turn over during the next two years. All of this information helps the lender assess the business. How well the borrower has performed in the past is a fair indicator of how well the borrower will operate in the future.

The lender has to be convinced that borrowers understand not only their products and services but also the factors that affect their businesses. The borrower must know not only the science of flipping hamburgers but also how traffic count on the street relates to sales.

A frequent complaint about lenders involves the time taken to evaluate a loan proposal. Although many lenders may seem inordinately slow, a thorough analysis of a business does require time. Mistakes are generally made by not taking enough time rather than taking too much. The loan officer's job performance will be graded more severely for loan losses than for loan successes.

Lenders may often seem disinterested in the critical time requirements of the borrower's loan request. But urgency does not relieve the loan officer of the inherent responsibilities of underwriting. When the borrower demands an answer too soon, that answer is always going to be negative.

The better prepared the borrower is with pertinent information, the faster the lender can address the loan request. Since the loan officer's job is not to organize the paperwork, delivering disarranged information to the lender will slow down the review or even cause the application to be rejected.

The borrower's loan request is similar to a company's effort to sell a product. In many respects, the lender is investing in people and in management. The personalities of the borrower and the lender must be compatible or the relationship will not last very long.

When listening to the comments of the loan officer, the borrower needs to be patient with the lender's lack of understanding, excitement, or enthusiasm. When the loan officer raises concerns, objections, or questions, the borrower needs to respond with measured information.

Although a commercial loan is a financial transaction, it is ultimately a relationship between lender and borrower. The key is the reciprocal comfort between the people involved.

The Five Cs of Lending

Commercial lending is an art, not a science. Based on the information provided and confirmed, lenders have a responsibility to make lending decisions that are consistent with the parameters and limitations of their institution and with the principals of prudent lending. Stretching these principals beyond their limitations is not good business and carries enormous risks that are not worth taking. Most denied loan requests lack a key ingredient that would make the lender confident that the funds could be repaid from the operations of the business.

Lenders test each loan application against five elementary lending criteria to determine the strength of the proposed deal. There is no magic formula or defined minimum standard of these criteria for the borrower to attain. In order to consider the loan request seriously, the lender has to be comfortable with the combined, subjective strength of these criteria.

If the borrower has an acute weakness in one of these criteria, then that deficiency may or may not be overcome with a stronger position in one of the remaining criteria. It depends on the relative strengths and weaknesses of the borrower. These five categories include *capacity, capital, collateral, credit,* and *character*.

Capacity

With this criteria, the lender attempts to determine whether the borrower has the qualification, wherewithal, or "capacity" to borrow the sum requested. Are borrowers operating within the confines of their abilities or are borrowers attempting to accomplish something beyond their limitations? Do the borrower's position in the market, experience in the industry, and track record in business make the lender confident that the loan proceeds will be capably used to produce the projected results?

The lender will carefully consider whether the borrower demonstrates sufficient effort, resolve, ingenuity, and perseverance to manage and coordinate the tasks necessary to generate profitable business revenues and repay the loan. If the borrower has previously obtained and

The Five Cs of
Commercial Lending:

✧ Capacity
✧ Capital
✧ Collateral
✧ Credit
✧ Character

repaid a loan of only $20,000, that accomplishment alone does not automatically justify the borrower's capacity for a subsequent loan of $200,000,000 in the same industry.

Sometimes borrowers fail to pass this test because they are more ambitious than talented. The lender must draw conclusions from the limited information provided within the application and from a few meetings with the borrower. A borrower's resume, past accomplishments, references, and ability to communicate a credible strategy, as well as a demonstration of prior financial successes, can contribute significantly to establishing the capacity to obtain a business loan.

Capital

When lenders are asked to be involved in a transaction, they must quantify the adequacy of the borrower's investment. The lender will always limit its leverage in a deal and require the borrower to have a meaningful amount of capital at risk, thereby ensuring the owner's commitment to the venture and reducing the lender's exposure to loss.

Capital is defined as the portion of the total business cost that must be contributed by the borrower. Different lenders have different requirements for the capital adequacy of a borrower in different situations. There are varying degrees of capitalization in which a lender may favorably view the borrower's position, depending on the use of proceeds, the availability and value of collateral, and the nature of the business operation.

As the company's profits grow, the lender will watch its equity or net worth position. Lenders expect that the company's owners will permit earnings to be retained by the business accordingly, rather than constantly drawing down all of the profits with dividends and distributions. While this equity-building process may cause the business owner to pay more taxes and limit the growth of personal income, it is a reasonable expectation if the business wants to borrow money to finance its growth. The business should provide a measure of its own financing to provide a growing revenue base. This strategy makes good long-term sense for the business and its owners.

Though generally unpopular with small businesses, the requirement to require internally generated capital is significant since growth will present a new set of financial demands on the company. As sales grow, businesses invariably need new locations, new equipment, or additional working capital to absorb increasing receivable and inventory balances.

Ability versus Ambition

Lender will have to judge whether borrower has the capacity to succeed.

◇ ◇ ◇

The business must always generate a portion of its capital funds internally—at any stage, it is smart for the business and required by the lender.

Retaining some of the profits in the business provides a vital part of this essential funding and reduces future borrowing requirements.

Collateral

This criteria quantifies the borrower's ability to support the loan request with tangible assets that will guaranty the loan by providing a secondary source of repayment. Lenders prefer that the loan be supported by assets valued on a discounted basis. This discounted value provides the lender with a safe margin to cover the time and costs of converting depreciated assets into cash, should that ever be necessary.

Typically, lenders will secure the loan at a minimum of the assets being financed. But often the lender is requested to finance a sum larger than the discounted value of the financed assets. Sometimes the loan is for even more than the actual cost of the financed assets, because the ancillary costs involved with the acquisition are part of the requested loan proceeds. Sometimes the borrower is purchasing an asset that the lender could not readily liquidate without incurring expenses.

In these circumstances, lenders will require borrowers to encumber other assets. This precaution ensures that the lender has a comfortable margin of value from which to be repaid if the business operations do not provide sufficient funds. The lender will discount the market value of the collateral assets so as to maintain an adequate excess margin to cover the loan balance at any point in the borrower's repayment schedule along with the cost necessary to convert the collateral to cash.

The excess margin is required to ensure that asset values always equal or exceed the balance of the loan, commensurate with the schedule on which the loan principal is repaid and the period over which the asset is normally depreciated. The borrower is generally required to provide a minimum of 100% collateral coverage over the entire term of the loan.

Credit

The lender must evaluate the applicant's previous experience as a borrower. Studying the borrower's credit history discloses whether the business or the owners have paid previous borrowings as agreed. The credit report also discloses whether the business or individuals have (or have had) civil judgments against them, unpaid tax liabilities, liens against their assets, or ever sought protection under bankruptcy proceedings.

> By getting a lien against the assets of the borrower, the lender ensures that they have more than one way to get the loan repaid in the event of default.
>
> ✧ ✧ ✧
>
> Lenders view how well the borrower's other loans have been repaid as indicative of how well the next one will perform.

While clearly not an exclusive indicator of how well the business will perform in the future, this information relates to how the borrower has performed in the past. Negative information in this category may be indicative that the borrower is unqualified for an extension of credit or reveal that the borrower has not overcome earlier difficulties. Poor performance with previous lenders may indicate that the borrower does not take the responsibility of repayment seriously.

Character

Character may be the most important assessment the lender can make about the loan applicant. Regardless of the positive attributes of the borrower's capacity, capital, collateral, and credit, if the borrower does not demonstrate integrity and appear trustworthy to the lender, any proposal will be refused.

Character is the most subjective criteria. Not only is the criteria difficult to define, it is difficult to assess. There is no checklist available to guide the lender's sensitivity to quantifying someone's good character, particularly when the other party is a new acquaintance.

The lender has to observe and study the borrower to evaluate the personal qualities and characteristics. The lender must watch for potential flaws in the attitude, conversation, perspective, or opinion of the borrower about business, ethics, responsibility, and commitment.

The borrower's character is important because it reveals intent. If the loan officer senses that the borrower is ambivalent toward fulfilling responsibilities under the proposed business deal, there is a character problem. The loan officer must believe that the borrower embraces a moral obligation to repay the loan, superseding even the legal agreement to do so.

When a lender does not feel comfortable with the character of a borrower, this information may not be directly communicated to the borrower. The loan request will often be denied for different reasons, because the loan officer may have difficulty defending a subjective decision without definitive proof. This ambiguity is part of the intangible matrix of underwriting commercial loans.

In the real world of a multicultural society such as ours, it is sometimes difficult for persons of different origins to communicate effectively to each other. This situation can lead to misinterpretations of words and actions, making it hard for one ethnic group to become comfortable with another. These culture differences certainly permeate the lending envi-

> The lender must be confident of the borrower's intention and commitment to repay a loan. Character counts.

ronment. The borrower and lender must be sensitive to such differences; they must invest extra time developing a business relationship to establish comfort and confidence in each other.

How Loans Are Approved

As financial institutions grow from hometown neighbors into national conglomerates, the ability of an individual to single-handedly approve a commercial loan has all but vanished. Loan authority—the internal lending capacity a financial institution assigns to an individual to approve loans—has virtually disappeared from any lending representative that interfaces directly with the borrower.

Most loan officers manage customer requests and originate loans for the lender. When an attractive loan request is submitted, the loan officer compiles the borrower's application data, evaluates it for eligibility, and verifies the accuracy of this information. If the loan officer concludes that the borrower's request has merit and is consistent with the lender's loan criteria, the deal is forwarded on for formal consideration by someone with the authority to make an actual credit decision.

Depending on the size of the organization and the size of the loan request, sufficient credit authority to make a decision may go through several layers of credit review to render a final answer. The two primary structures used by most lenders to make credit decisions are the loan committee and designated credit authority.

Loan committees are usually organized groups that meet regularly to consider various loan proposals offered by the lender's loan originators. The size of the lending institution usually determines the size and composition of the loan committee. In small-to-medium-sized institutions, the loan committee will be composed of the senior management, the senior credit officer, and often several outside directors.

The loan committee hears all proposals and discusses each one according to the merits of the information presented. The person sponsoring the loan application usually presents the loan request and defends it against any questions or critique from the committee. Although the presenter should be supportive of the transaction, this commitment may have its limitations.

The committee process can become somewhat political. Failure to support loan proposals introduced by other committee members can cost reciprocal support for one's own loan proposals. This system can obviously be

> Loan approval is rarely granted by the lender's representative. But getting a loan approved requires the successful presentation by the representative to the credit authority or loan committee.

❝ Lenders rarely get fired for being too conservative.❞

flawed with personalities, institutional hierarchies, and the dynamics of corporate ambitions.

With designated credit authority, experienced credit underwriters are vested with substantial credit authority and responsible to impartially evaluate and decide upon credit requests. There may be many levels of credit authority through which transactions must be approved, depending on the amount of money involved. Persons vested with credit authority are typically insulated from direct contact with borrowers and depend entirely on information filtered through the business development officer.

In too many lending institutions, the chances of deal success are disproportionately negatively affected by the poor communication skills of the individual sponsoring the loan request. Loan requests stand a better chance of success if the business development person can effectively articulate the positive attributes of the transaction to the credit authority. Often, ineffective translation of a loan proposal slows down or eliminates viable opportunities in the loan approval rituals. This weakness in the process is bad for both the borrower and the lender.

Lenders rarely get fired for being too conservative, and it is always easier to find a reason not to make a loan. Sometimes people who hold credit authority seem to actually compete with their peers to be the most conservative underwriter. In such cases, lending is unnecessarily restricted and the institution pays a heavy price—sluggish growth and substandard income.

With most lenders, credit authority is vested among underwriters or committees that are not personally involved with originating the transaction. This process has advantages and disadvantages.

On the positive side, the lender is able to evaluate the proposed loan on a purely factual basis without the bright lights, soothing sounds, and warm feelings often created by the borrower to convince the lender to approve the loan on other than prudent financial considerations. Lenders can make sound credit decisions in an emotive vacuum. Borrowers can be confident that an affirmative reply in such circumstances reflects the lender's recognition of a solid financial investment and commitment to a business relationship.

On the negative side, a laboratory approach to the borrower's loan request makes it difficult for the lender to consider legitimate contributing factors that may not be reflected on the financial ratios. Sometimes, extraneous factors off the balance sheet can compensate for a less than glorious financial history, when the lender is struggling through a review of the numbers. Businesses must start somewhere. A newer company may fail to earn money instantly for a variety of reasons; without taking those reasons into account, lenders sometimes miss opportunities to invest in good loan transactions. Emerging companies may not have sterling financial histories, but may have a bright future based on market factors, new products, or premier locations not accounted for on the financial statement of the business.

Getting SBA Approval

After the lender approves the credit request, the transaction still must be forwarded to the SBA in order for the loan guaranty request of the lender to be considered. The status of the lender with the SBA determines the method under which loan guaranty requests are treated. There are three distinct lender classifications utilized by the SBA.

Preferred Lender Program (PLP)

This designation is a special classification by which the SBA delegates the entire guaranty approval process to the lender. Using PLP, the lender notifies the agency of any loan approvals granted under the program and submits documentation describing the transaction and verifying compliance with all eligibility parameters. Utilizing this status, the lender is capable of reducing the processing time required to obtain the SBA authorization to one day.

Lenders qualify for PLP status by having an exceptional performance record with strong loan volume and low default rates. These attributes confirm that PLP lenders are better equipped to manage SBA loans than other participating lenders.

Certified Lender Program (CLP)

This designation a special classification by which the SBA agrees to provide accelerated processing of the lender's 7(a) loan guaranty requests. The lender agrees to provide the agency with more thorough financial analysis and to assume additional servicing responsibilities.

Lenders qualify for CLP status by having a consistent performance record of good loan volume and low default rates. Utilizing a CLP lender ensures the borrower of faster processing by the SBA and suggests that the borrower is dealing with a more experienced SBA lender.

SBA loan guaranty approval turnaround time (best case):

PLP lenders—24 hours
CLP lenders—3 days
GP lenders—5 to 21
   days (depending on
   District)

General Program Lender (GP)

All chartered banks and licensed SBLCs are eligible to participate in the SBA 7(a) loan guaranty program. Lenders are required to execute a standard agreement setting forth their covenant to comply with the program regulations of the SBA.

Most lenders participate under this classification of the program, which requires the lender to submit loan guaranty applications to the agency's district office for review on a first-come, first-served basis. Applications not completed according to agency requirements are screened out and returned to the lender for necessary modifications.

The SBA evaluates the transaction based solely on the merits demonstrated in the documentation prepared and submitted by the lender. SBA personnel usually make no visits to the business and conduct no interviews with the borrowers. The participating lender is required to respond to any questions the SBA may have regarding the guaranty application and provide any additional information requested.

While each SBA district office is somewhat different, all offices are generally reasonable in their loan approval. Except for lenders with a poor track record with the SBA, the agency usually assumes that the lender has the capacity to make prudent credit decisions. However, the SBA will review the lender's credit decision for reasonableness and accuracy.

In addition, the SBA will seek to ensure that the borrower is eligible for participation and that the proposed transaction is an acceptable use of proceeds under the SBA regulations as defined by the program's standard operating procedures.

Approval of the loan request by the lender does not guarantee automatic SBA approval. But if the lender is well acquainted with the SBA program, and if the lender does not make any substantive errors in qualifying the proposal, the borrower can assume that SBA approval is probable.

What Is the Business of the Borrower?

One of the fundamental determinants of the lender's review of the business loan request is evaluating the industry in which the business operates. There are many inherent characteristics in various business categories that create risks for a lender. Many lenders will actually avoid loans to specific industries if the relative risks are perceived to be beyond what the lender is willing to accept.

Before seeking financing, small businesses should understand internally how they will be viewed as an industry from the lender's perspective. For instance, small business lenders may feel more confident financing a convenience store that sells gasoline than financing an oil and gas exploration company. The risks associated with each of these businesses are dramatically different though both operate from the same industry.

Positioning the business in a more positive rank in its industry helps the borrower by elevating the lender's perception and magnifying the appeal of the transaction. For example, instead of limiting a company's description as a hamburger stand, the borrower should broaden the depiction to define the business as a food service provider.

This heightened characterization can effectively communicate the actual maneuverability of a business that owns a grill and a kitchen and has patrons regularly appearing to purchase food. As a food service provider, the borrower verifies that it has the flexibility to modify its business strategy and product mix according to unforeseen changes in the macro and micro economy. That is to say the borrower can switch from hamburgers to chicken sandwiches if necessary to follow current trends in dining preferences.

Knowing how lenders perceive and evaluate the borrower's industry and business can assist in planning the approach necessary to obtain credit. Where is the business within the life cycle of its industry? How will the business exploit its position and opportunity? This preparation will help the borrower define the risks that the lender will have to address. The borrower should have a strategy to reduce the obvious risks facing the lender. If the borrower incorporates these concepts into the loan application, the loan will be easier to approve.

Lenders will evaluate the borrower's industry life cycle to determine whether the business is beyond its financial peak (such as manufacturing buggy whips) or whether the business is too new to be an acceptable risk (such as manufacturing battery-operated automobiles). Lenders prudently prefer to finance an industry while it still possesses a strong growth potential for the products or services provided, before its marketing peak has occurred.

Lenders will be wary of the borrower if the business attempts to serve too many specialized markets from a limited operating base. For example, a dry cleaner/car wash/convenience store/cappuccino bar with

Always present a clear definition of the business in the broadest terms possible.

live music represents a unique business plan probably destined to fail. Such an operation could not have adequate focus, effective marketing, or sufficient profits. A business should be defined in specific terms so that the lender clearly understands what the borrower is trying to accomplish.

How Is the Business Organized?

Business entities may be organized in one of four different legal forms, which may affect how a lender analyzes a loan request. Each business form has distinct legal characteristics and tax attributes. Selecting the appropriate form of business entity is an important decision for the borrower and should be made when the company is begun, preferably with the advice of an attorney and an accountant. Each business form is eligible for financing assistance from the SBA.

Proprietorship

This form of business organization is for individuals who have chosen to sell products or provide services without the creation of a separate legal entity. The business is embodied in the efforts of the individual, who may use a distinctive business name or title, which is usually preceded with "d/b/a," which stands for "doing business as." The business name does not carry protection from duplication, and the individual carries full legal and financial liability for all acts of the enterprise. A proprietor's income is described as business income on Schedule C of the IRS form 1040.

Partnership

This form of business organization is for two or more individuals who choose to formalize their business relationship in a registered partnership. Partnerships may be defined as general or limited, each of which provides distinct definitions of the responsibilities of the individual partners.

In brief, general partnerships divide the responsibility of their activities equally among the partners on a prorated basis of ownership. Limited partnerships may limit the responsibility and liability of the limited partners for the activities of the partnership. Limited partnerships have a general partner who accepts the personal liability for the actions of the partnership.

Partnerships are usually taxed by prorating any gains or losses among the partners, as provided for in the partnership agreement.

Four types of business organization.

Proprietorship—doing business without protection of a legal entity.

Partnership—sets forth ownership and responsibility of each partner and pass-though taxation based on ownership.

Corporation—affords legal protection to owners but may create second level of taxation.

Limited Liability Company—combines best features of partnership and corporation which may benefit newer companies.

Corporation

This form of business organization is a distinct business entity organized by one or more individual "shareholders," who have certain rights under the protection of the corporate entity. Generally, shareholders are not exposed to any of the liabilities of the corporation unless they purposely elect to personally guaranty specific liabilities of the corporation.

The two primary forms of corporations are the C corporation and the S ("subchapter S") corporation. Although similar, these forms differ in that an S corporation is intended to provide smaller companies the advantage of lower tax obligations by passing profits or losses through to the shareholders on a pro rata distribution based on ownership, similar to a partnership. In contrast, C corporation earnings are taxable and the shareholders are also taxed on any distributions or dividends paid out by the corporation. Distributions and dividends paid by C corporations to shareholders are not deductible from the corporation's taxable income, thereby causing the distributed monies to be taxed twice.

Limited Liability Company

In recent years, many states have created an entity known as a Limited Liability Company (LLC), which combines the favorable liability protection of a corporation and the favorable taxation attributes of a partnership. Owners of LLC interests are known as "members," and the controlling members are described as "managing members."

Why Borrow Money?

Borrowed money is expensive and represents an additional business risk for the company seeking to obtain it. In conjunction with the normal business risks associated with building new facilities or launching new products, borrowing money involves a compound layer of management. The borrower's new partner (the lender) may not be as patient as is sometimes desired, particularly if plans do not go as projected. The lender may have higher expectations for the financial results than management or the market can deliver in a given time frame.

Careful consideration of the implications of debt is recommended for any business seeking to borrow funds, because of the potential risk of not succeeding. Rather than maximizing the available leverage, businesses should consider the advantages of minimizing the level of borrowed monies in order to reduce the company's exposure to default.

> *" Minimizing the amount of borrowing reduces the company's exposure to default. "*

Defining the exact reason a business requires a loan is the first step toward the application process. Qualified borrowers lose precious time and credibility by not establishing a succinct financing proposition to explain how much funding is needed and how it will be used. Unfocused borrowers make lenders nervous. It is impossible to feel confident about a business that wants to acquire a large, imprecise loan to sink into an enterprise without defining how it will be absorbed and what results are intended.

Business owners must be able to specify exactly why they need financing and exactly what impact it will have on the enterprise. Failure to articulate this information reflects either unprepared or inadequate management, or the existence of another agenda in which the lender should not participate.

Time is frequently wasted by small business owners seeking to borrow money from the wrong lender through their failure to define the kind of money they need. Too many institutions reject these inappropriate applications without referring borrowers to the correct lender.

Understanding that certain lenders service specific types of loans can make the search for financing much easier and more successful. There are four major reasons for a business to borrow money. Each of these reasons requires distinctive underwriting and repayment terms:

Real Estate Loans

Whether for acquisition, construction, or improvement, real estate loans are the most popular loans for most small business lenders. These are typically long-term loans that on the average have the safest collateral available to lenders. SBA-guaranteed loans for commercial real estate provide up to a twenty-five-year amortization of principal and interest.

Start-Up Loans

Start-up financing is needed by some borrowers to supplement their own equity contributions when purchasing a business operation or when launching a business. Most lenders require the borrower to have strong collateral or other compensating factors to justify the risks involved with this kind of financing. Start-up money is hard to obtain if the borrower cannot supply a sizable contribution of personal capital, usually a minimum of 25–30% of the total financing needed.

SBA financing for start-up businesses can be amortized over a long term, based on the use of loan proceeds, as described in other loan pur-

> Have a well thought out plan before borrowing money, including how much is needed, why it's needed, and precisely how it will create enough profits to repay the loan in a reasonable time.

poses discussed in this section. As the most difficult financing to obtain, start-up loans can test the new business owner's resolve to begin the business.

Loans to acquire a business are less difficult sometimes due to the track record established by the operation prior to acquisition. Generally, SBA business acquisition loans can be repaid over a ten-year term.

Equipment Loans

Equipment loans are intermediate-term loans that provide funds to purchase equipment assets. They are usually repaid over a term of no more than the expected useful life of the equipment assets financed. SBA loans for equipment usually offer a ten-year amortization of principal and interest, although loans may be amortized for up to fifteen years for certain major equipment assets.

Working Capital Loans

Monies used by the business as operating cash to produce profitable revenues is called "working capital." If the borrower can provide assets as collateral, loans can sometimes include funds for working capital, which are repaid over a long term. Loans for this purpose essentially a substitute for capital. SBA loans for working capital are amortized over a maximum of seven years.

Adjusting the Borrower's Attitude

Borrowers are better prepared when they recognize the dynamics of the loan application process. Approaching the process with a realistic attitude enhances the borrower's loan application and increases the chances of success.

Borrowers should understand the basic concept described in an old banker's axiom called the "Golden Rule." It simply says, "those with the gold make the rules." During the application process, the borrower provides an enormous volume of information, answers many laborious questions, and is scrutinized over trivial details of the company's financial affairs. This repetitive and tedious process is not personal in intent but, rather, a necessary procedure required to define the lender's risk.

The borrower is asking for a service that requires subjective qualification and objective quantification. One business (the borrower) is asking

❝ Start-up loans and working capital are the most difficult to get approved by most lenders. ❞

PART 1

another business (the lender) for an investment of time and funds. The application process, by necessity, is arduous but meaningful. Most lenders see many hundreds of loan requests every year.

A borrower should plan ahead and initiate the loan request before it is needed. By rushing the process, the borrower dampens the lender's enthusiasm about the loan request and creates suspicions that facts are being distorted or concealed. Even if the borrower is approved for a loan, missteps in the application or approval process can weaken the relationship with the lender from the beginning, which may haunt the borrower later.

Information is a powerful tool for supporting the business loan application. The borrower's understanding of the industry, the competition, the market, and even the economy can support the representations the borrower may be depending on to boost the loan request. This pertinent data will make the lender more confident about the borrower's capability to repay the loan.

The frontline personnel with whom the borrower directly interfaces may not possess the same business acumen and often will not have as much business experience as a more seasoned borrower. But the lender has chosen this person to perform an important screening process for eliminating the numerous proposals that are undefined or unrealistic.

Recognizing the difficulty of the lender's role does not ease the effort that may be required to educate a novice lender, but the borrower will benefit from approaching the relationship understanding the dynamics of the lender's role. Cooperation and patience throughout this process are necessary for successfully obtaining a loan.

Banker's Golden Rule: Those with the gold make the rules.

Researching the Lending Market

Too many small business owners watch television. The best source of information to find small business financing is definitely not creative TV advertising, clever radio ads, or glossy magazine ads.

A practical rule is that the lenders with the fanciest advertising may be the most difficult lenders to get a loan from. Why do the largest banks spend so much money on advertising when they already have a high public profile and their branches seem to be everywhere? One reason is that, in comparison to their smaller competitors, these larger banks have more stringent credit standards and they turn down a higher percentage of loan applications. Therefore, these lenders need a larger stream of applications in order to find the loan requests they will approve.

How should a borrower find a lender that is interested in small businesses? Borrowers need to research the market for lenders that address the small business sector. The best place to begin this research is at the nearest SBA District Office. A complete list of SBA District Offices is included in the Appendix.

The SBA can provide information about local lenders that participate in the SBA loan guaranty program. The SBA can also disclose the total dollar amount of loans made by any specific lender in that district in preceding periods. Evaluating this information along with other public information will reveal if SBA lending is important to a prospective lender.

For example, all federally and state regulated banks are required to make copies of their financial statement available to the public. Comparing the total commercial loan volume to the total SBA loan volume will be indicative of how significant SBA lending is to the bank's commercial loan portfolio.

Another important factor is the size of the bank relative to the size of its SBA portfolio. If a $2 billion bank can deliver only $10 million in SBA loans, and a $70 million bank can make $15 million in SBA loans, it is obvious which lender has the stronger interest in the small business market.

A borrower should interview the commercial loan officers from several local lenders to determine if they make small business loans. Prior to applying for a loan, the borrower needs to determine if the lender would seriously consider the specific kind of transaction the borrower is seeking. Which lender would be most likely to favorably consider the loan proposal?

The borrower should be aware that some lenders may not be in optimum financial condition. For a variety of reasons some banks perform inadequately and even fail. Poor management, bad investments, and unsound business practices are problems encountered by banks as well as other businesses.

Bank financial problems do not occur suddenly. Since regulated either by federal or state banking supervisors, a bank's performance is a matter of public record. There are many sources of information about a

> **The best source of SBA-guaranteed loans is generally from middle-sized ($100 million–$800 million in assets) community banks and SBA-licensed small business lending companies (SBLCs) that specialize in SBA lending.**

particular bank to which the borrower may refer. One source is Bauer Financial Reports, Inc., which monitors the performance of banks and rates them according to their financial condition and performance. These reports are available to the public by calling Bauer at 800-388-6686.

Other sources of information on potential lenders may be the borrower's CPA, other business owners, or even business competitors. Virtually every small business needs financing at some time. Establishing a prospective list of lenders early in the process is well worth the effort.

Getting a Second Opinion

It is wise to test the loan application on the borrower's closest advisors before taking it to a lender for review. Sometimes in the rush to complete the voluminous set of documents, the preparer can lose sight of errors in providing support information or omissions in detailing plans and projections. Having other parties review this data before it is submitted to the lender can reduce the chances of mistakes and hopefully eliminate embarrassing inaccuracies.

Larger borrowers may have employees from the appropriate departments review specific sections of the information to proof the work for errors or omissions. For example, the marketing department can review the presentation of the company's marketing plan, while the operations department can review a description of the company's production details. This exercise will separate the preparer from the documentation for a few days, improving the preparer's focus, and ensuring the inclusion of important details.

After each section has been reviewed by the various departments of the company, the financial or accounting personnel should review the entire set of data for completeness and accuracy. These employees will usually have a high degree of familiarity with the entire business operation and will be capable of reviewing the big picture.

If a business does not have people in positions capable of providing this review, the application information might be reviewed by the company's CPA, business advisor, or a loan consultant. The proposal should always be given a second opinion before it leaves the borrower's office.

> **Have associates review the loan application before submission for a second opinion to ensure accuracy, completeness, and focus.**

Giving the Application a Trial Run

In its formative stages an application can be tested in a preliminary interview with a lender. This exploratory meeting is not intended to establish a banking relationship between the borrower and lender; rather it is used to define general parameters of the proposed loan.

In these discussions, the borrower should talk (not write) about the proposed loan, regarding its size, term, use of proceeds, and collateral. In response, the lender will indicate the feasibility and limitations of the loan transaction.

Since this preliminary discussion is designed to assist with preparation of a final proposal, the borrower need not select the most appropriate lender. Nor should the borrower leave any written information in the lender's files that may affect how the lender would structure the proposed loan or that could be compared to an amended application.

If there are any special circumstances that would need to be explained or that would require additional attention, this information should be saved for the end of the discussion. The focus of the conversation should be on the positive: how the lender would approach the deal and what could be done. Once the potential for a deal is determined, other conditions can be introduced to determine how the lender can work with or around them.

Because this exercise is intended to be a trial run to access the lending community, the borrower should avoid committing to a particular loan request until learning how the lender reacts. The borrower thereby gains insight and information about changes that would strengthen a particular application strategy.

Sometimes, understandably, lenders refuse to be specific about transactions until borrowers provide more information in writing. This reaction need not eliminate a lender from the prospect list but, rather, prompts the borrower to interview a different lender from whom information might be obtained.

> Practice makes perfect. Trying the draft proposal out on different lenders increases borrower's confidence and provides information about various policies, practices, and preferences of the local lending market.

Timing Is Important

To maximize the impact of the borrower's presentation of a loan proposal, smart scheduling is important and is based on calculated criteria. Serious borrowers make an appointment to see the lender, rather than arriving unexpectedly. Without discussing the proposal over the phone, the borrower should tell the loan officer the purpose of the appointment and how much time is needed to present the loan request. A prepared borrower needs a minimum of an hour of the loan officer's full attention without interruption. Timing the presentation is essential to maximizing its impact and increasing the borrower's chances of approval.

Most loan officers appreciate this planning in order to reserve sufficient time to focus on what the borrower wants to discuss. Requesting an appointment will communicate that the borrower is serious about the presentation and that the loan officer's undivided attention is expected.

When setting an appointment with a loan officer, recognize that some meeting times can be better than others. For example, if the lender is a bank, the first and fifteenth days of the month may be disadvantageous if the lending officer also has other banking operation responsibilities. Those two days are the busiest days of the month for retail banks, due to payroll deposits, government check cashing, and benefit payment receipts. The lender could be constantly interrupted with frivolous questions and check approvals for other clients.

Meet with the lender when they can most likely give you unhurried, uninterrupted time.

Mondays and Fridays should also be avoided. Loan officers are often subjected to more demands on these days, due to the natural interruption of work flow caused by the weekend. They seem to have more continuous control of their time Tuesday through Thursday. Within this time frame, morning meetings are more favorable than afternoon meetings.

Although many people are impressed when treated to lunch by a banker, the invitation does not indicate any elevation of the borrower's desirability to the lender. In addition, lunch meetings are usually too congested with the distractions of people movement, food service, and the lack of privacy to get the full attention the borrower needs for the loan proposal. Trying to share any written information in that scenario is haphazard. At this stage of a loan proposal, the borrower needs the quiet and seclusion of an office.

It is possible to determine—and avoid—time periods when lenders are being audited by regulators. During the audit, which usually lasts from two to three weeks, the lender is often deluged with requests for information from the auditors, which could make this period a difficult one for the borrower to get the lender's full attention.

Of course, the primary determinant of when the applicant can meet with the loan officer is when the borrower's business permits. Important duties at the business must be the primary and controlling priorities.

Projecting the Revenues, Expenses, and Income

Financing is based on a simple principle: Lenders always require the borrower to agree that the loan will be repaid. At the time the loan request is submitted, the lender will evaluate the borrower's ability to repay the loan with funds generated by the business. This analysis is integral to the borrower's ability to get a loan.

The lender will expect the borrower to provide realistic projections about how the proceeds of the loan will be invested to generate revenues for the borrower. Further, the borrower should identify the costs the business will incur to produce these revenues, and calculate the resulting profits from which the borrower will repay the loan.

The integrity and reasonableness of these projections are often the most important factors in granting loan approval. In constructing these financial projections, management must be honest not only with the lender but also with themselves; representing unrealistic figures is unethical and also self-defeating.

The lender is usually not an expert in the borrower's field and may not recognize exaggerated revenue projections or inadequate expense estimates. Failure to be prudent and exercise good judgment can place the company and the owner's financial stability at risk if money is borrowed that cannot be paid back as scheduled.

Financial projections take into account the estimated operating results of the business for a defined period in the future. Most lenders require operating results projected for a minimum of two years. It is useful to project the first twelve months on a month-to-month basis, in order to demonstrate the immediate effects of the borrowed money on the current business cash cycle. Projecting financial results beyond twenty-four months is difficult, due to multiple factors and economic cycles that may not be anticipated or easily predicted.

In developing the operating projections, the borrower should use a model that resembles the business profit/loss statement (sometimes referred to as a pro forma) and insert the estimated figures accordingly. The starting date should coincide with the date the borrower would reasonably expect the loan to be funded. The projections should be aligned with the beginning of the company's next fiscal year.

Written details are necessary to explain and substantiate estimates of the revenues and expenses. Rather than overloading this worksheet with

Realistic, detail-driven revenue/expense projections will define the feasibility of the loan proposal to the borrower and lender.

❝ Borrowers should be honest with lenders and themselves about financing projections. Unrealistic estimates are unethical and self-defeating. ❞

rows of itemized minutia, the projection model should be streamlined by combining the many small detail accounts into larger revenue and expense categories.

For example, the many different expenses of hiring, compensating, motivating, providing benefits to, and paying taxes for employees should be projected as "Salaries" rather than detailed into several line items. This larger, general category would include all related expenses such as actual salaries, payroll taxes, unemployment insurance premiums, employee benefits, employee insurance costs, payroll processing costs, and other direct expenses attributable to the payroll of the business.

Specific accounts of the "Salaries" expense category can be detailed in the footnotes, readily found if requested but not distracting from the main text. This exercise helps the borrower organize information better and keeps the lender focused on the big picture of the financial projections.

Providing the lender with line-by-line calculations of the expected revenues or expenses could create many unnecessary, extraneous questions. The borrower does not want the lender to micromanage the business or to lose sight of the overall projected results.

Producing this projection model will assist in the borrower's planning and subject the proposal to a financial litmus test. The most important guideline is to be realistic. The borrower needs to demonstrate confidence in the projected revenues and costs necessary to produce business income.

A simple profit/loss projection model is shown in Illustration 2-A. It is easy to use this model to estimate the borrower's results by adding the specific revenue and expense estimates. Most projection models include these categories:

Income:

Sales/Revenues—Monies expected to be received by the business in payment for services provided or products sold to its customers.

Cost of Goods Sold (COGS)—Expenses that represent a direct cost associated with producing or acquiring the products sold by the business. (If the borrower is not sure about which expenses to include here, consult the company's CPA.)

Gross profit—The result of subtracting the COGS from the Sales/Revenues.

Profit/Loss Projections

Business Name:_____

	Interim Period Ending	Proforma Year 1	Proforma Year 2
TOTAL REVENUES	$ _____	$ _____	$ _____
COST OF GOODS	_____	_____	_____
GROSS PROFIT	$ _____	$ _____	$ _____

EXPENSES:

Officer's Salaries	_____	_____	_____
Salaries & Payroll Taxes	_____	_____	_____
Other Payroll Expenses	_____	_____	_____
Repairs/Maintenance	_____	_____	_____
Bad Debts	_____	_____	_____
Rents	_____	_____	_____
Taxes & Licenses	_____	_____	_____
Depreciation & Amortization	_____	_____	_____
Advertising & Marketing	_____	_____	_____
Employee Benefits	_____	_____	_____
Telephone	_____	_____	_____
Utilities	_____	_____	_____
Accounting & Legal Expenses	_____	_____	_____
Insurance	_____	_____	_____
Miscellaneous	_____	_____	_____
Total Expenses	_____	_____	_____
TOTAL OPERATING PROFIT	$ _____	$ _____	$ _____
Interest-SBA loan	_____	_____	_____
Interest- All Other	_____	_____	_____
Total Interest Expense	_____	_____	_____
NET INCOME	$ _____	$ _____	$ _____

ILLUSTRATION 2-A

Monthly Cash Flow Projection

Name of Business

MONTH NUMBER	Pre Start-up Estimate	1 Jan. Estimate	2 Feb. Estimate	3 March Estimate	4 April Estimate	5 May Estimate	6 June Estimate	7 July Estimate	8 August Estimate	9 Sept. Estimate	10 Oct. Estimate	11 Nov. Estimate	12 Dec. Estimate	Total Estimate
MONTH NAME														
YEAR:														
1. Cash On Hand														
2. Cash Receipts														
Cash sales														
Collections from credit accounts														
Loan or other cash injection														
3. Total Cash Receipts														
4. Total Cash Available														
5. Cash Paid Out														
Purchases														
Gross wages														
FICA & Workers Comp.														
Benefits														
Outside services														
Supplies														
Repairs/maintenance														
Advertising														
Car, delivery, & travel														
Accounting & legal														
Rent														
Telephone														
Utilities														
Insurance														
Taxes														
Interest-SBA loan														
Interest-Other Loans														
Other (specify)														
Miscellaneous														
Subtotal of expenses														
Principal repay-SBA														
Principal repay-Other Loans														
6. Total Cash Paid Out														
7. Cash (end of month)														

Date

ILLUSTRATION 2-B

Expenses:

Salaries—Labor costs (except direct labor costs included in the COGS), the company's FICA tax contributions, unemployment taxes, benefit insurance, and other costs incurred by the business to acquire labor.

Management salaries—Optional entry to define the labor expense of the company's management. Lenders are often interested in how well the borrower plans to reward management and owners.

Administrative—Costs associated with managing the operation, such as office supplies, petty cash, refreshments, light equipment maintenance, copier supplies, and other small expenses associated with the administrative functions of the borrower.

Advertising—Costs of marketing and advertising the business, such as brochures, newspaper ads, radio spots, television commercials, yellow pages ads, corporate gifts, direct mail, telemarketing, and other promotion efforts.

Bank fees—Costs of banking fees (except interest on loans). Typically, a business that might incur large bank fees is one that issues a large number of checks, requires a significant volume of cash inventory, makes frequent deposits, or utilizes a merchant account for credit card processing. This line item should be used only if the estimated expenses are expected to exceed 5% of the company's total expenses. Otherwise, they should be included in administrative expenses.

Depreciation/Amortization—Noncash expenses based on the useful life of capital assets or the acceptable amortization period recommended by the CPA. These expenses affect the profitability of the business, but not the cash flow. The sum of these entries is added back to the company's net income when projecting the operation's cash flow.

Entertainment/Travel—Costs of entertaining prospective clients, traveling on sales calls or to trade conferences, or other general purposes not attributable to the direct production of income. This line item should be used only if the estimated expenses are expected to exceed 5% of the company's total expenses. Otherwise, they should be included in administrative expenses.

Equipment—Costs of purchasing light equipment assets that are acquired with the entire expense recognized in the same year, or equipment leasing costs. Equipment maintenance and repair

❝ Streamline expense categories to keep the lender focused on the big picture. ❞

PART 1

expenses should be included in this sum. This line item should be used only if the estimated expenses are expected to exceed 5% of the company's total expenses. Otherwise, they should be included in administrative or miscellaneous expenses.

Insurance—Expenses for general liability insurance, workers' compensation, and other insurance expenses of the business (except employee benefit insurance). This line item should be used only if the estimated expenses are expected to exceed 5% of the company's total expenses. Otherwise, they should be included in administrative expenses.

Postage/Courier—Costs of postage, postage equipment, courier fees, and special handling costs (such as certified mail). This line item should be used only if the estimated expenses are expected to exceed 5% of the company's total expenses. Otherwise, they should be included in administrative expenses.

Professional fees—Costs of any professional services anticipated for the business, such as legal, accounting, or tax.

Rent/Occupancy—Costs of occupancy, CAM (Common Area Maintenance) charges, and other expenses associated with the business premises, such as utilities, repairs, and real estate taxes.

Telephone—Costs of the basic telephone service, long distance, and answering services, communication equipment rental, and other expenses related to providing telephone communication for the business.

Miscellaneous—Various costs that are not defined in the other categories but that must be recognized. This entry should be relatively small. If it exceeds 10% of the expenses projected, then additional categories should be introduced for any group of costs that total comparably with the other categories used in the projections.

Total operating expenses—Total the sum of projected expenses.

Operating Profit—Gross profit minus total expenses—also referred to as Earnings Before Interest and Taxes (EBIT).

Interest—Interest costs expected to be incurred for all debt balances during the period. Be sure to use the actual interest rate and loan amortization schedule for all balances, and calculate the proposed financing according to the terms requested.

Income taxes—Federal and state income taxes, based on expected profits. (*Note*: Most lenders are not interested in income tax projections, due to many variables that make reliable estimates difficult to calculate.)

Net Profit—operating profit less interest and income taxes

Projecting Cash Flow

Income projections will provide the borrower with the expected profits (or losses) of the business. The next step is to develop a cash flow projection. How much cash will be available to cover the debt service required on the proposed loan?

In a basic cash flow model, the noncash expenses (depreciation and amortization) and interest expenses are added to the company's net profit. This calculation provides a quick summary of the total cash available to service the projected debt. This figure is derived as follows:

Net Profit + Depreciation & Amortization + Interest Expenses

With this calculation, the lender will be primarily interested in determining the ratio of the borrower's available cash to the total debt payments required to make payments on the proposed loan. The *Debt Service Coverage Ratio* is calculated as follows:

$$\frac{\text{Cash Available for Debt Service}}{\text{Total Principal \& Interest Payments}}$$

This ratio measures the company's ability to meet its scheduled obligations and to service its debt. By comparing cash available to the required debt payments, this ratio indicates how well a business is managing its existing debt and its capacity to take on new loans. If this ratio is less than 1.0x, then the company is not projected to have sufficient cash to meet its existing or projected payments.

Most lenders require this ratio to be 1.2x, or higher, depending on their loan policy and the borrower's situation. If the cash flow projections do not result in an adequate Debt Service Coverage Ratio, it is important to review all of the borrower's revenue and expense estimates.

“ Lenders focus on the ratio between net cash available from operations to service debt and the payment amount of the requested loan.”

PART 1

If the borrower cannot reconcile these figures according to the company's true estimates, then the loan request will probably have to be reduced to a level that can be serviced by the profits produced with a smaller loan.

A more sophisticated management tool is to utilize a month-to-month cash flow projection model, which tracks revenues and expenses in monthly increments. The elementary example discussed above does not account for accounts receivable (credit sales), trade accounts (credit purchases), and other variables that will affect the company's cash flow.

Using a month-to-month pro forma enables the borrower to account for all such variables and to be more accurate in predicting the cash flow of the business. A detailed legend is necessary for explaining the borrower's assumptions in developing the pro forma.

A commonly used cash flow projection model is shown in Illustration 2-B. It is easy to modify this model to match the borrower's financial reporting, simply by making changes to the revenue or expense entries to match the company's financial statement. Other variables that have an impact on the borrower's cash flow should also be demonstrated.

Other Financial Analysis

Lenders may use a number of financial ratios in analyzing the borrower's financial position to determine the relative strength of the company. Various calculations are used to measure the liquidity, leverage, coverage, and operating performance of the business in comparison to a composite of other businesses of similar size in the borrower's industry.

Depending on the borrower's financial acumen and the level of analysis the borrower wants to perform, these ratios can calculated on the company's financial results to learn what should be expected from the lender's evaluation. Inclusion of positive results in the application will be helpful to the loan proposal by accentuating the financial strength of the business and demonstrating the sophistication of the borrower's financial management.

The most common financial ratios are discussed below with an explanation of how they are calculated and what information they provide. There are no right or wrong answers; these figures measure the borrower's financial position in relative terms, which can be compared to other businesses. Most lenders use the Robert Morris Associates (RMA) Annual Statement Studies as a guideline for industry norms in comparatively analyzing financial ratios.

The RMA Studies gather voluntary submissions of financial statements from thousands of businesses in every industry, as defined by the SIC. These financial statements are compiled and averaged to determine the median and mean of operating standards for every industry each year. These results are published by SIC category in order to provide information about the relative financial condition and performance of each industrial sector.

❝ Liquidity ratios examine the adequacy of working capital in the business. ❞

Liquidity Ratios

Current Ratio—This ratio is calculated as follows:

$$\frac{\text{Total Current Assets}}{\text{Total Current Liabilities}}$$

The Current ratio is a rough measurement of the company's ability to pay its current liabilities with its current assets. It reveals the relative strength or weakness of the working capital, which is the result of subtracting current liabilities from current assets. A higher current ratio is the result of stronger working capital, indicating the excess of current assets over current liabilities. The composition and quality of current assets are critically important to understanding the liquidity of a business.

Quick Ratio (Acid Test)—This ratio is calculated as follows:

$$\frac{\text{Cash \& Equivalents \& Receivables}}{\text{Total Current Liabilities}}$$

Dubbed the "acid test," the Quick ratio provides a more difficult test of liquidity, based on existing cash assets and those assets likely to be converted to cash in the current period. A result totaling significantly lower than the current ratio might mean that the business is relying on the conversion of inventory or other assets to liquidate current liabilities.

Sales/Receivables Ratio—This ratio is calculated as follows:

$$\frac{\text{Net Sales}}{\text{Trade Receivables}}$$

The Sales/Receivables ratio measures the number of times the accounts receivable are fully collected, or "turn over," during the year. If a company's ratio equals twelve, that means that the receivables turn over twelve times a year. A higher ratio means a shorter time between sales and cash collection. If a company's ratio is smaller than the rest of its industry, then the quality of the company's receivables or the company's credit and collection policies may need to be examined.

Day's Receivables—This ratio is calculated as follows:

$$\frac{365}{\text{Sales/Receivables Ratio}}$$

The Day's Receivables ratio expresses the Sales/Receivables ratio in the average number of days required to collect an account receivable. This ratio may be indicative of the control a company has over its credit policy or the quality of its account receivables.

COGS/Inventory—This ratio is calculated as follows:

$$\frac{\text{Cost of Sales}}{\text{Inventory}}$$

The COGS/Inventory ratio measures the number of times the inventory is completely used, or "turns over," during the year. If a company's ratio equals twelve, that means that the inventory turns over twelve times a year. A higher ratio indicates that the inventory is turning over more often, which usually means the company has better liquidity or good merchandising. If a company's ratio is smaller than the rest of its industry's, then the company's inventory may not be selling, may be obsolete, or may be overstocked.

Day's Inventory—This ratio is calculated as follows:

$$\frac{365}{\text{COGS/Inventory Ratio}}$$

The Day's Inventory ratio expresses the COGS/Inventory ratio in the average number of days required to use the inventory on hand. This ratio may be indicative of the quality of inventory management or the quality of the inventory.

COGS/Payables—This ratio is calculated as follows:

$$\frac{COGS}{Trade\ Payables}$$

The COGS/Payables ratio measures the number of times the company's trade payables are paid off, or "turn over," during the year. The larger this ratio, the shorter the time between the company's purchases and subsequent payment for goods. If the company's ratio is lower than the industry average, then there may be a liquidity problem causing the company to pay its bills slowly.

Leverage Ratio

Debt/Worth—This ratio is calculated as follows:

$$\frac{Total\ Liabilities}{Net\ Worth}$$

The Debt/Worth ratio measures the size of the owner's equity capital relative to the lender's debt capital. By determining the relative investment provided by the owners, it defines the degree of risk assumed by the lenders.

"Figures never lie, so figure a lot of liars."

—Unknown

Operating Ratios

% Profit Before Taxes/Total Assets—This ratio is calculated as follows:

$$\frac{Profit\ Before\ Taxes}{Total\ Assets}$$
$$X\ 100$$

The % of Profits Before Taxes/Total Assets ratio measures the pretax return against total assets, which reflects the efficiency with which management is employing the company's assets. Lower-than-average ratios may suggest a problem with the company's profitability.

Sales/Total Assets—This ratio is calculated as follows:

$$\frac{Net\ Sales}{Total\ Assets}$$

The Sales/Total Assets ratio measures the company's ability to generate sales based on its total asset strength. It is useful in comparing the effectiveness of a company's management and sales effort relative to other companies in the industry.

A problem with many of these ratios is that they compare one day's financial position in annualized terms. Because they cannot take a company's seasonality into account, they may be skewed by circumstances that distort the results.

Be mindful (and remind your lender) that there are no good or bad ratios; they are always relative. Even if the borrower's particular financial performance is very impressive, the company may not compare well with the results of the RMA study because of extraordinary, local reasons. These studies should not solely determine that the loan proposal is approved or rejected. The information is useful for understanding how the company compares to other companies in the same business. Based on this data, the borrower can explain differences between the company's performance and the industry norms, good or bad.

While there is additional ratio information published by the RMA, the ratios included above will give the borrower a general understanding of the information the lender is using to evaluate the business. A more thorough explanation of the ratios and a current edition of the RMA Annual Statement Studies, can be requested through Robert Morris Associates at (215) 446-4000.

CHAPTER 3

Preparing a Loan Application

The most dreaded part of applying for a loan is the mountain of paperwork requested by the lender—most of which seems redundant, unnecessary, and unread. This chapter defines most of the information being sought and explains why it's necessary. Learn:

✧ What is needed and why
✧ How to organize it
✧ How to recognize your limitations

Getting Organized

When applying for a business loan, people are often surprised about the extensive degree of information that the lender will require. This information provides the lender with details about such items as the amount of the borrower's loan request, status of the business, use of the loan proceeds, value of collateral assets, and financial condition of the business and business owners.

The size of the loan proposal will not necessarily enlarge or reduce the list of required information. The necessity of the lender to understand the borrower's situation, financial condition, and prospects for repayment is constant, whether the loan is for thousands or millions of dollars. The degree of scrutiny could be greater on larger transactions, but the borrower's command of this information is important, regardless of the size of the loan proposal.

There is no comprehensive list of required application information since every deal is different. The list of suggested information presented in this chapter is fairly complete, but may be either too inclusive or perhaps exclusive of items needed for any particular loan application. That is because no two loans are alike—the lender, the borrower, the business, and the situation are all unique in every transaction, with very little duplication.

There are hundreds of variables that can change the comprehensive information requirements of the lender. Even the lender will not know everything that is needed until the review process begins.

Applying for a business loan requires the borrower to educate the lender about the business and its owners with a customized set of standard documentation, much of which is prepared specifically for each particular application. These documents will disclose an enormous amount of information from which the lender will determine whether the borrower qualifies for a loan in accordance with the lender's criteria.

This chapter defines many items frequently requested by lenders, describes exactly what the lender is looking for, and discusses why this information is needed. Further, it will suggest how to anticipate questions and be prepared to answer them in advance. Attention to the details of this process will enhance the loan application and accelerate the lender's response.

Be Prepared

—Scout Motto

Most of the information, documents, and records needed by the borrower are detailed in this chapter, organized in specific categories and in the logical order for discussing these topics with the lender when the borrower presents the loan proposal. It is recommended that the proposal be introduced to the lender in person in order to benefit from the most effective and persuasive technique for obtaining loan approval—the impressive selling skills of the borrower. However, it is necessary to leave the lender with a written summary of the proposal to document exactly what the borrower is seeking. The lender can refer back to the written information when beginning to review the specifics of the request, to answer questions from the decision makers.

The borrower's level of preparation and the borrower's degree of cooperation will determine how desirable the applicant will be as a customer to the lender. If it is difficult to get the borrower to respond to the lender's request for additional documentation and information before the loan is closed, then the lender will assume that it will be even more difficult to get such information after the loan is made. When the borrowers are responsive and cooperative in meeting these requests for information, they demonstrate management capabilities, they bolster their efforts to receive a loan, and they facilitate consideration of the proposed loan.

Much of the data suggested in this chapter does not exist in the form of a specific document. For purposes of supplying this required information to the lender, memoranda can be designed to document the facts, figures, and information in writing. Emphasis should be on completeness, conciseness, logical sequence, accuracy, and clarity.

Submitting information to promote the business is undermined when there are grammatical errors, misspelled words, and incoherent ideas. With the availability of high-quality word processing software, many of these errors can be eliminated. There is no excuse for poorly written information communicated incorrectly and haphazardly.

When supplying information to the lender, the borrower should assume that the lender does not understand the industry jargon or abbreviations. Technical terms and methodologies should be explained to ensure that the lender can follow the reasoning of the loan proposal. For example, if a lender doesn't understand how local health ordinances mandate certain minimum standards for food processing, then they may not recognize how the borrower can justify the costly expenditures required to build a commercial kitchen. By assuming that the lender has no familiarity with the business, the application will need to communicate precisely what plans the borrower wants to accomplish and how the borrower proposes to pay for these plans.

Too many small businesses pay thousands of dollars annually for the preparation of financial statements without truly understanding what this information discloses. The lender will carefully study the borrower's balance sheet, income statement, and statement of the changes in financial position. By analyzing financial trends and ratios, the lender will assess the strength of the company and will even compare it to other companies in the industry. After determining the positive (or negative) trends of these results, the lender must weigh the risks of lending money to the borrower. The lender is primarily interested in the borrower's ability to produce future funds to repay the lender.

In addition, the lender will check the company's credit history, appraise the collateral, check references, verify account balances, and test the reasonableness of financial projections of future performance in order to quantify the risk associated with providing capital to the applicant.

When initiating the application process for a business loan, it is essential for the borrower to know the fine details of all of the requested documentation but also what the lender's analysis will conclude. Sometimes a business will have periods of lower performance or other

> The lender will ask for an immense volume of documentation without regard to the effort needed to provide it or its usefulness once obtained. Just get it and eliminate one reason the lender could turn down the request.

❝Incorrect, incomplete, poorly reproduced, or out-of-sequence documentation speaks volumes about the borrower's management skill.❞

events occur that will raise the concern of the lender. The borrower should be prepared to discuss those exceptions and to produce documentation to support the explanation. By anticipating the need for these items, the borrower can demonstrate the relevant skills of organization and competence in financial affairs.

The lender will need information in several distinct categories. Although there is no official format, the borrower's assemblage should be organized to assist the lender in cataloging the information easier and evaluating it quickly. This compilation method is more efficient and in better sequence than submitting information in a business plan.

Due to the typically large volume of material, it is more useful to arrange the information in a series of large open-ended folders, rather than using ring binders, clamps, or color-coded tabs. This system permits the lender to access and to file each section independently. Much of the information will have to be copied for various parties to review it, and this duplication can be done more easily if the documents are not bound in any way.

It is important to provide clean, clear documents that are entirely legible. Everything should be reviewed prior to submission to eliminate incorrect compilation, incomplete pages, poor copy reproduction, or out-of-sequence documentation. These logistic errors cause confusion and distract the lender from the business information being submitted by the borrower.

Original documents such as the company's financial statement should not be submitted unless there are several copies. Any copied document may be authenticated, if necessary, with a dated original signature on the margin of the cover page.

Finally, if the borrower cannot produce a particular document or other information requested by the lender, an honest explanation is important to provide a legitimate reason and a timeframe for availability. If, for example, company operations are overloaded at that moment and no one can stop to prepare the information, the borrower will be demonstrating that the business priorities are in correct order.

It is a mistake for the borrower to blame the unavailability of information on the company's accountant, attorney, bookkeeper, or any other party. If these parties cannot be managed by the borrower, who is paying them for professional assistance, how can the borrower manage other operations to repay the lender's loan?

If information is not available due to reasons that cannot be resolved immediately, then the borrower should consider delaying the initiation of the loan application. For example, if the borrower is not able to obtain the most recent financial statements because the accountant has not been paid for last year's financial statement, then the borrower is wise to wait. The borrower's credibility would be significantly damaged if the lender were to learn that the company's invoices are past due.

Categorized organization of information will permit the lender to absorb as much or as little information as needed. The format suggested below accommodates further evaluation and consideration in the loan review process.

Does the Borrower Need a Business Plan?

How do companies use business plans? Too often, borrowers put a business plan together only when seeking to borrow money from lenders or investors. Business plans should provide information on the short-term strategies for accomplishing long-term goals. Business plans should detail how the human resources will convert the marketing, operational, and financial resources into a successful venture. Business plans should be used to measure results against projections.

Many people are obsessed with business plans, particularly those who charge exorbitant fees to prepare them. Business plans are good, even necessary, in many situations (such as for a start-up business operation); but they are over-used as a financing tool. When an existing business is seeking to obtain additional financing, a business plan can be a duplication of efforts, considering the documentation requirements of the lender.

If a business plan is contrived merely to justify financing, then it has limited utility or value for the borrower or the lender. If the lender requires a business plan, then the borrower should justify the investment of time by producing a plan that will benefit the business and that will continue to be used after the financing is obtained.

This chapter outlines at least 98% of all possible information that could be requested for a commercial loan—information that is more pertinent and detailed than is usually included in any business plan. This chapter also suggests the format preferred by most lenders for this information.

Ensure that all documentation is easily accessed without binding or staples. Use clamps or paper clips to make duplication easier.

Borrower Beware!

Many lenders have had the unfortunate experience of entering into discussions with a borrower who was using false, exaggerated, or misleading information to obtain credit. Whether or not the ploy succeeded, the effects are often felt by legitimate borrowers, whose applications are subsequently scrutinized with even more suspicion. While under normal circumstances there is a natural inclination toward trusting people, be prepared to confirm everything.

Unless actual loan losses have been incurred, many lenders may be hesitant to prosecute loan applicants found to have used false information to obtain their loan. The federal government is not so hesitant, and the agency's Inspector General is available to investigate any attempt to defraud the SBA with false or misleading information. These cases are prosecuted by a U.S. attorney, who has unlimited resources to pursue such matters. Most federal prosecutors have almost perfect conviction rates.

For those individuals who are flippant about the integrity of their business dealings, or who willingly try to obtain an SBA loan with fraudulent information, these actions can carry heavy penalties. It is a federal crime to submit false information in order to induce a lender and the SBA to provide business financing. If caught in such an attempt, one can be sure of criminal prosecution. If convicted, one may be punished with up to twenty years in prison and a fine of as much as $1,000,000.

Borrowers certify the accuracy and completeness of the information they submit in the SBA Business Loan Application. This covenant acknowledges that the information is provided by the borrower in order to obtain loan approval. Borrowers also affirm that they have not made payments to anyone within the government for assistance with the loan application, nor will they hire anyone employed by the agency for a period of two years after the loan is approved.

In 1994, the SBA began to verify each borrower's personal and business income tax returns with the Internal Revenue Service. There have been many instances of fictitious tax returns submitted to the agency by fraudulent loan applicants, resulting in significant loan losses. Lenders now confirm that the income tax returns submitted with loan applications are the same as those income tax returns submitted to the IRS to report income.

"The only good loan is one that's paid back."

E. Guice Potter, Sr.
(1907 – 1994)
President
Commercial National Bank
Anniston, AL

Business Loan Proposal

The borrower should produce information addressed to the lender that clearly sets forth the exact loan proposal being requested by the borrower.

Many items are suggested that involve professional preparation, such as appraisals or special reports. Lenders will generally approve loans subject to these items, if not previously available, so that the borrower won't be required to spend a lot of money for this information until they are assured that the loan will be granted. These items are marked below with an asterisk (*).

At a minimum, the loan proposal should included the following components:

General Information
Loan purpose
Loan justification
Proposed loan structure
Use of proceeds
Collateral information
Application form

Personal Information
Date of birth
Social security number
Place of birth
Citizenship
Current/previous address
Military record
Spouse information
Other business interests
Regulatory questions

Business Information
Business name
Address
Taxpayer ID
Date established
Number of employees
Name of bank
Previous SBA debt

Business indebtedness
Business owners
Regulatory questions
Business history
Organizational chart
Key employee resumes
Credit authorization
Lease agreements
Business organization
    documentation
Identification of loan consultant

For Partnerships:
    Partnership agreement
    List of partners
    Certificate of good standing
    Certificate as to partners

For Corporations:
    Articles of incorporation
    By-laws
    Corporate seal
    Corporate resolution
    List of corporate officers
    Certificate of good standing

For LLCs:
    Articles of organization
    LLC operating agreement
    List of LLC members

Financial Information
Personal financial statement
Personal tax returns, 3 yrs.
Year end financial statements,
   3 yrs.
Interim financial statement
Net worth reconciliation
Financial statement analysis
A/R aging report
Inventory aging
A/P aging report
Business tax returns, 3 yrs.
2 yrs. P/L projections
12 month cash flow pro forma
Balance sheet pro forma

Collateral Information
Real Property Collateral
Legal description
Appraisal (*)
Property
Survey (*)
Location map
Engineering reports (*)
Environment report (*)
Environment questionnaire
Photographs
Lease agreements
Sales contracts
Insurance coverage

Personal Property Collateral
Description
   Manufacturer

Date acquired
Cost
Serial numbers
Location
Appraisal (*)
Photographs
Price quotations

Automotive Collateral
Description
   Manufacturer
   Date acquired
   Cost
   Serial numbers
   Mileage (or log hours)
   Registration no.
Title
Appraisal (*)
Photographs

Securities Collateral
Brokerage statements
Schedule of closely held securities

Notes Receivable Collateral
Description
   Name of debtor
   Balance of the note
   Interest rate
   Repayment terms
   Collateral
   Current status
Collateral values
Copy of notes

Depository Account Collateral
Description
   Name of depository
   Name on account

Type of account
Account balances
Interest rate on account
Maturity of account
Account statements

Accounts Receivable/Inventory
  Collateral
A/R aging
Bad debt schedule
Inventory report
Obsolete inventory
Inventory valuation
Borrowing base certificate
Customer lists

Cash Surrender Value Collateral
Copy of policy
Policy declaration
Assignment form

Marketing Information
What are the products or services
  of the business?
How does the business operate?
Who is the typical customer for
  products or services?
How does the business advertise?
Who is the competition?
How will the borrower increase
  revenues?

Miscellaneous Information
Affiliates
Year end financial statements,
  3 yrs.
Interim financial statement

Construction Loans
Performance bond (*)
AIA contract
Cost breakdown
Boundary survey (*)
Sealed construction plans (*)
Construction specifications
Soil reports (*)
Construction schedule
Curb cut permits (*)
Building permit (*)
Insurance (*)
Utility service confirmation
Zoning verification letter

Franchise Businesses
Franchise information
Franchise agreement (*)
Uniform franchise offering circular

Special Assets
Contracts
Lottery awards
Trusts
Tax exempt bonds

SBA Documents
Business loan application
Statements required by law
Statement of financial need
Statement of personal history
Compensation agreement
Assurance of compliance. for
  nondiscrimination
Certificate for regarding debar-
  ment
Request for transcript of tax form
Justification

" In direct terms,

inform the lender:

• *the purpose of the*

  loan

• *the justification for*

  an SBA loan

• *the proposed structure*

  of the loan"

A detailed discussion of each of these documentation requirements is contained in the following pages. If any of the recommended items are not applicable to the borrower's business or loan request, disregard it when compiling this information.

General Information

Purpose of the loan. The lender wants a concise statement of exactly why the borrower wants to borrow money. It is important to provide the lender with an explanation of the purpose of the loan and where all of the funds will be spent. Do not be surprised if the lender is not satisfied with the borrower's statement of merely wanting to purchase an asset.

The lender will require a thorough explanation as to what the borrower is seeking to accomplish with the asset. The borrower may want to buy a new forklift, in order to increase productivity in warehouse operations by lowering labor costs and reducing the exposure to job-related injuries. It is important for the lender to understand the costs savings that may effectively pay for the forklift.

Justification of the loan. A prepared borrower will produce a statement of how a business loan is the best source of the funds being requested. The lender may be aware of alternative sources for the financing and will want to test whether the borrower has considered them as well. The borrower should be prepared to explain why this loan is the most advantageous source of financing, due to more reasonable costs, better terms, higher leverage, or other factors that made the borrower choose to apply for the loan.

Be specific as to how the borrower has determined how much equity to contribute in the transaction. If there is a logical reason to limit the company's investment, be sure to identify it to the lender. Otherwise, be prepared for the lender to insist that the borrower contribute a minimum sum into the transaction.

Proposed structure of the loan. The borrower should propose how the loan should be structured at the time the loan request is submitted. Loan structure refers to the conditions and terms that define the transaction between the lender and borrower.

The borrower has the best opportunity to influence the loan structure at the opening of negotiations. By introducing the borrower's preferences up front, the borrower sets the tone for discussions and is likely to get a better deal by demonstrating concern on these issues than by waiting to allow the lender to offer its own terms.

Lenders often do not appreciate the borrower's desire to maintain cash reserves, especially when part of the loan request is specified for that purpose. Be prepared to walk away from that part of the proposal, since most lenders do not feel it is prudent to fund cash that they cannot be assured is used in the manner requested and may wind up enlarging the lender's loss exposure.

The lender will always have the ultimate leverage in determining the loan terms. But the borrower's suggestion of reasonable terms in the proposal is an important communication to the lender that influences the tone for the loan negotiations. Components of the loan structure should include:

66 Interest rates should be determined by the level of risk accepted by the lender.99

◆ *Loan amount*—Specify exactly how much money the borrower wants, and be ready to defend it with supporting information.

◆ *Loan term*—Define the period over which the borrower wants to repay the loan. Remember, maximum terms are established by the SBA.

◆ *Interest rate*—It never hurts to ask, but be realistic about how much risk your deal presents to the lender. Real estate loans are generally safer than equipment loans; equipment loans are generally safer than working capital loans. Interest rate should be a function of the lender's risk.

Be sure to know how to calculate the loan payment using the amount, interest rate, and repayment term requested, before initiating negotiations about the loan structure. Being able to accurately determine the payment is essential so that the borrower can identify an acceptable or unacceptable amount. There is no sense in agreeing to terms under which the borrower cannot perform.

There are several financial software programs that provide loan amortization formulas, such as Lotus 123 or Microsoft Excel. Alternatively, the borrower may choose to invest in a business calculator to accomplish this task.

Use of loan proceeds. The borrower's loan proposal must include a specific schedule that defines how the proceeds of the loan will be used. If the borrower does not specifically declare exactly how much is needed,

Lenders will expect borrowers to provide a detailed explanation of exactly how all of the loan proceeds will be employed.

the lender will decide based on limited information, which will slow down the approval process.

The lender deserves to know precisely where every dollar goes. When the borrower is purchasing an asset, this number is easy to define. But, if the borrower seeks to borrow a portion of the funds for working capital, specifying where these funds will be applied is a little more difficult.

The borrower should produce a detailed month-to-month cash flow projection for working capital financing, predicting how and when the cash proceeds will be used, and describe the expected expenses or purchases that will be paid. It is easier for the borrower to restrict the use of working capital proceeds to larger-ticket items such as inventory, contracted services, or other major costs that the lender can identify without as much documentation.

The borrower should produce accurate documentation that details how the loan will be used. The SBA requires lender verification of the use of proceeds, such as copies of notes being refinanced (along with the original settlement statement or security agreement), purchase contracts, construction contracts, bills of sale, price quotes, or other documents that back up the uses of funds.

If there is working capital in the transaction, prepare a schedule of where these funds will be applied. Most lenders require borrowers to provide paid receipts to justify working capital needs and will hold back loan funds to reimburse the borrower after the costs are incurred. The borrower requesting to finance the transaction costs associated with the loan should seek assistance from the lender to determine exactly what these costs will be.

Collateral. The borrower should define what assets are available to reasonably secure the loan. Collateral is very important to the lenders because it defines a tangible alternative to the normal liquidation of a loan. The lender will typically require coverage for 100% of the loan, with assets valued on a discounted basis.

For example, if the borrower is purchasing a building with the loan proceeds, the lender will discount the value of the property in order to determine a collateral value. If the lender's loan policy defines an advance rate of 75% on commercial real estate, the lender will reduce the value of the borrower's real property by 25% to determine the collateral value. On that basis, the lender will lend the borrower up to 75% of the cost of the building. Should the borrower require a greater sum, the lender may consider more money but will require the borrower to pledge additional assets in order to secure the excess loan.

Most lenders margin real estate at 80%, but that figure varies, depending on the loan policy of each specific lender and the condition of the local real estate market. Unimproved real estate is usually margined at 50%.

Lenders generally value equipment and furniture at 50% of cost, and give little or no value to leasehold improvements or fixtures unless the real estate also secures the loan. Accounts receivable and inventory (current assets) are of little, if any, value to the lender unless these assets are regularly monitored. Current assets can disappear too fast to be considered dependable secondary sources of repayment.

Loan application form. Some lenders require that the borrower submit a loan application form that is unique to the lender. This application is not to be confused with the SBA Business Loan Application. Many lenders choose to use an in-house application form that requests basic information from the borrower.

This document is probably used by the lender as an internal document to move the loan into its loan approval process. The borrower should be cooperative with such requests, even if compliance duplicates information already provided. The information gathered on such forms generally assists the lender in an orderly movement of information to other parts of its organization.

Special information. If there are special circumstances, negative or positive, that affect the borrower's access to financing, these circumstances should be presented to the lender at an early stage of the application process. With increasing frequency, borrowers have extraordinary conditions that require special handling by the lender on a case-by-case basis.

During the past several years, thousands of persons with great character and impeccable credit have encountered conditions beyond their control that have tarnished otherwise perfect financial histories. The unpredictable economy, some unavoidable bankruptcies, and soaring divorce rates have damaged thousands of borrowers while not necessarily reflecting their character or capability to repay a loan.

Lenders will discover these conditions early during the due diligence procedures, so it is better for the borrower to introduce the topic and provide a full explanation. This voluntary revelation removes any suspi-

" Providing all of the anticipated information up front helps the lender act on a loan request more quickly and with more enthusiasm. "

PART 2

cion of the lender that the borrower may have attempted to hide this information, and provides a legitimate forum in which to enhance the lender's understanding of any such events.

First, get the lender interested in the deal. Introduction of any special information too early may end the chances of getting fair consideration. Once the lender has enough data to be genuinely interested in a deal, introduce any unrelated but relevant features that need explanation and initiate a dialog about how a loan can be granted in light of the former situation.

There is a more detailed discussion about several different circumstances that may need explanation by borrowers in Chapter 4.

Personal Information

The lender will require personal information about each individual who owns an interest in the business entity and each party offering to guaranty the proposed loan. This information is designed to assist the lender and the SBA in confirming that each individual is eligible for SBA participation.

The information covers a broad range of facts that are pertinent to the borrower's capability of obtaining SBA financing. Certain disclosures could result in further review by other government agencies. Specifically, if the borrower or any of its owners have been arrested for or convicted of a crime, other than minor traffic offenses, SBA regulations require an FBI review of this information to confirm that the borrower has completed all sentencing requirements. Prior conviction of a felony does not deem an individual ineligible for SBA financing. But all terms of the sentencing must have been completed, including probation and payment of fines, in order for financing to be considered.

The information required on each individual involved includes:

Date of birth. Federal law prohibits a person's age from being used as a qualification (or disqualification) for obtaining a loan. The individual's date of birth is used as a verification of identification.

Social security number. This information is required for identification.

Place of birth. This information is required to confirm identification.

Declaration of citizenship. The individuals are required to declare their country of citizenship. If any individual is not a U.S. citizen, proof of alien status must be provided. Foreign citizens must have at least a resident alien status (green card) to qualify for SBA assistance.

Current home address and occupancy dates. This information is required for lender and SBA protection.

Previous home address and occupancy dates. This information is required as per SBA regulations.

Declaration of military service. This information is required as per SBA regulations.

Name of spouse and spouse social security number. This information is required as per SBA regulations.

List of affiliated business interests (in which a 20%+ interest is owned). This information is required as per SBA regulations to confirm the eligibility of the borrower. If any such interests exist, it will be necessary to produce financial information for each such business to determine the cumulative effect these other businesses have on the eligibility of the proposed transaction.

Regulatory questions. A written response is required to answer any affirmative replies:

◆ Are you presently under indictment, on parole, or probation?

◆ Have you ever been charged with or arrested for any criminal offense other than a minor motor vehicle violation?

◆ Have you ever been convicted, placed on pretrial diversion, or placed on any form of probation, including adjudication withheld pending probation, for any criminal offense other than a minor motor vehicle violation?

◆ Have you ever been involved in bankruptcy or insolvency proceedings?

◆ Are you involved in any pending lawsuits?

◆ Do you or your spouse or any member of your household, or anyone who owns, manages, or directs your business or their spouses or members of their households work for the Small Business Administration, Small Business Advisory Council, SCORE or ACE, any federal agency, or the participating lender?

Most of this information is required to complete the SBA Form 4 (the Business Loan Application) and Form 912 (the Statement of Personal History), which are found in Illustrations 3-H and 3-J, respectively.

" Adverse answers to regulatory questions do not disqualify borrowers, but will trigger a more in-depth examination. "

PART 2

Business Information

The lender will require administrative information about the borrower in order to evaluate the proposed loan. This information is designed to help the lender establish the eligibility of the borrower for SBA participation.

The information covers a broad range of facts that are pertinent to the borrower's capability of obtaining SBA financing. It also provides the lender with information from which can be determined how the borrower is organized and the depth of the borrower's operations.

Registered business name. The lender needs to know the exact legal name under which the business is legally registered, along with any trade names or d/b/a under which the company operates. This information applies to all businesses that operate under a name different than that under which they are legally organized. Such registration is typically required with the local superior court.

Address(es) of business. The lender will need to know the exact mailing address and principal location of the business, as well as a list of any other offices, stores, plants, warehouses, or other sites used by the business in the course of normal operations. Principal telephone numbers of the business must also be submitted.

Taxpayer identification number (TIN). Lenders need this information for verification of the business identification.

Date established. The borrower should identify the date on which the business was established.

Number of employees. The lender will require that the borrower define how many persons the company employs, including all affiliated businesses and subsidiaries. In addition, the borrower will be requested to estimate the number of employees that will be added by the borrower if the proposed financing is approved. This information may be necessary to ensure the borrower's eligibility.

Name and address of principal bank. The lender will request the name and address of the principal depository bank used by the borrower.

Previous SBA/government debt. The borrower must disclose any previous loans requested or obtained through the SBA or other federal agencies, the amount, the date of request, whether or not it was approved, what the current balance is, and what the loan's current status is.

Identify professionals assisting the borrower. If the borrower is using any professional assistance for the preparation of the SBA application, this information must be disclosed to the SBA, along with an estimate of any fees paid for these services. This requirement includes "packaging fees" or any consulting charges incurred for the gathering or preparing of the borrower's information or identification of a lender by a third party. Points, referral fees, and arbitrary fees determined solely by the loan balance and not determined by specified hourly, detailed duties provided on the borrower's behalf are usually not permitted in conjunction with SBA loans.

Schedule of business debt. The borrower must provide a schedule of all business loans, which should reconcile with the most recent interim financial statement submitted to the lender.

List of business owners. The lender needs a complete list of the individual owners of the business, with names, social security numbers, addresses, and their respective percentage of ownership. In addition, the SBA requests to know whether the named individuals completed any military service (along with the period of service). The SBA is interested in the voluntary ethnic and gender classifications of the individuals it serves.

Regulatory questions. A written response is required to answer any affirmative replies:

- ✧ Has any officer of the business ever been involved in bankruptcy or insolvency proceedings?
- ✧ Is the business involved in any pending lawsuits?
- ✧ Does the business own a 20 percent or more interest in other businesses?
- ✧ Does the business presently engage in export trade?
- ✧ Does the business intend to begin exporting as a result of this loan?

History of the Business. The lender can understand the business better if the borrower can provide some narrative about the history of the business. The borrower should discuss what led to the founding of the company and some of the achievements that have been accomplished since the business opened.

Some relevant information includes the revenue growth record of the company, business locations, key employees, and historical profitability. This section should detail the products or services offered by the company, describe the market the company seeks to address, and identify the company's competition.

Organizational chart. This document will provide a graphic demonstration that defines the business entity's chain of command or lines of

‘‘ Business information will be used to help establish eligibility to participate in the SBA program.’’

PART 2

authority. It is important to the lender to understand the flow of authority and the various positions used by the company to accomplish its mission.

Resumes of key employees and owners. The lender can have more confidence in the borrower's plans if provided with good information about the key people in the organization who will direct the company's efforts. This information should provide details that go beyond the organizational chart and identify the specific functions of each person as they relate to the borrower's operation.

A resume quantifies the background, education, and experience of each individual on hand at the business to accomplish its mission. This information is easier to interpret if prepared in a standard format with the same layout and style.

In larger transactions, particularly since SBA loans have longer terms, the lender will be concerned about executive management succession, which can be addressed with this section of information.

Credit authorization. The borrowers must provide the lender with written authorization to obtain a credit report about each owner, shareholder, or partner who will be guaranteeing the requested loan. An example of such an authorization can be found in Illustration 3-A.

The credit report is intended to disclose to the lender the past credit history of the individuals. This information is needed for the lender to determine whether the individuals have satisfactorily managed earlier credit relationships, or whether there are unresolved issues or problems that would cause the lender to question the likelihood of being repaid. The credit report also reveals if there are any matters of public record regarding the individuals, such as judgments, tax liens, bankruptcies, or debts under collection.

Lease agreements. If the borrower occupies leased premises, the lender will require a copy of the lease agreement. The lender will require the borrower's lease to either have term remaining or have an option to renew for a period for not less than the maturity date of the loan.

Business organization documentation. The lender needs documentation that describes any legal registration under which the borrower has organized to conduct business. There are four primary legal structures under which a commercial business can organize: a sole proprietorship (which may require no registration), partnership, corporation, and limited liability company.

If the borrower is operating as a *sole proprietorship*, a distinct legal entity has not been created to distinguish the individual owner from the business enterprise. Therefore, the business does not require any administrative or legal filing, except a name registration if the business operates under a name different from its owner.

If the business is organized as a *partnership*, the following documentation is required:

✧ *Partnership agreement*—The lender will require that the borrower provide a copy of the partnership agreement with any amendments.

✧ *List of partners*—The lender will require a complete list of the partners that is representative of 100% ownership of the partnership. This list should include the names, addresses, percentage of ownership, and status of the interests (general or limited).

✧ *Certificate of good standing*—The lender will require a certificate of good standing for the partnership, which is usually issued by the state. This certificate provides confirmation that the partnership is duly recognized by the state and authorized to conduct business.

✧ *Certificate as to partners*—The borrower should provide the lender with a Certificate as to Partners, which attests to the authority of the partnership to enter into the loan agreement. SBA Form 160A can be used to satisfy this requirement. A copy of this form is found in Illustration 3-B.

If the business is organized as a *corporation*, the following documentation is required:

✧ *Articles of incorporation*—This document is used to register a corporation with the state, to be legally recognized as a legal entity.

✧ *By-laws*—This document is adopted at the time of incorporation to set forth the official rules that govern the corporation.

✧ *Corporate seal*—Many states require that a corporation have an embossed seal that produces a distinctive imprint of the corporation's name and organization date. In states where required, lenders will direct corporate borrowers to use their seal on particular documents in order to confirm the corporate authority of any signer.

❝Documentation detailing the legal organization is essential, since the entity will be a component of the organization.❞

PART 2

✧ *Corporate resolution*—The lender will request a corporate resolution confirming that the corporation's Board of Directors has authorized the company to enter into the proposed loan. SBA Form 160 can be used to satisfy this requirement. A copy of this form is found in Illustration 3-C.

✧ *List of corporate officers*—The lender will require a current list of corporate officers (those persons who hold a legal corporate position as defined in the by-laws).

✧ *Certificate of good standing*—The lender will require a certificate of good standing issued by the state. This certificate provides confirmation that the corporation is duly recognized by the state and authorized to conduct business.

Financial Information

It is a federal crime to submit false information in order to induce a lender to provide a loan.

The lender will require complete financial disclosure on the borrower in order to fairly evaluate the proposed loan. This information will help the lender and the SBA confirm that the borrower is eligible for SBA participation.

Financial information is pertinent to the borrower's eligibility for SBA assistance, since it will establish how the borrower (and any related interest) measures against maximum financial qualifications. Financial information also informs the lender about how the borrower has and is performing, which may have a bearing on the prospects of future success.

Personal financial statements. The lender will require a personal financial statement from every business owner and from any other party that has been proposed to personally guaranty the loan. The personal financial statement will provide the lender with an accurate summary of the individual's assets, liabilities, income, and other pertinent data.

Sometimes prospective borrowers submit inaccurate financial information that either understates or overstates the borrower's financial position. Some of these erroneous submissions are made due to genuine confusion or lack of understanding of how to define the requested financial information. Others try to inflate the appearance of the financial wherewithal being disclosed, so as to convince the lender that a more qualified application is being considered. These efforts are usually easy for the lender to recognize.

Authorization to Release Information

TO: _____ (the "Lender")

The undersigned grants the Lender authority to investigate and verify any bank account information, deposit balance(s), employment information, and credit history; to obtain a consumer or business credit report; to make any other inquires pertaining to my qualifications for the requested loan; and authorizes the recipient of this document to release to the Lender any and all information that may be requested by the Lender for the purpose of considering my application for a credit transaction. This document may be reproduced as often as needed to acquire references from more than one source and any reproduction will have the same effect as the original document.

NAME_____   S.S. #_____

DATE OF BIRTH____/____/____

HOME ADDRESS

_____

_____

_____
CITY   STATE   ZIP CODE

_____   _____
        SIGNATURE   DATE

SPOUSE INFORMATION (if spouse has any ownership in business enterprise)

NAME_____   S.S. #_____

DATE OF BIRTH____/____/____

_____   _____
        SIGNATURE   DATE

ILLUSTRATION 3-A

U.S. SMALL BUSINESS ADMINISTRATION

RESOLUTION OF BOARD OF DIRECTORS OF

SBA LOAN NO

(For Corporate Applicants)

_____
(Name of Applicant)

(1) RESOLVED, that the officers of this corporation named below, or any one of them, or their, or any one of their, duly elected or appointed successors in office, be and they are hereby authorized and empowered in the name and on behalf of this corporation and under its corporate seal to execute and deliver to the _____
(hereinafter called "Lender") or the Small Business Administration (hereinafter called "SBA"), as the case may be, in the form required by Lender or SBA, the following documents: (a) application for a loan or loans, the total thereof not to exceed in principal amount $ _____ , maturing upon such date or dates and bearing interest at such rate or rates as may be prescribed by Lender or SBA; (b) applications for any renewals or extensions of all or any part of such loan or loans and of any other loans, heretofore or hereafter made by Lender or SBA to this corporation; (c) the promissory note or notes of this corporation evidencing such loan or loans or any renewals or entensions thereof; and (d) any other instruments or agreements of this corporation which may be required by Lender or SBA in connection with such loans, renewals, and/or extensions; and that said officers in their discretion may accept any such loan or loans in installments and give one or more notes of this corporation therefor, and may receive and endorse in the name of this corporation any checks or drafts representing such loan or loans or any such installments;

(2) FURTHER RESOLVED, that the aforesaid officers or any one of them, or their duly elected or appointed successors in office, be and they are hereby authorized and empowered to do any acts, including but not limited to the mortgage, pledge, or hypothecation from time to time with Lender or SBA of any or all assets of this corporation to secure such loan or loans, renewals and extensions, and to execute in the name and on behalf of this corporation and under its corporate seal or otherwise, any instruments or agreements deemed necessary or proper by Lender or SBA, in respect of the collateral securing any indebtedness of this corporation;

(3) FURTHER RESOLVED, that any indebtedness heretofore contracted and any contracts or agreements heretofore made with Lender or SBA on behalf of this corporation, and all acts of officers or agents of this corporation in connection with said indebtedness or said contracts or agreements, are hereby ratified and confirmed;

(4) FURTHER RESOLVED, that the officers referred to in the foregoing resolutions are as follows:

_____	_____	_____
(Typewrite name)	(Title)	(Signature)
_____	_____	_____
(Typewrite name)	(Title)	(Signature)
_____	_____	_____
(Typewrite name)	(Title)	(Signature)
_____	_____	_____
(Typewrite name)	(Title)	(Signature)
_____	_____	_____
(Typewrite name)	(Title)	(Signature)

(5) FURTHER RESOLVED, that Lender or SBA is authorized to rely upon the aforesaid resolutions until receipt of written notice of any change.

CERTIFICATION

I HEREBY CERTIFY that the foregoing is a true and correct copy of a resolution regularly presented to and adopted by the Board of Directors of _____
(Name of Applicant)

at _____ on the _____ day of _____ , 19 _____ , at which a quorum was present and voted, and that such resolution is duly recorded in the minute book of this corporation; that the officers named in said resolution have been duly elected or appointed to, and are the present incumbents of, the respective offices set after their respective names; and that the signatures set opposite their respective names are their true and genuine signatures.

_____
Secretary

(Seal)

SBA FORM 160

ILLUSTRATION 3-B

U.S. SMALL BUSINESS ADMINISTRATION

CERTIFICATE AS TO PARTNERS

SBA LOAN NO.

We, the undersigned, are general partners doing business under the firm name and style of _____ and constitute all the partners thereof.

Acts done in the name of or on behalf of the firm, by any one of us shall be binding on said firm and each and all of us. This statement is signed and the foregoing representations are made in order to induce the _____ (hereinafter called "Lender") or the Small Business Administration (hereinafter called "SBA"):

1. To consider applications for a loan or loans to said firm when signed by any one of us.
2. To make a loan or loans to said firm against a promissory note or promissory notes signed in the firm name by any one of us.
3. To accept as security for the payment of such note or notes any collateral which may be offered by any one of us.
4. To consider applications signed in the firm name by any one of us for any renewals or extensions for all or any part of such loan or loans and any other loan or loans heretofore or hereafter made by Lender or SBA to said firm.
5. To accept any other instruments or agreements of said firm which may be required by Lender or SBA in connection with such loan, renewals, or extensions when signed by any one of us.

Any indebtedness heretofore contracted and any contracts or agreements heretofore made with Lender or SBA on behalf of said firm and all acts of partners or agents of said firm in connection with said indebtedness or said contracts or agreements are hereby ratified and confirmed, and we do hereby certify that THERE IS ATTACHED HERETO A TRUE COPY OF OUR AGREEMENT OF PARTNERSHIP.

Each of the undersigned is authorized to mortgage and/or pledge all or any part of the property, real, personal, or mixed, of said firm as security for any such loan.

This statement and representations made herein are in no way intended to exclude the general authority of each partner as to any acts not specifically mentioned or to limit the power of any one of us to bind said firm and each and every one of us individually.

Lender or SBA is authorized to rely upon the aforesaid statements until receipt of written notice of any change.

Signed this _____ day of _____ , 19 _____ .

_____	_____
(Typewrite Name)	(Signature)
_____	_____
(Typewrite Name)	(Signature)
_____	_____
(Typewrite Name)	(Signature)
_____	_____
(Typewrite Name)	(Signature)
_____	_____
(Typewrite Name)	(Signature)
_____	_____
(Typewrite Name)	(Signature)
_____	_____
(Typewrite Name)	(Signature)
_____	_____
(Typewrite Name)	(Signature)

State of _____)

County of _____)ss:

On this _____ day of _____ , 19 _____ , before me personally appeared

_____ and _____ and _____ and

_____ and _____ and _____ and

_____ and _____ and _____

to be known to be the persons described in an who executed the foregoing instrument, and acknowledged that they executed the same as their free act and deed.

My commission expires _____

_____
Notary Public

NOTE: If this form of notarial certificate cannot be used in the State in question, the form should be properly modified.

SBA FORM 160A

ILLUSTRATION 3-C

While there are many financial statement forms available, the SBA's form is the preferred form to submit. A copy of the SBA Form 413 (the Personal Financial Statement) is found in Illustration 3-D.

To clarify questions that may arise while preparing the personal financial statement, remember the following guidelines:

✧ Establish a date of the report and describe the various asset and liability accounts at their approximate value as best known. For simplicity, round entries to the nearest $100.

✧ This report is not an audit, so each entry will not be scrutinized to the penny. But be assured that the lender can spot exaggerations and will question the borrower about any entries that seem out of context or unrealistic. Credit reports are also used to compare the report liabilities to the debt disclosed by the individual.

✧ Liquid asset accounts (including cash, accounts receivable, and marketable securities) should be listed according to the most recent balance the depositor can document. If the transaction depends on the borrowers injecting cash as part of the settlement, the lender will ask for verification of these funds at the application stage.

✧ Real estate, automobiles, and other major assets should be valued at the likely price at which they could be sold in a reasonable time. The financial statement provides space for more details about real estate assets, such as the address, the title names, the purchase date, the purchase price, the present market value, and the present mortgage balance. This additional information is necessary since real estate comprises a majority of many individuals' net worth.

✧ The borrower should remember to include the value of any closely held stock or partnership interests owned, particularly in the subject business. These assets should be valued according to the percentage of ownership, based on a reasonable assessment of the market value of the company or the company's actual book value.

✧ Under "Other Assets," borrowers should record the value of personal household assets such as furniture, art, silverware, furs, jewelry, antiques, silver, and other personal effects. The lender will not seek to use these assets to secure the loan, but inclusion of the value of these assets ensures that any assets acquired with consumer debt is offset. Also, the net value is a relevant disclosure of the individual's wealth accumulation.

✧ Borrowers should segregate liabilities into distinct categories, including bank notes (i.e., car loans, personal notes, and student loans), credit accounts (i.e., Visa, MasterCard, Discover, and other retail accounts), and real estate debt (any debt that encumbers the borrower's real property, including equity lines of credit).

✧ The personal financial statement form provides a space in which the individual subtracts the total liabilities from the total assets to calculate the net worth of the individual.

✧ The individual will be requested to estimate total annual income and identify the primary sources, such as salaries, real estate, investment, interest, or other. These various sources should be detailed separately on an annualized basis.

✧ The personal financial statement form provides a space for the disclosure of any contingent liabilities that may include potential taxes or fines, guaranteed or cosigned obligations, or other special debts that are not direct obligations as of the date of the financial statement.

✧ Any asset or liability entry that needs explanation should be listed in specified sections on page two. These sections are provided for individuals to disclose information that assists the lender's understanding of specific entries. In addition, there is a section for the details about life insurance owned by the individual, including the insurer, amount of coverage, beneficiaries, cash surrender value, and the name of any assignees.

✧ Be sure to sign and date the financial statement. The individual's social security number is usually required in order to verify identification.

Copies of personal income tax returns. The lender will require individuals to provide copies of personal income tax returns along with all schedules for the past three years. And, in compliance with SBA rules, the borrower will need to execute IRS Form 4506 to authorize the lender to obtain a transcript of each tax return from the IRS for verification. This requirement is in response to many past unscrupulous applicants who used fictitious tax returns to qualify for SBA loans. A copy of IRS Form 4506 (Request for Copy or Transcript of Tax Form) is found in Illustration 3-E.

❝ Don't forget to add the value of ownership in the subject business on the personal financial statement. ❞

PART 2

PERSONAL FINANCIAL STATEMENT

U.S. SMALL BUSINESS ADMINISTRATION

As of _____ , 19 ____

Complete this form for: (1) each proprietor, or (2) each limited partner who owns 20% or more interest and each general partner, or (3) each stockholder owning 20% or more of voting stock, or (4) any person or entity providing a guaranty on the loan.

Name	Business Phone
Residence Address	Residence Phone
City, State, & Zip Code	
Business Name of Applicant/Borrower	

ASSETS	(Omit Cents)	LIABILITIES	(Omit Cents)
Cash on hands & in Banks	$	Accounts Payable	$
Savings Accounts	$	Notes Payable to Banks and Others	$
IRA or Other Retirement Account	$	(Describe in Section 2)	
Accounts & Notes Receivable	$	Installment Account (Auto)	$
Life Insurance-Cash Surrender Value Only	$	Mo. Payments $	
(Complete Section 8)		Installment Account (Other)	$
Stocks and Bonds	$	Mo. Payments $	
(Describe in Section 3)		Loan on Life Insurance	$
Real Estate	$	Mortgages on Real Estate	$
(Describe in Section 4)		(Describe in Section 4)	
Automobile-Present Value	$	Unpaid Taxes	$
Other Personal Property	$	(Describe in Section 6)	
(Describe in Section 5)		Other Liabilities	$
Other Assets	$	(Describe in Section 7)	
(Describe in Section 5)		Total Liabilities	$
		Net Worth	$
Total	$	**Total**	$

Section 1. Source of Income		Contingent Liabilities	
Salary	$	As Endorser or Co-Maker	$
Net Investment Income	$	Legal Claims & Judgments	$
Real Estate Income	$	Provision for Federal Income Tax	$
Other Income (Describe below)*	$	Other Special Debt	$

Description of Other Income in Section 1.

*Alimony or child support payments need not be disclosed in "Other Income" unless it is desired to have such payments counted toward total income.

(Use attachments if necessary. Each attachment must be identified as a part of this statement and signed.)

Name and Address of Noteholder(s)	Original Balance	Current Balance	Payment Amount	Frequency (monthly, etc.)	How Secured or Endorsed Type of Collateral

SBA FORM 413

ILLUSTRATION 3-D

Section 3.

Number of Shares	Name of Securities	Cost	Market Value Quotation/Exchange	Date of Quotation/Exchange	Total Value

Section 4. (List each parcel separately. Use attachment if necessary. Each attachment must be identified as a part of this statement and signed.)

	Property A	Property B	Property C
Type of Property			
Address			
Date Purchased			
Original Cost			
Present Market Value			
Name & Address of Mortgage Holder			
Mortgage Account Number			
Mortgage Balance			
Amount of Payment per Month/Year			
Status of Mortgage			

Section 5. (Describe, and if any is pledged as security, state name and address of lien holder, amount of lien, terms of payment and if delinquent, describe delinquency)

Section 6. Unpaid Taxes. (Describe in detail, as to type, to whom payable, when due, amount, and to what property, if any, a tax lien attaches.)

Section 7. Other Liabilities. (Describe in detail.)

Section 8. Life Insurance Held. (Give face amount and cash surrender value of policies - name of insurance company and beneficiaries)

I authorize SBA/Lender to make inquiries as necessary to verify the accuracy of the statements made and to determine my creditworthiness. I certify the above and the statements contained in the attachments are true and accurate as of the stated date(s). These statements are made for the purpose of either obtaining a loan or guaranteeing a loan. I understand FALSE statements may result in forfeiture of benefits and possible prosecution by the U.S. Attorney General (Reference 18 U.S.C. 1001).

Signature: Date: Social Security Number:

Signature: Date: Social Security Number:

PLEASE NOTE: The estimated average burden hours for the completion of this form is 1.5 hours per response. If you have questions or comments concerning this estimate or any other aspect of this information, please contact Chief, Administrative Branch, U.S. Small Business Administration, Washington, D.C. 20416, and Clearance Officer, Paper Reduction Project (3245-0188), Office of Management and Budget, Washington, D.C. 20503.

ILLUSTRATION 3-D CONTINUED

Lenders will require that borrowers certify the submitted tax returns (and financial statements) with either an attached statement of authenticity or with an original signature on the document. The latter is certainly easier, but make sure not to sign on the form's signature line when signing a copy of a tax return. It could be technically viewed as an original form if obtained by the IRS and create many problems. Use a colored pen such as blue or red, so that the signature is easy to find and obviously is not copied.

Business financial statements. The lender will require the borrower to submit the past three years' business financial statements. This information permits the lender to examine the borrower's recent financial performance and evaluate results during each period. The lender will compare many components from each year to analyze a number of factors that describe the company's success.

If practical, the borrower should have its financial statements prepared by a certified public accountant (CPA). Depending on the size of the business and the amount of capital financing requested, a CPA can provide a more credible financial report than other preparers without a professional designation. The accreditation of the accountant can add to the lender's confidence about the financial statements.

There are three general levels of financial reporting:

1. *Compilation.* This financial report has the lowest level of confirmation, since the CPA merely reviews the internally generated report of receipts and payments, and compiles a financial statement based on the account classifications defined by the business. The accountant will correct any blatant errors discovered but will typically depend on the client to provide most of the information, which is reported in a standardized format.

2. *Review.* This financial report is prepared by compiling information and conducting several tests to assure accuracy and consistency. The CPA accepts a greater responsibility in issuing a review statement and is obligated to report inconsistencies found in the accounting methods or in preparation of the financial statements. Further, the CPA confirms to the company's owners that the information has been prepared in accordance with generally accepted accounting principles (GAAP).

SBA
U.S. Small Business Administration

Form **4506**
(Rev. May 1997)
Department of the Treasury
Internal Revenue Service

Request for Copy or Transcript of Tax Form
ı **Read instructions before completing this form.**
ı **Type or print clearly. Request may be rejected if the form is incomplete or illegible.**

OMB No. 1545-0429

Note: *Do not use this form to get tax account information. Instead, see instructions below.*

1a Name shown on tax form. If a joint return, enter the name shown first.	1b First social security number on tax form or employer identification number (See instructions.)
2a If a joint return, spouse's name shown on tax form	2b Second social security number on tax form

3 Current name, address (including apt., room, or suite no.), city, state, and ZIP code

4 Address, (including apt., room, or suite no.), city, state, and ZIP code shown on the last return filed if different from line 3.

5 If copy of form or a tax return transcript is to be mailed to someone else, enter the third party's name and address.

6 If we cannot find a record of your tax form and you want the payment refunded to the third party, check here .... ı ☐

7 If name in third party's records differs from line 1a above, enter that name here (see instructions) ı

8 Check only one box to show what you want. There is no charge for items 8a, b, and c:

  a ☐ Tax return transcript of Form 1040 series filed during the current calendar year and the 3 prior calendar years. (see instructions).

  b ☐ Verification of nonfiling.

  c ☐ Form(s) W-2 information (see instructions).

  d ☐ Copy of tax form and all attachments (including Form(s) W-2, schedules, or other forms). **The charge is $23 for each period requested.**
      Note: *If these copies must be certified for court or administrative proceedings, see instructions and check here* .... ı ☐

9 If this request is to meet a requirement of one of the following, check all boxes that apply.

  ☐ Small Business Administration   ☐ Department of Education   ☐ Department of Veterans Affairs   ☐ Financial institution

10 Tax form number (Form 1040, 1040A, 941, etc.)	12 Complete only if line 8d is checked. Amount due:	Does not apply to SBA transcript requests
	a Cost for each period	
11 Tax period(s) (year or period ended date). If more than four, see instructions.	b Number of tax periods requested on line 11	
	c Total cost. Multiply line 12a by line 12b .... $	
	Full payment must accompany your request. Make check or money order payable to "Internal Revenue Service."	

Caution: *Before signing, make sure all items are complete and the form is dated.*

I declare that I am either the taxpayer whose name is shown on line 1a or 2a, or a person authorized to obtain the tax information requested. I am aware that based upon this form, the IRS will release the tax information requested to any party shown on line 5. The IRS has no control over what that party does with the information.

Please Sign Here

Signature. See instructions. If other than taxpayer, attach authorization document.	Date	Telephone number of requester
Title (if line 1a above is a corporation, partnership, estate, or trust)		Best time to call
Spouse's signature	Date	**TRY A TAX RETURN TRANSCRIPT** (see line 8a instructions)

Instructions
Section references are to the Internal Revenue Code.

TIP: If you had your tax form filled in by a paid preparer, check first to see if you can get a copy from the preparer. This may save you both time and money.

Purpose of Form.—Use Form 4506 to get a tax return transcript, verification that you did not file a Federal tax return, Form W-2, information, or a copy of a tax form. Allow 6 weeks after you file a tax form before you request a copy of it or a transcript. For W-2

information, wait 13 months after the end of the year in which the wages were earned. For example, wait until Feb. 1999 to request W-2 information for wages earned in 1997.

Do not use this form to request Forms 1099 or tax account information. See this page for details on how to get these items.

Note: *Form 4506 must be received by the IRS within 60 calendar days after the date you signed and dated the request.*

How Long Will It Take?—You can get a tax return transcript or verification of nonfiling within 7 to 10 workdays after the IRS receives your request. It can take up to 60 calendar

days to get a copy of a tax form or W-2 information. To avoid any delay, be sure to furnish all the information asked for on Form 4506.

Forms 1099.—If you need a copy of a Form 1099, contact the payer. If the payer cannot help you, call or visit the IRS to get Form 1099 information.

Tax Account Information.—If you need a statement of your tax account showing any later changes that you or the IRS made to the original return, request tax account information. Tax account information lists

(Continued on back)

For Privacy Act and Paperwork Reduction Act Notice, see back of form.   Cat. No. 41721E   Form **4506** (Rev. 5-97)

ILLUSTRATION 3-E

3. *Audit.* This financial report is the highest level of financial reporting, where the CPA prepares the financial statement after testing every revenue, expense, asset, and liability classification and confirming the validity of all entries. The report is issued with an opinion of the CPA as to its accuracy, disclosing any exceptions or inconsistencies.

There are no formal standards with which to qualify when a business should use one financial accounting report or another. This decision should be made based on the particular needs of the business and who is requiring the information. A compilation is fine for a company with $20 million in sales if there is only one shareholder who does not plan to borrow money. However, a company with sales of $3 million desiring to make a public equity offering must have three years of audited financial statements.

The lender should inform the borrower which level of financial reporting is preferred by the lender. If there are several shareholders or the company's borrowing requirements are expected to exceed $500,000, it is a good idea to consider a review-level financial report. The review statement will provide sufficient credibility of the company's financial controls, without the high cost of audit.

Recognize that the financial statements are probably the most important part of the application that determines whether or not the borrower will qualify for financing. Therefore, the quality of preparation is germane to the company's ability to obtain a loan. Many businesses utilize an in-house bookkeeper to organize their financial records and produce a basic financial statement for operations. A capable person in this role is essential since this information is usually the basis for the work performed by the company's CPA for the annual financial and tax reports.

Many companies pay for monthly compiled financial statements. Such an effort is usually a waste of money unless required by a lender or if the owner wants an independent report of the monthly financial results. A small business generally does not need independent monthly financial statements.

If the loan request is approved, lenders will require the borrower to submit annual financial reports, as of the last day of the company's fiscal year. Regardless of the type of financial statement prepared for the company, the report should be completed within ninety days after the end of the reporting period.

Interim financial statement. The lender will require the loan application to include an interim financial statement no more than ninety days old. Updated financial information is particularly important during the last half of the year, when more time will have elapsed since the previous year end report. The need for an interim report is accentuated by an SBA requirement that the loan guaranty application include updated interim financial statements.

Reconciliation of net worth. Provide the lender with a reconciliation of net worth, if needed. Often, there are adjustments made to the retained earnings, or other equity accounts, that will render the net worth out of balance with previous reporting periods. These adjustments are not always obvious and can slow down the lender's analysis of the financial statements. Prepare a reconciliation of any such changes ahead of time and provide a detailed explanation of all adjustments.

Analysis of financial statements. It is beneficial for the borrower to provide the lender with a detailed narrative of the business financial reports, describing the results of each reporting period. This analysis permits the borrower to influence the lender's interpretation of the financial statements and ensure a complete understanding and perspective of the operating results.

Emphasis should be placed on information that favorably explains any negative results or highlights the positive results. If appropriate, the borrower may even prepare a separate restatement of the financial results with any particular adjustments reflected to demonstrate the full impact of the noted information.

Some of the financial ratios explained in Chapter 2 may also assist the borrower in preparing an analysis for the lender's review.

Accounts receivable aging report. The lender will require an accounts receivable aging report as of the date of the latest interim or year end financial statement. The total balance of this report should be reconciled to the accounts receivable balance on the most recently submitted interim financial statement. This information provides the lender with an indication of the strength of the company's working capital position.

Inventory aging report. If inventory represents a significant asset of the business, it is helpful to provide the lender with an inventory aging report so that components of the company's inventory (raw materials, work-in-process, or finished goods) can be evaluated and the aging of each of these categories defined. This report should also be dated and

❝ Companies paying for monthly independent financial statements could be wasting money—few lenders require them. ❞

reconciled to the inventory balance stated on the most recent interim or year end financial statement.

If inventory is an important component of the company's assets, the lender will be interested in the valuation method used by the company to account for the value of inventory. There are two methods by which companies can assess the inventory value:

1. First In—First Out (FIFO). This method values inventory based on the cost of the inventory unit when acquired—units are expensed out as used, based on the original price paid per unit. This method is the more aggressive of the two methods, because it permits the business to retain higher-valued units on the books while expending typically lower-cost units. This method results in a higher inventory valuation.

2. Last In—First Out (LIFO). This method values inventory based on the latest cost of inventory units—units are expensed out based on the latest market price without regard to the actual price paid for the particular units. FIFO is the more conservative of the two methods because it requires the business to expense the higher-price units first as depleted, which results in a lower inventory valuation.

Accounts payable aging report. The lender will require an accounts payable aging report as of the date of the latest interim or year end financial statement. The total balance of this report should be reconciled to the accounts payable balance on the most recently submitted interim financial statement. This information provides the lender with an indication of the strength of the company's working capital position and how well it manages trade debt.

Copies of business income tax returns. The lender will require copies of business income tax returns along with all schedules for the past three years. And, in compliance with SBA rules, execute IRS form 4506 to authorize the lender to obtain a transcript of each tax return from the IRS for verification. This requirement is in response to many past unscrupulous applicants who used fictitious tax returns to qualify for SBA loans. A copy of IRS Form 4506 (Request for Copy or Transcript of Tax Form) is found in Illustration 3-E.

It may be helpful to prepare a memorandum discussing the tax reporting methods and procedures employed by the business. Some lenders may not be very sophisticated in interpreting income tax returns, especially when compared directly to the business financial statements. Most businesses tend to reduce profits where possible on income tax reports in order to reduce taxes. Financial statements may be a better indication of the company's true financial results.

Providing information about the obvious differences between the borrower's tax returns and financial statements will help the lender reconcile the differences and reduce the lender's concerns.

Financial projections—The lender will be interested in the company's projections of future financial performance for at least two years following the proposed loan. The company's ability to accurately project these figures and justify the basis for these predictions is an important component of the loan application.

The borrower should provide the following financial projections to support the loan application:

✧ *Balance sheet pro forma.* Using the most recently submitted interim balance sheet, the borrower should demonstrate the immediate effect the loan proceeds would have on the company's balance sheet. This projection is best demonstrated by a comparative spreadsheet showing the present (preloan) balance sheet with appropriate debits and credits detailing the effects of the loan transaction to the right of each affected account; then a summation of the pro forma balance sheet in the last column, reflecting the post-loan financial position. An example of this balance sheet projection format is found in Illustration 3-F.

✧ *Profit/loss statement projections.* Prepare a detailed income projection for the company for two years based on the existing financial trends and the changes that are expected to result directly from the proposed loan. There are additional suggestions about how to develop profit/loss projections in Chapter 2. An example of a profit/loss pro forma is found in Illustration 2-A.

✧ *Cash flow projections.* Using the first year's income projections, prepare a monthly cash flow projection to demonstrate the company's cash cycle during the first year following the loan transaction. Be sure to reflect the principal and interest payments of the requested loan as scheduled.

❝ Accurately projecting financial performance will be an important component of a loan application. ❞

PART 2

Balance Sheet Projections

Business Name: _____

	For the Interim Period Ending	Debits	Credits	Pro Forma Balance
ASSETS				
Current Assets:				
Cash	_____	_____	_____	_____
Accounts Receivable	_____	_____	_____	_____
Inventory	_____	_____	_____	_____
Total Current Assets:	$ _____	_____	_____	$ _____
Fixed Assets:				
Land	_____	_____	_____	_____
Building(s)	_____	_____	_____	_____
Machinery & Equipment	_____	_____	_____	_____
Less: Accum. Depreciation	- _____	_____	_____	- _____
Total Fixed Assets:	$ _____	_____	_____	$ _____
Other Assets:				
Intangible Assets	_____	_____	_____	_____
Deposits	_____	_____	_____	_____
Total Other Assets:	$ _____	_____	_____	$ _____
Total Assets	$ _____	_____	_____	$ _____
LIABILITIES & EQUITY				
Current Liabilities:				
Notes Payable - Short Term	_____	_____	_____	_____
Current Maturities - LTD	_____	_____	_____	_____
Accounts Payable - Trade	_____	_____	_____	_____
Accrued Expenses	_____	_____	_____	_____
Total Current Liabilities	$ _____	_____	_____	$ _____
Long Term Liabilities:				
Long Term Debt	_____	_____	_____	_____
Other	_____	_____	_____	_____
Total Long Term Liabilities	$ _____	_____	_____	$ _____
Total Liabilities	$ _____	_____	_____	$ _____
Owner's Equity:				
Stock	_____	_____	_____	_____
Paid-In Capital	_____	_____	_____	_____
Retained Earnings	_____	_____	_____	_____
Total Owner's Equity	$ _____	_____	_____	$ _____
Total Liabilities & Equity	$ _____	_____	_____	$ _____

ILLUSTRATION 3-F

More sophisticated borrowers will even account for the timing of revenues generated on a receivable basis, goods purchased on trade credit, and seasonal changes in sales. There is additional information about how to develop cash flow projections in Chapter 2. An example of a month-to-month cash flow pro forma is found in Illustration 2-B.

Collateral Information

It is helpful to the lender—and accelerates consideration of the loan application—if the borrower provides information about the assets to be offered to the lender as collateral to secure the loan. This data helps the lender assess collateral adequacy, understand the borrower's predisposition to secure the loan, and evaluate the loan proposal with these factors. This section outlines a number of items the lender can use to evaluate the specifics of the borrower's proposed collateral.

Generally, borrowers will not have the professional reports suggested at the time of loan application, particularly for real property collateral. But any available collateral information will assist the lender's understanding of exactly how the borrower can secure the loan.

Most of the valuation or analytical information will have to have been prepared very recently if the borrower is to use it for the present loan. Appraisals, environmental reports, and even surveys more than six months old are useful as a guideline but are stale in terms of the lender being able to rely on this information.

There may be a significant difference between the lender's and the borrower's impression of the valuation of collateral assets. Lenders discount the market or cost values of collateral assets when determining the adequacy of collateral against the requested loan. This discount is understandable, since the lender has to maintain a safety margin to hedge on possible depreciation and cover possible liquidation costs.

Sometimes the lender is too conservative in determining a prudent advance rate on specific collateral assets. Borrowers may be able to address this problem with more information demonstrating the actual value of the asset in question. For example, providing the lender with recent comparable sales records, advertisements, or other data that may have been overlooked can help establish the value of similar assets to those offered as collateral. This supporting information may give the borrower the opportunity to negotiate better leverage for the collateral.

Anticipate how much collateral may be required
Decide which assets are off-limits in advance
Confer with spouse concerning assets which are owned jointly

Lenders use the lower cost or appraised value, as a basis for calculating the discount of collateral.

In determining liquidation or collateral value, lenders will use the lower of cost or appraised value of an asset. If the borrower is acquiring an asset at a price significantly lower than an appraiser's opinion of the market value, the reality is that the lender will still base their credit decision on the actual sales price. The borrower will not be allowed to leverage against "phantom" equity. Expect lenders to assert the collateral base as the lower of appraised value or sale price.

When a loan proposal is approved, lenders will offer terms based on the requirement of certain assets being encumbered as collateral. Sometimes lenders go beyond prudence and suggest an absurd amount of collateral just because there are assets on the borrower's balance sheet that can virtually eliminate any potential risk of the loan (and prevent the borrower from obtaining another loan).

Loan commitments do not have to be the final word. The borrower can always refuse the lender's offer and try to convince the lender to amend the deal to reflect more reasonable terms. *Everything is negotiable*. Often, qualified borrowers can find other lenders hungrier for business.

The borrower should resist the lender's inclination to secure too much collateral. Challenge the lender to justify the quantity of collateral requested and the method used to determine the adequacy of that collateral.

Ultimately, this exercise may not change the lender's requirements, but it may cause the lender to either (1) reconsider the leverage (how much advanced) of certain assets, or (2) give the borrower a better interest rate to reflect lower risk on the deal.

Before entering into serious negotiations for a loan, the borrower should decide exactly which assets available and unavailable to pledge as collateral. In the detailed categories of assets described below, some suggestions are made concerning their suitability and exposure as collateral. There are recommendations about how to manage some of the situations the borrower may face if certain assets are requested as collateral. But be prepared with an answer before questions are posed, so as to keep priorities straight and eliminate regret as an outcome of your loan terms.

Additionally, it may be useful to disclose that the SBA cannot refuse to guaranty a loan due to insufficient collateral. Conversely, in an ironic twist of the regulations, if the borrower possesses enough assets to fully secure the loan, the lender is obligated to at least cover 100% of the loan amount with collateral.

Another point to remember when negotiating collateral is the lender's "golden rule." Know exactly what the company's and individual's limits are before negotiations begin.

Depending on the nature of the borrower's collateral being offered, the following information can assist the lender in understanding these assets:

Real property collateral. If the borrower chooses to pledge a mortgage interest in a parcel of real property to secure the loan, the following documentation is helpful to evaluate and assess this collateral:

✧ *Legal description*—The lender should receive a metes and bounds description of the property, if available, or at least the district and land lot number of the property. This information may be found on the warranty deed, or mortgages, or it may be attached to the property's purchase contract.

✧ *Appraisal*—The lender should receive a copy of a current or aged property appraisal on the subject property, if one exists.

✧ *Description of property improvements*—The lender should receive a list of the various improvements on and features of the property that may increase its value (such as extra curb cuts, zoning classifications, and adjacent development).

✧ *Survey*—The lender should receive a copy of a survey or plat of the property. A survey was probably obtained when the property was purchased. A plat of the property can usually be obtained in the county tax assessor's office.

✧ *Location map*—The lender should receive a portion of a local city or county map that depicts the general area containing the property site, including an indication of the exact position of the property.

✧ *Engineering reports*—The lender should receive any available engineering studies, especially for older facilities. These reports reflect an engineering inspection of the structure and discussion of the general condition of the structure.

✧ *Environmental reports*—The lender should receive any Phase 1, Phase 2, or other environmental inspection reports that may have been previously prepared for the property. If the property contains underground storage tanks (USTs), the lender should be given copies of any testing or inspection results of the USTs.

❝ Lenders are wary to the risks of real property contamination due to much case law which has held them liable for the cleanup. ❞

PART 2

✧ *Environmental questionnaire*—The borrower should be prepared to assist the lender with the completion of the Environmental Questionnaire and Disclosure Statement, which details pertinent information about real property that will secure the loan. If the property has never been used for commercial or agricultural purposes, there may be sufficient grounds for the lender to waive the requirement of a Phase 1 survey, based on the responses to this questionnaire. A copy of this form can be found in Illustration 3-G.

✧ *Photographs*—The lender should receive photographs of the property and its improvements. Visualization of the property can reinforce the lender's recognition of the value of the asset.

✧ *Lease agreements*—The lender should receive copies of leases for tenants who occupy part or all of the subject property. The lender may give the borrower credit for the income generated from renting portions of the property, but the SBA will not recognize that income—the borrower must generate sufficient income from operations to repay its debt. This rule is necessary since the SBA cannot finance an investment property operation, which would be the source of such income.

✧ *Insurance*—The borrower should provide the lender with information describing insurance coverage provided for the real property improvements. While insurers do not insure unimproved property, all improvements should be insured against fire or other hazards to the extent of their replacement costs. Lenders will mandate such coverage as a condition of extending credit using real estate assets as collateral.

✧ *Sales contracts*—If the borrower is acquiring the subject real property as part of the total transaction, the lender should receive a copy of the executed sales contract.

Concerning personal residences. A frequent conflict arises between lenders and borrowers, concerning the lender's requirement that individual business owners encumber their personal residences. The lender justifies this requirement by seeking to secure the personal guaranty of the business loan. Sometimes the equity value of the individual's residence is needed to provide adequate collateral for the loan, but sometimes this equity is not needed.

Environmental Questionnaire and Disclosure Statement

The undersigned, as owner or buyer of the Property described on Exhibit "A" attached hereto, is familiar with the operations presently conducted on the Property, has made a reasonably diligent inquiry into the former uses of the Property and hereby declares and certifies that to the best of its knowledge the following information is true and correct.

A response is required for each item. Please note and continue answers on a separate sheet, if necessary.

COMMERCIAL REAL ESTATE

Current/Former Uses of the Property:

1. Provide dates of current improvement construction and any improvements that have been demolished or removed.

   _____

   _____

2. Description of current uses.

   _____

   _____

3. Names of all owners since 1940.

   _____

   _____

4. Names of previous occupants.

   _____

   _____

5. Description of all previous uses since 1940.

   _____

   _____

6. Current and past uses of adjacent property.

   _____

   _____

ILLUSTRATION 3-G

7. Was the Property ever parceled differently?

(_____) Yes (_____) No – to the best of my knowledge

8. Were there ever-different addresses for the site?

(_____) Yes (_____) No – to the best of my knowledge

If yes, please give full details.

_____

_____

9. Are there, or have there ever been any disposal facilities, dump sites or facilities involving hazardous waste within 2,000 feet of the site?

(_____) Yes (_____) No – to the best of my knowledge

If yes, describe.

_____

_____

Asbestos

1. Is there asbestos currently in any of the construction materials contained in the building?

(_____) Yes (_____) No – to the best of my knowledge

If so, Where?

_____

_____

2. If so, has a survey been conducted to assess the type, amount, location and condition of asbestos on the site?

(_____) Yes (_____) No – to the best of my knowledge

If so, please attach a copy of any survey report.

ILLUSTRATION 3-G CONTINUED

3. Have asbestos air samples been taken?

(_____) Yes   (_____) No – to the best of my knowledge

If so, what were the results?

_____

_____

Polychlorinated Biphenyl's ("PCBs")

1. Have PCBs been used in electrical transformers, capacitors or other equipment at the property?

(_____) Yes   (_____) No – to the best of my knowledge

If so, please describe the use and quantity of PCBs used on the property.

_____

_____

Fuel/Chemical Storage Tanks, Drums, and Pipelines.

1. Are there any above ground or underground gasoline, diesel, fuel oil, chemical storage tanks, or other hazardous materials on the Property?

(_____) Yes   (_____) No – to the best of my knowledge

If so please describe substances stored and capacity of tank(s).

_____

_____

2. Are any of the tanks known to leak now or to have leaked in the past?

(_____) Yes   (_____) No – to the best of my knowledge

When was the most recent test? _____

Results?

_____

_____

ILLUSTRATION 3-G CONTINUED

3. Provide an inventory of materials, quantity, age, construction material, and leak protection systems on each tank.

_____

_____

4. Are any other chemicals stored on the Property in drums or other containers?

    (_____) Yes   (_____) No – to the best of my knowledge

    If so, please describe the substances, quantities stored, and types and conditions of container.

_____

_____

5. Have there been any spills, leaks, or other releases of chemicals on the Property?

    (_____) Yes   (_____) No – to the best of my knowledge

    If so, please describe the chemicals and quantities released, any cleanup measures taken, and the results of any soil or ground water samples performed to detect the presence of the chemicals spilled, leaked, or released on the Property.

_____

_____

6. Please attach copies of any permits or licenses pertaining to the use, storage, handling, or disposal of chemicals on the Property.

7. Are any of the tanks known to leak now or to have leaked in the past?

    (_____) Yes   (_____) No – to the best of my knowledge

Water Discharges

1. List all sources of wastewater discharges to surface waters, ground waters, septic systems, or holding ponds.

_____

_____

ILLUSTRATION 3-G CONTINUED

2. List all sources of wastewater discharges to public sewer systems and storm collection systems.

   _____

   _____

3. Please attach copies of any water discharge permits, licenses, or registration pertaining to operations on the Property.

Air Emissions

1. Describe air emissions from each source of air pollutants, including fuel-burning equipment. Describe type of fuel burned.

   _____

   _____

2. Describe air pollution control equipment used to reduce emissions for each source of air emissions.

   _____

   _____

3. Are air emissions monitored?

   (_____) Yes   (_____) No – to the best of my knowledge

   If so, please indicate frequency of monitoring and attach results.

   _____

   _____

4. Please attach copies of any air permits, licenses, or registrations pertaining to operations on the Property.

Waste Disposal

1. Describe the types of liquid wastes, other than wastewater described above, and solid wastes generated at the Property.

   _____

   _____

ILLUSTRATION 3-G CONTINUED

2.　Describe how the liquid and solid wastes generated at the Property are disposed.

_____

_____

3.　Please attach copies of any waste disposal permits or licenses pertaining to operations on the Property.

Soil Contamination

1.　Have there been any spills, leaks or other releases of hazardous materials on the Property?

(_____) Yes　　　　　　　　(_____) No – to the best of my knowledge

If so, describe the materials and quantities released, any mitigation measures, and the results of soil or ground water samples performed.

_____

_____

2.　Are there any known spills, leaks or other releases on adjacent sites?

(_____) Yes　　　　　　　　(_____) No – to the best of my knowledge

3. Is there evidence of contamination plumes moving onto the site from adjacent sites?

(_____) Yes　　　　　　　　(_____) No – to the best of my knowledge

Agricultural Property

If the property has been or is used for agricultural purposes, the following additional information should be provided.

1.　Have pesticides, herbicides, or other agricultural chemicals been applied to the Property?

(_____) Yes　　　　　　　　(_____) No – to the best of my knowledge

If so, please describe the locations where such pesticides or chemicals were applied, the type of pesticides or chemicals applied in each area, and the results of any soil or ground water analyses performed to detect pesticides or chemicals used at the site.

_____

_____

ILLUSTRATION 3-G CONTINUED

2. Have pesticides, herbicides or other agricultural chemicals been mixed, formulated, rinsed, or disposed of on the Property?

(_____) Yes   (_____) No – to the best of my knowledge

If so, please describe the locations where such pesticides were mixed, formulated, rinsed, or disposed, the type of pesticides or chemicals mixed, formulated, rinsed, or disposed of at each location, and the results of any soil or ground water analyses performed to detect pesticides or chemicals mixed, formulated, rinsed, or disposed at the site.

_____

_____

Industrial Property

If the Property has been or is used for industrial purposes, the following additional information should be provided:

1. Has the Property been used for disposal of any liquid or solid waste?

(_____) Yes   (_____) No – to the best of my knowledge

If so, describe the location of all disposal sites, the type of wastes disposed at each site, the results of any soil or groundwater samples taken in the vicinity of each site, and the manner in which each site not presently in use was closed.

_____

_____

2. Have evaporation or storage ponds been located on the Property?

(_____) Yes   (_____) No – to the best of my knowledge

If so, describe the location of all ponds, the type of wastes placed in each pond, the results of any soil or ground water samples taken in the vicinity of each pond, and the manner in which each pond not presently in use was closed.

_____

_____

ILLUSTRATION 3-G CONTINUED

3. Have wastewater treatment facilities, such as acid neutralization vaults, been located on the Property?

(_____) Yes   (_____) No – to the best of my knowledge

If so, please describe the location of all facilities, the types of wastes treated in each facility, the results of any soil or ground water samples taken in the vicinity of each facility, and the manner in which each facility not presently in use was closed.

_____

_____

4. Are there raw chemicals or waste chemical storage areas on the Property?

(_____) Yes   (_____) No – to the best of my knowledge

If so, please describe the location of all such areas, the type of products or wastes stored in each area, the amount of products or wastes stored in each area, the results of any soil or ground water samples taken in the vicinity of each area, and the manner in which each are not presently in use was closed.

_____

_____

STUDIES, REPORTS, CITATIONS, ENFORCEMENT

1. Attach a copy of each environmental study, report, or assessment that has been performed on the Property's soil, air, or water conditions.

2. Have any federal, state, or local agencies ever investigated cited or been involved on the Property for violations of any environmental law?

(_____) Yes   (_____) No – to the best of my knowledge

If so, describe in full.

_____

_____

ILLUSTRATION 3-G CONTINUED

3. Has any public agency listed the Property as a site requiring or qualifying for cleanup under any environmental law?

    (_____) Yes   (_____) No – to the best of my knowledge

    If so, describe in full

    _____

    _____

ADJOINING PROPERTY

1. Are there any of the above-referenced hazardous substances or pollutants present on adjoining properties or properties in the immediate area of the Property?

    (_____) Yes   (_____) No – to the best of my knowledge

Date: _____   _____

                                      _____

                                      _____

                                      Buyer(s) Signature

                                      _____

                                      _____

                                      _____

                                      Seller(s) Signature

Attachment: Exhibit "A" - Legal Description

ILLUSTRATION 3-G CONTINUED

If the transaction requires the personal equity to secure the loan, the borrower may have to choose whether to pledge the house or pass on the loan commitment. If the individual is married, the spouse is usually a 50% co-owner of the residence and will have to consent to any such encumbrance.

If the transaction does not require the individual's residential equity in order to provide sufficient collateral for the loan, then the lender is seeking "psychological collateral." This collateral position is intended to remind borrowers of their personal commitment to ensuring the lender that the loan will be repaid. While the SBA rarely forecloses on a personal residence, that is the ultimate risk of allowing the lender to place a mortgage on it.

The lender and the SBA want the borrowers to provide some assurance that repayment of the loan will be a high priority with them, regardless of the success of the business operations. Lenders also want to protect their position in the individual's net worth. A personal guaranty can be worthless if unsecured. The individual can obtain additional financing that could lead to other lenders with claims against the unencumbered equity in the personal residence.

This requirement has killed many transactions, because some borrowers are simply not willing to meet this condition. It is a business decision that has to be faced when obtaining small business financing.

There are some strategies to employ in attempting to convince the lender to waive or modify the requirement of using an individual's personal residence as collateral. These suggestions may or may not be applicable, depending on the individual's situation.

✧ The borrower can offer to substitute other assets not previously requested by the lender to replace the personal residence collateral requirement.

✧ The borrower can explain to the lender that the spouse will absolutely not permit such an encumbrance. This position may prove to be an effective negotiating ploy if the equity is not needed to fully secure the loan.

✧ The borrower can offer to pledge a 50% undivided interest in the personal residence. This scenario reduces the individual's exposure, limiting the borrower to having a 50% partner in the residential property.

✧ Before the loan application begins, the borrower can execute a quit claim deed to the spouse for the 50% interest in the personal residence. Because the individual can then legally and morally exclude the residence from the personal financial statement, the lender cannot require it as collateral. This tactic carries a number of potential legal and tax consequences and should be considered only after careful evaluation and counsel from an attorney and CPA.

✧ If the residential equity is not needed to fully secure the loan, the borrower can sometimes get the lender to agree that, upon successful completion of three or four years of loan payments, the lender will release the mortgage against the personal residence. This compromise will demonstrate a good faith effort on both parties to accommodate this sensitive requirement.

If real estate assets to be used as collateral have been owned more than three years, and have likely appreciated in value, insist on an appraisal to establish the collateral value, if it is expected to be significantly higher than cost.

Sometimes the borrower will have to agree to this requirement in order to obtain the business loan. In fact, most small business owners have pledged their residences against business financing at one time or another. If the house has a large first mortgage, it is not likely that the business lender would ever foreclose on the house and take on another large obligation of the individual's.

The borrower usually need not be concerned about the risks of personal financial planning involved with a second lien on the residence. During periods of dropping residential interest rates, most lenders will accommodate a refinance of a residence if it will save the borrower money. The lender will generally agree to subordinate to the new lender or cancel the second lien, so long as the individual executes a new lien to keep the lender in the same position after the new mortgage is obtained.

Personal property collateral. If the borrower chooses to pledge a lien interest in personal property to secure the loan, the following documentation is helpful to evaluate these assets:

✧ *Description*—The lender should receive a schedule of the personal property assets that includes the following information:
  Asset description
  Name of manufacturer
  Date acquired
  Cost

❝ Lenders discount the value of assets used as collateral so to provide for a margin to cover depreciation and liquidation costs.❞

Model and serial numbers

Location (if the borrower has more than one location)

✧ *Appraisal*—The lender should receive a copy of a current or aged appraisal of the subject assets, if one exists. Or, the borrower should assemble relevant quotations of what the assets are currently being marketed for, if this information will demonstrate their relative value.

✧ *Photographs*—If these assets comprise a major portion of the collateral value to be used by the borrower, the lender should receive photographs of the personal property assets. Visualization of the personal property can reinforce the lender's recognition of the value of these assets.

✧ *Price quotations*—If the borrower is planning to acquire personal property assets as part of the total transaction, the lender should receive a price quotation that details the costs of the assets being acquired.

Automotive collateral. If the borrower chooses to pledge a security interest in automotive assets to secure the loan, the following documentation is helpful to evaluate and assess these assets:

✧ *Description*—The lender should receive a schedule of the automotive assets that includes the following information:

Asset description

Name of manufacturer

Date acquired

Cost

Model and serial numbers

Mileage (or log hours)

State of registration and license number

✧ *Title*—The lender should receive copies of the title of the vehicles, if available.

✧ *Appraisal*—The lender should receive a copy of a current or aged appraisal of the subject assets, if one exists. Or, the borrower should assemble relevant quotations of what the assets are currently being marketed for, if this information will demonstrate their relative value.

✧ *Photographs*—If these assets comprise a major portion of the collateral value to be used by the borrower, the lender should receive photographs of the automotive assets. Visualization of the vehicles can reinforce the lender's recognition of the value of these assets.

Securities collateral. If the borrower chooses to pledge a security interest in listed securities to secure the loan, the following documentation is helpful to evaluate these assets:

✧ *Brokerage statements*—The lender should receive copies of recent brokerage account statements or a schedule of the securities portfolio with updated market price quotes if the securities are not held by a brokerage firm. (It is a federal crime to make copies of the share certificates or bonds.)

✧ *Schedule of closely held securities*—If using closely held securities as collateral, the borrower should prepare a memorandum describing the securities. This information should include the borrower's valuation and method of valuation, the relative stake of the entity represented by the borrower's securities, and a recent financial statement of the entity. The borrower will be required to deliver the actual securities to the lender at loan closing for safekeeping during the loan term.

The use of listed securities by the borrower as collateral for a commercial loan is discouraged. The lender will be restricted by Regulation U to value any listed security used as collateral at only 50% of its current market value. Securities priced under $5 per share are generally not accepted by most lenders. And since the lender cannot control the borrower's brokerage account, the lender will have to hold the borrower's bonds or share certificates for safekeeping during the term of the loan.

These securities cannot be pledged or assigned to another entity or person per se. The borrower is required to actually execute a blank sales receipt to the secured party that is relying on these securities as collateral. Language in most collateral agreements permits the lender to actually initiate a trade of these securities if there is a change in the valuation of the securities that diminishes the lender's collateral position.

That is, the lender can sell the securities and liquidate the loan with the borrower's collateral at any time—regardless of whether the borrower is actually in default or the length of the remaining term. Obviously, this act could have significant tax implications for the borrower.

" Resist the lender's efforts to negotiate for too much collateral. 100% coverage with discounted values is enough. "

PART 2

This requirement can also be very risky for the borrower if the need to trade the securities arises in order to respond to changes in the market value of a specific asset. The lender will become part of that potential decision if the borrower decides to pledge these securities as collateral.

Even if the lender is amenable to working with the borrower in such a scenario, the time required to get the lender's consent or to actually obtain possession of the securities can be delayed. The borrower risks that the lender's decision period can lead to additional market losses (or missed opportunities for the borrower to profit).

Delays in getting possession of the securities can interfere with the borrower's ability to meet the delivery requirements of the rigid securities market. The borrower should not risk its portfolio assets in this manner unless there is a written agreement as to how these situations will be handled.

An alternative is to approach the borrower's brokerage firm for a loan on the borrower's portfolio and to substitute these funds for the portion of the loan that would have been obtained using the securities as collateral. Most major brokerage firms make loans on very reasonable terms against listed securities because they are better positioned to monitor the market changes than other lenders.

The individual security holder should be comfortable with the brokerage firm's ability to make a short-notice margin call. The borrower must understand that these loans are subject to being liquidated quickly if the value of the portfolio falls suddenly.

Notes receivable collateral. If the borrower chooses to pledge any notes held in order to secure the loan, the following documentation is helpful to evaluate these assets:

✧ *Description*—The lender should receive a schedule of any notes held by the borrower or business owners, including the following information:

Name of debtor
Principal amount of the note
Interest rate
Terms of repayment
Collateral
Current status of the account (current, past due, etc.)

✧ *Collateral values*—The lender should receive any information available to identify and justify the value of the collateral.

✧ *Copy of notes*—The lender should receive a copy of each note.

Depository account collateral. If the borrower chooses to pledge a security interest in a depository account or deposit certificates to secure the loan, the following documentation is helpful to evaluate these assets:

✧ *Description*—The lender should receive a schedule of all such accounts, including the following information:

Name of depository and name in which the account is identified

Type of account

Account balances

Current interest rate paid on account

Maturity of each account

✧ *Depository account statements*—The lender should receive a copy of recent account statements that confirm the balances listed in the schedule.

The borrower should be aware that IRA accounts, Keogh accounts, and 401(k) accounts are prohibited by law from being used as collateral to secure a loan for any purpose.

Accounts receivable/Inventory collateral. If the borrower chooses to pledge a security interest in the current business assets to secure the loan, the following documentation is helpful to evaluate these assets:

✧ *Accounts receivable aging*—The lender should receive a current aging of accounts receivable.

✧ *Bad debt schedule*—The lender should receive a current schedule of bad debts, with an explanation of each account and the borrower's efforts to recover any sums outstanding.

✧ *Inventory report*—The lender should receive a current detailed report of the borrower's inventory, segregating raw materials, work-in-process, and finished goods.

✧ *Obsolete inventory*—The lender should receive a schedule of the borrower's obsolete inventory and disclosure of the borrower's current book value of those assets.

❝IRA, Keogh, and 401(k) accounts are prohibited by law from being used as collateral to secure a loan for any purpose.❞

PART 2

✧ *Inventory valuation*—The lender should receive a narrative report detailing how the borrower values the inventory and whether any particular components of the inventory may be subject to volatile price risks.

✧ *Borrowing base certificate*—The lender will require the borrower to prepare and submit a borrowing base certificate at regular intervals. This form is used to define the periodic balances and changes in the borrower's eligible collateral for asset-based loans. This form is usually updated on a daily or weekly basis, depending on the specific arrangement between the lender and borrower.

✧ *Customer lists*—The lender should receive a list of the names, addresses, and telephone numbers of the regular customers of the business. The lender needs this information in the event it is ever necessary to attempt to collect the accounts directly from the customers.

Cash surrender value. If the borrower chooses to pledge a security interest in the cash surrender value of a life insurance policy held to secure the loan, the following documentation is helpful to evaluate these assets:

✧ *Copy of policy*—The lender should receive a copy of the insurance policy that has accrued the cash surrender value being offered as collateral.

✧ *Policy declaration*—The lender should receive a recent statement or declaration from the insurance carrier, affirming the balance of the policy's cash surrender value.

✧ *Assignment form*—The borrower should determine whether the insurance carrier requires a specific document to be executed in order to pledge the proceeds of the cash surrender value of the particular policy. If so, the borrower should obtain it from the insurance company.

Marketing Information

The lender should be provided with marketing information about the borrower to understand what the business contributes to the economy and how the borrower attracts other parties to pay for that contribution. In this category, the borrower defines the business, describes how it is marketed, and details future plans for continuing or expanding the revenue base of the business. This information should be compiled in a marketing summary or even a business plan.

What are the products or services of the business? The borrower should define exactly what and how products or services are provided by the business. It is easy to understand a company that sells radios, but it takes a greater study to relate to a company that manufactures digitized, variable overdrive power systems.

The lender should be told what the borrower does with those products or services. Does the borrower manufacture, distribute, retail, resell, liquidate, remodel, recover, research, or remanufacture the products? If the company sells services, is it providing research, information, analysis, advice, or solutions?

The lender should be able to completely understand what specific niche the borrower serves and what particular market the business addresses. And if the borrower can distinguish business as unique, the lender should be able to understand why the business is discernibly different from the competition in the market.

How does the business operate? The lender should be given an idea as to how the business operates. After defining the products or services, the borrower should explain how the business uses them, sells them, manufactures them, or provides them. In addition, the borrower should explain the logical sequence of events that defines the normal course of the business operation. Again, the purpose is to educate the lender about what the borrower does, so that the lender can be more responsive to what the borrower wants to do.

For example, the lender needs to understand that it takes the borrower twenty minutes to prepare, fry, and glaze ten dozen doughnuts, but the borrower can sell fifteen dozen doughnuts in twelve minutes. With this perspective, the lender will appreciate why the borrower wants to acquire a larger capacity to produce doughnuts.

Who is the typical customer for the products or services? Two of the most important management tools available to a business owner are knowing who the customer is and who the customer can be. This information is crucial in the design of the product or service, pricing, business location, capability to perform, and strategic planning to determine and achieve the business goals.

By sharing this information with the lender, the borrower communicates strength as a manager. In addition, this information supports the

❝ Borrowers should be able to provide a concise statement of exactly who, what, how, and where it produces a product or service. ❞

PART 2

request for financing because it will give the lender confidence that the borrower understands the dynamics of the market in which the company operates.

How does the business advertise? Included in the loan application package should be a description of the ways in which the borrower markets and advertises the business. There is not necessarily a right or wrong way to raise awareness about the business, but explaining the activities and media through which the borrower promotes the business provides more credibility for the operation.

The lender should receive copies of any print ads, flyers, brochures, specialty products, or other tangible items that have been distributed to advertise the business. The borrower can also produce a detailed report about media advertising such as radio, television, cable, yellow pages, billboards, or signage. Also important are the civic organizations, trade associations, community activities, contributions, sponsorships, youth sports leagues, fund-raising events, and other involvements through which the borrower has promoted the business.

Who is the competition? Identify the other businesses that provide the same products or services and that are trying to attract the same customers. The borrower should be honest in assessing the competitor's strengths, weaknesses, and advantages. The borrower should be specific about the position of each competitor in the market. In explaining where the borrower stands in comparison, the borrower can describe the plan to maintain or increase market share. The lender needs to know the unique features of the market the borrower is operating within and the opportunities the borrower sees there.

How will the borrower increase revenues? Some of the most important information the borrower can give to the lender is a marketing plan to describe how the business will increase its revenues. If the loan proposal is to provide additional assets or capital to directly increase revenues, the borrower has to support that proposal with a plan detailing exactly how such increases will be accomplished.

The financial projections will provide a numerical measure of the revenue increases the borrower predicts, but the marketing plan has to define the basis for those predictions. In other words, the borrower has to relate to specific numerical increases by describing what causes them. If the loan enables the borrower to make twenty more dozen doughnuts per hour and the borrower can sell these doughnuts for eight hours at

$3.00 per dozen, it stands to reason that the revenues will increase by $480 per day, or $14,400 per month.

This detailed explanation and reasoning lends credibility and rationality to the borrower's financial projections. The process of dissecting and describing the correlation between the marketing efforts and financial results also communicates to the lender that the borrower understands the operational capabilities and limitations of the business.

Miscellaneous Information

Many categories of information are going to relate specifically to the borrower's particular situation, depending on the nature of the business or purpose of the loan. Several of these categories of information are included in this section. Listed here in alphabetical order, they should be used if the business situation applies to them.

Affiliates. Affiliated companies affect a borrower's participation in the SBA loan guaranty programs. Affiliates are defined as any other business entity in which the borrower, or any holder of at least 20% of the borrower's business, own at least a 20% interest. The affiliated companies are considered collectively with the enterprise that the borrower is seeking to finance for purposes of determining eligibility under the SBA loan guaranty program.

That is, any and all business interests in which the borrower and any of the borrower's partners or shareholders, individually or collectively, own at least a 20% stake, are considered along with the entity seeking to borrow money. The purpose is to determine the total sales, number of employees, net income, or net worth to compare to the eligibility limitations for obtaining a loan guaranty.

The lender will be required to confirm the borrower's eligibility if affiliated companies exist, so the borrower should be prepared to provide the lender with the following information. This documentation will be provided to the SBA as well.

- ✧ *Year end financial statement*—The most recent year end financial statement of each affiliated company.
- ✧ *Interim financial statement*—The most recent interim financial statement, if the year end statement provided is more than 90 days old at the time this information is forwarded to the SBA.

❝ There are no two loan applications exactly alike. Every borrower and business have specific, distinguishable attributes. ❞

PART 2

If eligibility is subjected to close scrutiny due to the relative size of any affiliate, it may be necessary to provide the past two years of financial statements in order to permit the lender to average the statements, as provided for in the regulations.

Construction loans. Borrowers seeking to obtain financing for the construction of improvements to real property will be required to have an additional layer of documentation. These documents are specifically intended to satisfy the lender that the business risks are not compounded by any extraordinary risks associated with the construction aspect of the transaction.

The format of a normal construction loan requires the lender to make an initial advance of loan proceeds for the purchase of real property (if necessary) and to make additional draws on an "as completed" basis. In other words, the lender will provide the borrower with enough funds to pay for 20% of the construction costs after 20% of the construction is completed.

This type of lending carries additional risks due to the involvement of a third party who is responsible for the management of the construction project. The building contractor has to get the project started and keep the project moving between the draws of borrowed funds. Contractors use either their own working capital or the borrower's equity, which is advanced through the lender.

In addition, the contractor has to be able to complete the project for the predetermined amount, or the borrower could run short of funds without having a completed building. With the advent of new building standards, zoning codes, and environmental regulations, the lender must be diligent in ensuring that the proposed structure will be constructed in compliance with all applicable laws.

Most lenders wisely use a construction consultant who specializes in monitoring projects to administer the lender's construction loan. This consultant will review the pertinent information before the loan closes in order to assure the lender that the project is feasible, is in compliance with applicable laws, and can be completed within the approved financing.

After loan closing, the consultant will monitor the progress of the project and inspect the site when the contractor requests a loan draw. This inspection will determine whether the contractor has made sufficient progress on the structure to justify the requested loan advance, in accordance with the agreed-upon terms governing the lender's construction loan. By working strictly for the lender, the consultant protects the lender's interest on the project site.

The extraordinary risk faced by the borrower and lender is that the financial condition of the contractor can create serious problems if the contractor cannot keep the project going between loan draws. A stalemate occurs if the contractor draws all of the loan funds available, but cannot pay for labor or materials necessary to get to the next stage of the project.

If the borrower is seeking construction financing, the lender will likely require that the borrower provide the following documentation in order to close the loan, or at least before the first loan draw is approved. References below to the lender may be applicable to the lender's construction consultant, who will supervise the project on behalf of the lender. References to the borrower may be applicable to the contractor, who will likely interface directly with the construction consultant for the transmission of much of this information.

" Construction loans present a new layer of risk to the lender, which involves a third party empowered to spend the loan proceeds on behalf of the borrower. "

PART 2

 ◆ *Performance and material bonds*—Lenders usually will require that the borrower's building contractor provide some form of financial guaranty in order to assure the lender that the contractor's financial condition will not pose a threat to completing the project. This bond, a financial surety given to the lender on behalf of the contractor, ensures that funds will be available to complete the project should the contractor's financial condition interrupt the job.
 ◆ *Executed AIA construction contract*—This contract is a widely accepted standard to define the expectations and requirements of a contractor. It should be submitted with *any and all attachments, amendments, or addendum*, in order for the lender to know the complete agreement and specifications agreed to by the borrower and the contractor. Most lenders require the borrower to enter into these contracts with at least a 10% retainage allowance. The borrower is able to accrue up to 10% of the total amount owed under the contract until final inspection of the project has been approved by the lender.
 ◆ *Cost breakdown*—The lender will require a schedule of values, which defines each component of cost assigned by the contractor for the project. This information is relevant on either a contracted price or cost plus contract. It permits the lender to test

the reliability of the contractor's estimates for the cost of completing the project.

✦ *Boundary survey*—The lender will require a boundary survey to show the parameters of the property and will want to see exactly where the building is to be built. This survey should also demonstrate compliance with local set-back lines and denote any easements on the property.

✦ *Complete set of sealed construction plans*—The lender will require the borrower to provide a full set of blueprints imprinted by the architect. In evaluating the project, the lender and the consultant will compare these plans with the other information that has been submitted.

✦ *Complete set of construction specifications*—The lender will require the borrower to provide a full schedule of specifications.

✦ *Soil reports*—The lender will require the borrower to provide copies of any soil tests completed on the site for the purpose of evaluating the percolation, compression, or contamination.

✦ *Construction schedule*—The lender will require the borrower to provide the construction schedule agreed upon between the contractor and borrower. By confirming that the construction schedule conforms to the term of the proposed loan schedule, the lender can monitor progress after construction begins.

✦ *Curb cut permits*—Where applicable, the lender will require the borrower to provide copies of any curb cut permits that have been obtained from the appropriate government subdivision.

✦ *Building permit*—The lender will require the borrower to provide a copy of the building permit that has been obtained from the appropriate government subdivision.

✦ *Proof of insurance*—The lender will require the borrower to provide a declaration of insurance form confirming that the contractor has liability, workers' compensation, and builder's risk insurance. This insurance has to name the lender as the additionally insured, with written notice required to the lender prior to cancellation.

✦ *Utility letters*—The lender will require the borrower to provide copies of letters obtained from various utility companies, confirming to the borrower that these utilities have agreed to furnish their services to the subject property. At a minimum, these letters should be obtained from the providers of electricity, natural gas, telephone service, water, and the sanitary/storm sewer.

✦ *Zoning letter*—The lender will require the borrower to provide a copy of a letter from the appropriate government subdivision responsible for zoning, confirming the zoning code of the subject property and defining the specific use permitted on the property.

Franchise businesses. Many small business owners choose to affiliate with franchised businesses. There are many advantages to this strategy, such as the access to proprietary products, methods, and services for the business to sell. Also, name recognition in the public marketplace is easier to promote with the backing of a national organization. Although all of these advantages come with a price, franchised businesses generally have a lower failure rate than nonfranchised businesses.

If the borrower is seeking to finance a franchised business, the lender will need the following information in order to precede with the loan request:

✦ *Information on franchisor*—The lender will want to be familiar with the franchisor, particularly with lesser-known ones that may not yet have national recognition. The lender should be given the informational brochures and marketing materials that the borrower received in selecting the particular franchisor.

✦ *Franchise agreement*—The lender will require a copy of the borrower's signed franchise agreement, including all attachments and exhibits. The lender needs to know how the franchisor operates, in the event of a possible disposal of the borrower's franchised operation. Determining which party would control the continued use of the trade name, proprietary equipment, and methods directly affects the franchise's value to the lender as collateral and the lender's risk in dealing with the specific franchisor.

✦ *Franchise disclosure statement*—The Federal Trade Commission requires a franchisor to publish a disclosure report to provide the franchisee with specific operational and financial information about the franchisor and its management. This report is intended to protect prospective buyers from receiving dishonest or fraudulent information from unscrupulous franchise operators or sales representatives. A copy of this report should be submitted to the lender for review and a second opinion.

❝ The contractor's financial condition can be pivotal to the success of a construction loan.❞

PART 2

Special assets. Some borrowers possess certain assets that require extraordinary consideration when offered as collateral for a proposed loan. Although there is no asset that assures the borrower of loan approval, some assets definitely strengthen the chances of loan approval. Lenders relish the opportunity of lending money that is obtainable even if not readily accessible.

These special assets might include any of the following categories detailed below. Included here are suggestions about how borrowers might use such assets to obtain business loans. For any of these options, the borrower should insist that the lender provide financing at a lower interest rate, since the nature of the asset will virtually assure the lender's repayment.

The borrower should seek advice from an attorney before executing any documents pledging these kinds of assets to a lender. With common assets, such as real property or equipment, the Uniform Commercial Code provides the lender with standard language, forms, and precedent to perfect the lender's interest in the borrower's assets. When pledging these special assets, a custom agreement will be written to provide for the lender's security. The borrower's attorney must be involved to protect the borrower's interests in a situation where lenders and their attorneys probably have very little experience. Failure to evaluate such an agreement adequately could lead the borrower to granting rights to the lender that could prove disastrous in the event of default.

The borrower must ensure that the lender's liquidation of the loan would be conducted in a specified manner. Liquidation should not threaten the future value of these special assets nor create unnecessary conflicts that damage the residual value of the asset after the loan has been satisfied.

- ✧ *Contracts*—One special asset is the long-term payout provisions of a deferred contract to which the borrower has satisfied the obligation. Common for former sports professionals, this type of asset is also being seen as the settlement for a job buyout from many Fortune 1000 companies. The contracts often guaranty the recipient a fixed sum to be paid out over a specified term, ensuring an income stream over that period.
- ✧ *Lottery awards*—As more states and sales promotions utilize lotteries, there are more winners. Most of the major awards pro-

vided in these contests are paid out over a twenty-year period and can be assigned to a third party.

◆ *Trusts*—Many persons have the benefit of a trust that has been established to administer either an inheritance or a large financial settlement. These trusts specify to whom, under what conditions, and when the proceeds are to be distributed to the beneficiary.

Unless prohibited by the trust, the income stream can generally be assigned to a third party. The lender will need assurances that there are no special conditions that could alter or cease the income stream. Usually, the corpus assets of the trust cannot be pledged to a third party. This situation may not be true for smaller trusts or for those with a limited number of beneficiaries.

◆ *Tax exempt bonds*—Many tax-exempt securities cannot be used as collateral because they are restricted from third party assignment by the issuer. However, the income stream and final proceeds of the matured securities can be pledged by the holder. The trustee of the bond issuer can be directed to send interest payments and principal proceeds to any party designated by the beneficiary. This arrangement effectively allows the beneficiary to use the corpus of these investments to secure a commercial loan.

❝ Borrowers may find that certain non-traditional assets can be used to secure financing. ❞

SBA Documents

Depending on how active the borrower's lender is in the SBA program, the borrower may be as familiar with SBA documents as the lender. The application for a loan guaranty is typically prepared by the lender or a consultant engaged either by the lender or the borrower. Although the SBA loan application has a bad reputation, it is not really very complicated.

Lenders who process a relatively high volume of SBA-guaranteed loans may have software that produces SBA-approved application documents. Lenders who do not handle many SBA loans may be struggling to manually prepare a seemingly intimidating set of forms, with many unfamiliar pages and blanks.

The application consists of relatively few SBA forms. It is the additional information required to accompany these SBA application forms that seems to create a lot of work for the borrower and lender. The challenge for the lender is to determine the exact set of information needed for a specific transaction before it is submitted to the SBA. No two loans are alike.

There is an advantage to the borrower's drafting and providing the basic SBA application documents to the lender together with the loan proposal. The borrower benefits by providing the requested information in the format that the lender will have to use. Optional but recommended, this presentation can save the lender some work and will hopefully decrease the time required to process the application.

If the lender does not process many SBA applications, the borrower's assistance can be particularly helpful. The lender may actually utilize the documents the borrower prepares, if typed neatly. Whether or not the borrower chooses to complete these documents, it is helpful to understand the purpose of each document and the information being requested.

The following documentation comprises a standard SBA loan guaranty application:

> ✧ *Form 4: Application for business loan*—This SBA form contains much of the basic information requested on the business, including a proposed allocation of the loan proceeds, a detailed schedule of the existing business liabilities, and covenants binding the borrower to specific SBA rules and regulations. A copy of this form can be found in Illustration 3-H.
>
> Most of the additional information requested to support the loan proposal is defined as an exhibit to this document and is intended to accompany the application when submitted to the SBA. Detailed earlier in this chapter these items include:

Exhibit A	Schedule of collateral
Exhibit B	Personal financial statement (Form 413, see Illustration 3-D)
Exhibit C	Business financial statements for the past three years, including balance sheet, profit and loss statement, and reconciliation of net worth; also an interim financial statement no more than 90 days old, with a current aging of accounts receivable and accounts payable; also earnings projections for at least two years.
Exhibit D	Statement of history of the business

Exhibit E	Resumes of the business managers and owners
Exhibit F	Names, social security numbers, and personal financial statements of any identified guarantors
Exhibit G	List of any equipment to be acquired with loan proceeds, and name and address of seller
Exhibit H	Details of any bankruptcy proceedings of any company officers
Exhibit I	Details of any pending lawsuits involving the business
Exhibit J	Names and addresses of any related parties employed by the SBA, a federal agency, or the lender
Exhibit K	Details of any affiliated interests (20% or more) of the owners of the business applicant, along with recent financial statements on their affiliated entities
Exhibit L	Details of any related party from which the business applicant regularly buys products or services, or to which the business applicant regularly sells products or services
Exhibit M	For franchised business applicants, a copy of the franchise agreement and the FTC disclosure statement
Exhibit N	Estimated construction costs and a statement of the source of any additional funds
Exhibit O	Preliminary construction plans and specifications

The volume of SBA loans handled by a lender will dictate how proficient they are at preparing SBA guaranty applications.

✧ *Statements required by law and executive order*—This statement is an attachment to Form 4 and requires applicants to acknowledge their intention to comply with several federal laws and executive orders. This acknowledgment is documented with the applicant's signature on an attached form.

These particular laws and executive orders include the Freedom of Information Act (5 U.S.C. 552), the Freedom of Financial Privacy Act of 1978 (12 U.S.C. 3401), the Flood Disaster Protection Act (42 U.S.C. 4011), the Executive Orders—Floodplain Management & Wetland Protection (42 F.R. 26951 & 42 F.R. 26961), the Occupational Safety and Health Act (15 U.S.C. 651 et seq.), Civil Rights Legislation, the

OMB Approval No. 3245-0016
Expiration Date: 10-31-98

U.S. Small Business Administration

APPLICATION FOR BUSINESS LOAN

Individual	Full Address

Name of Applicant Business	Tax I.D. No. or SSN

Full Street Address of Business	Tel. No. (inc. A/C)

City	County	State	Zip	Number of Employees (including subsidiaries and affiliates)
Type of Business		Date Business Established		At Time of Application
Bank of Business Account and Address				If Loan is Approved
				Subsidiaries or Affiliates (Separate from above)

Use of Proceeds: (Enter Gross Dollar Amounts Rounded to the Nearest Hundreds)	Loan Requested		Loan Requested
Land Acquisition		Payoff SBA Loan	
New Construction/ Expansion Repair		Payoff Bank Loan (Non SBA Associated)	
Acquisition and/or Repair of Machinery and Equipment		Other Debt Payment (Non SBA Associated	
Inventory Purchase		All Other	
Working Capital (Including Accounts Payable		Total Loan Requested	
Acquisition of Existing Business		Term of Loan - (Requested Mat.)	___ Yrs.

PREVIOUS SBA OR OTHER FEDERAL GOVERNMENT DEBT: If you or any principals or affiliates have 1) ever requested Government Financing or 2) are delinquent on the repayment of any Federal Debt complete the following:

Name of Agency	Original Amount of Loan	Date of Request	Approved or Declined	Balance	Current or Past Due
	$			$	
	$			$	

ASSISTANCE   List the names(s) and occupations of any who assisted in the preparation of this form, other than the applicant.

Name and Occupation	Address	Total Fees Paid	Fees Due
Name and Occupation	Address	Total Fees Paid	Fees Due

PLEASE NOTE: The estimated burden hours for the completion of this form is 19.8 hours per response. If you have any questions or comments concerning this estimate or any other aspect of this information collection please contact, Chief Administrative Information Branch, U.S. Small Business Administration, Washington, D.C. 20416 and Gary Waxman, Clearance Officer, Paperwork Reduction Project (3745-0016), Office of Management and Budget, Washington, D.C. 20503.

SBA FORM 4

ILLUSTRATION 3-H

ALL EXHIBITS MUST BE SIGNED AND DATED BY PERSON SIGNING THIS FORM

BUSINESS INDEBTEDNESS: Furnish the following information on all installment debts, contracts, notes, and mortgages payable. Indicate by an asterisk(*) items to be paid by loan proceeds and reason for paying same (present balance should agree with the latest balance sheet submitted).

To Whom Payable	Original Amount	Original Date	Present Balance	Rate of Interest	Maturity Date	Monthly Payment	Security	Current or Past Due
Acct. #	$		$			$		
Acct. #	$		$			$		
Acct. #	$		$			$		
Acct. #	$		$			$		

MANAGEMENT (Proprietor, partners, officers, directors all holders of outstanding stock - <u>100% of ownership must be shown</u>). Use separate sheet if necessary.

Name and Social Security Number and Position Title	Complete Address	% Owned	*Military Service From	To	*Race	*Sex

*This data is collected for statistical purpose only. It has no bearing on the credit decision to approve or decline this application.

THE FOLLOWING EXHIBITS MUST BE COMPLETED WHERE APPLICABLE. ALL QUESTIONS ANSWERED ARE MADE A PART OF THE APPLICATION.

For Guaranty Loans please provide an original and one copy (Photocopy is Acceptable) of the Application Form, and all Exhibits to the participating lender. For Direct Loans submit one original copy of the application and Exhibits to SBA.

1. Submit SBA Form 912 (Personal History Statement) for each person e.g. owners, partners, officers, directors, major stockholders, etc.; the instructions are on SBA Form 912.

2. If you collateral consists of (A) Land and Building, (B) Machinery and Equipment, (C) Furniture and Fixtures, (D) Accounts Receivable, (E) Inventory, (F) Other, please provide an itemized list (labeled Exhibit A) that contains serial and identification numbers for all articles that had an original value greater than $500. Include a legal description of Real Estate offered as collateral.

3. Furnish a signed current personal balance sheet (SBA Form 413 may be used for this purpose) for each stockholder (with 20% or greater ownership), partner, officer and owner. Social Security number should be included on personal financial statement. It should be as of the same date as the most recent business financial statements. Label the Exhibit B.

4. Include the statements listed below: 1,2,3 for the last three years; also 1,2,3,4 as of the same date, which are current within 90 days of filing the application; and statement 5, if applicable. This is Exhibit C (SBA has Management Aids that help in the preparation of financial statements.) All information must be **signed and dated**.

1. Balance Sheet   2. Profit and Loss Statement
3. Reconciliation of Net Worth
4. Aging of Accounts Receivable and Payable
5. Earnings projects for at least one year where financial statements for the last three years are unavailable or where requested by District Office.
  (If Profit and Loss Statement is not available, explain why and substitute Federal Income Tax Forms.)

5. Provide a brief history of your company and a paragraph describing the expected benefits it will receive from the loan. Label it Exhibit D.

6. Provide a brief description similar to a resume of the education, technical and business background for all the people listed under Management. Please mark it Exhibit E.

SBA FORM 4

Page 2

ILLUSTRATION 3-H CONTINUED

ALL EXHIBITS MUST BE SIGNED AND DATED BY PERSON SIGNING THIS FORM

7. Do you have any co-signers and/or guarantors for this loan? If so, please submit their names, addresses, tax id Numbers, and current personal balance sheet(s) as Exhibit F.

8. Are you buying machinery or equipment with your loan money? If so, you must include a list of equipment and cost as quoted by the seller and his name and address. This is Exhibit G.

9. Have you or any officer of your company ever been involved in bankruptcy or insolvency proceedings? If so, please provide the details as Exhibit H. If none, check here: ☐Yes ☐No

10. Are you or your business involved in any pending lawsuits? If yes, provide the details as Exhibit I. If none, check here: ☐Yes ☐No

11. Do you or your spouse or any member of your household, or anyone who owns, manages, or directs your business or their spouses or members of their households work for the Small Business Administration, Small Business Advisory Council, SCORE or ACE, any Federal Agency, or the participating lender? If so, please provide the name and address of the person and the office where employed. Label this Exhibit J. If none, check here: ☐Yes ☐No

12. Does your business, its owners or majority stockholders own or have a controlling interest in other businesses? If yes, please provide their names and the relationship with your company along with a current balance sheet and operating statement for each. This should be Exhibit K.

13. Do you buy from, sell to, or use the services of any concern in which someone in your company has a significant financial interest? If yes, provide details on a separate sheet of paper labeled Exhibit L.

14. If your business is a franchise, include a copy of the franchise agreement and a copy of the FTC disclosure statement supplied to you by the Franchisor. Please include it as Exhibit M.

CONSTRUCTION LOANS ONLY

15. Include a separate exhibit (Exhibit N) the estimated cost of the project and a statement of the source of any additional funds.

16. Provide copies of preliminary construction plans and specifications. Include them as Exhibit O. Final plans will be required prior to disbursement.

DIRECT LOANS ONLY

17. Include two bank declination letters with your application. (In cities with 200,000 people or less, one letter will be sufficient.) These letters should include the name and telephone number of the persons contacted at the banks, the amount and terms of the loan, the reason for decline and whether or not the bank will participate with SBA.

EXPORT LOANS

18. Does your business presently engage in Export Trade?
Check here: ☐Yes ☐No

19. Do you have plans to begin exporting as a result of this loan?
Check here: ☐Yes ☐No

20. Would you like information on Exporting?
Check here: ☐Yes ☐No

AGREEMENTS AND CERTIFICATIONS

Agreements of non-employment of SBA Personnel: I agree that if SBA approves this loan application I will not, for at least two years, hire as an employee or consultant anyone that was employed by the SBA during the one year period prior to the disbursement of the loan.

Certification: I certify: (a) I have not paid anyone connected with the Federal Government for help in getting this loan. I also agree to report to the SBA office of the Inspector General, Washington, D.C. 20416 any Federal Government employee who offers, in return for any type of compensation, to help get this loan approved.

(b) All information in this application and the Exhibits are true and complete to the best of my knowledge and are submitted to SBA so SBA can decide whether to grant a loan or participate with a lending institution in a loan to me. I agree to pay for or reimburse SBA for the cost of any surveys, title or mortgage examinations, appraisals, credit reports, etc., performed by non-SBA personnel provided I have given my consent.

(c) I understand that I need not pay anybody to deal with SBA. I have read and understand SBA Form 159 which explains SBA policy on representatives and their fees.

(d) As consideration for any Management, Technical, and Business Development Assistance that may be provided, I waive all claims against SBA and its consultants.

If you make a statement that you know to be false or if you over value a security in order to help obtain a loan under the provisions of the Small Business Act, you can be fined up to $5,000 or be put in jail for up to two years, or both.

If Applicant is a proprietor or general partner, sign below.

By: _____
                                              Date

If Applicant is a Corporation, sign below:

_____
Corporate Name and Seal   Date

By: _____
              Signature of President

Attested by: _____

Signature of Corporate Secretary

SBA FORM 4   Page 3

ILLUSTRATION 3-H CONTINUED

U.S. SMALL BUSINESS ADMINISTRATION

SCHEDULE OF COLLATERAL
Exhibit A

OMB Approval No.: 3245-0016
Expiration Date: 10-31-98

Applicant		
Street Address		
City	State	Zip Code

LIST ALL COLLATERAL TO BE USED AS SECURITY FOR THIS LOAN

Section I - REAL ESTATE

Attach a copy of the deed(s) containing a full legal description of the land and show the location (street address) and city where the deed(s) is recorded. Following the address below, give a brief description of the improvements, such as size, type of construction, use, number of stories, and present condition (use additional sheet if more space is required).

LIST PARCELS OF REAL ESTATE

Address	Year Acquired	Original Cost	Market Value	Amount of Lien	Name of Lienholder

Description(s)

SBA FORM 4 SCHEDULE A

ILLUSTRATION 3-H CONTINUED

SECTION II - PERSONAL PROPERTY

All items listed herein must show manufacturer or make, model, year, and serial number. Items with no serial number must be clearly identified (use additional sheet if more space is required).

Description - Show Manufacturer, Model, Serial No.	Year Acquired	Original Cost	Market Value	Current Lien Balance	Name of Lienholder

All information contained herein is TRUE and CORRECT to the best of my knowldege. I understand that FALSE statements may result in forfeiture of benefits and possible fine and prosecution by the U.S. Attorney General (Ref. 18 U.S.C. 100).

_____ Date _____

_____ Date _____

SBA FORM 4 SCHEDULE A

ILLUSTRATION 3-H CONTINUED

Equal Credit Opportunity Act (15 U.S.C. 1691), the Executive Order 11738—Environmental Protection (38 F.R. 25161), the Debt Collection Act of 1982, Deficit Reduction Act of 1984 (31 U.S.C. 3701 et seq. and other titles), the Immigration Reform and Control Act of 1986 (Pub. L. 99-603), and the Lead-Based Paint Poisoning Prevention Act (42 U.S.C. 4821 et seq.).

This list contains references to several laws that average citizens may not be familiar with. A summary of each executive order and law is provided with the form so that the borrower can review the specifications before executing the form.

◇ *Statement of financial need*—This document describes the proposed financial transaction, defines the entire costs or expenses involved, and identifies the source of funds for each cost or expense. A copy of this form can be found in Illustration 3-I.

◇ *Form 413: Personal financial statement*—This document is described earlier in this chapter in the section discussing personal financial information. It is usually included as Exhibit B to the business loan application. A copy of this form can be found in Illustration 3-D.

◇ *Form 912: Statement of personal history*—This document is described earlier in this chapter in the section discussing personal administrative information. A copy of this form can be found in Illustration 3-J.

◇ *Form 159: Compensation agreement*—This document is needed to disclose to the SBA any professional fees that have been or will be paid by the borrower in connection with the SBA loan. This form is to be used for any consultants, accountants, attorneys, or other parties who have provided specific services or supporting documents to the borrower in preparing the SBA application or closing the SBA loan. A copy of this form can be found in Illustration 3-K.

◇ *Form 652: Assurance of compliance for nondiscrimination*—This document is required to attest that the borrower and any subsequent recipients of the SBA-guaranteed loan proceeds agree to comply with SBA regulations pertaining to discrimination. These regulations require that no person be excluded from participation in, or be denied the benefits of, any federal financial assistance from

❝ Borrowers can submit information to the lender on SBA forms which streamline the lender's job.❞

PART 2

Statement of Financial Need

	Funds Provided By Owners	Use of Loan Proceeds	Total Funds Required
A. Fixed Assets Acquisition/Repair			
Automotive	_____	_____	_____
Furniture and Fixtures	_____	_____	_____
Land	_____	_____	_____
Building Construction / Purchase	_____	_____	_____
Building Improvements	_____	_____	_____
Leasehold Improvements	_____	_____	_____
1. Other:_____	_____	_____	_____
2. Other:_____	_____	_____	_____
Total Fixed Asset Acquisition	_____	_____	_____
B. Debt Repayment			
Accounts Payable (Attach List)	_____	_____	_____
Notes Payable (Complete "Indebtedness" SBA Form 4)	_____	_____	_____
Total Debt Payment	_____	_____	_____
C. Working Capital			
Operating Cash	_____	_____	_____
Inventory	_____	_____	_____
Prepaid Expenses (Attach List)	_____	_____	_____
Advertising	_____	_____	_____
Deposits (Attach List)	_____	_____	_____
Training	_____	_____	_____
Accounts Receivable Financing	_____	_____	_____
Organizational Costs (Attach List)	_____	_____	_____
Other (Specify) Soft Costs	_____	_____	_____
1 Other:_____	_____	_____	_____
2 Other:_____	_____	_____	_____
3 Other:_____	_____	_____	_____
Total Working Capital	_____	_____	_____
TOTAL FUNDS	_____	_____	_____

Source of funds provided by owners:

1.
2.
3.

Signature:_____   Date:_____

ILLUSTRATION 3-1

Return Executed Copies 1, 2, and 3 to SBA

OMB APPROVAL NO.3245-0178
Expiration Date:7/31/2000

United States of America

SMALL BUSINESS ADMINISTRATION

STATEMENT OF PERSONAL HISTORY

Please Read Carefully - Print or Type

Each member of the small business concern or the development company requesting assistance must submit this form in TRIPLICATE for filing with the SBA application. This form must be filled out and submitted by:

1. If a sole proprietorship by the proprietor.
2. If a partnership by each partner.
3. If a corporation or a development company, by each officer, director, and additionally by each holder of 20% or more of the voting stock.
4. Any other person including a hired manager, who has authority to speak for and commit the borrower in the management of the business.

Name and Address of Applicant (Firm Name)(Street, City, State, and ZIP Code)

SBA District/Disaster Area Office

Amount Applied for (when applicable)   File No. (if known)

1. Personal Statement of: (State name in full, if no middle name, state (NMN), or if initial only, indicate initial.) List all former names used, and dates each name was used. Use separate sheet if necessary.

First   Middle   Last

Name and Address of participating lender or surety co. (when applicable and known)

2. Date of Birth (Month, day, and year)

3. Place of Birth: (City & State or Foreign Country)

4. Give the percentage of ownership or stock owned or to be owned in the small business concern or the Development Company

Social Security No.

U.S. Citizen?   ☐ YES   ☐ NO
If no, give alien registration number:

5. Present residence address:
From:
To:
Address:

Most recent prior address (omit if over 10 years ago):
From:
To:
Address:

Home Telephone No. (Include A/C):

Business Telephone No. (Include A/C):

IT IS AGAINST SBA'S POLICY TO PROVIDE ASSISTANCE TO PERSONS NOT OF GOOD CHARACT ER; THEREFORE, CONSIDERATION IS GIVEN TO A PERSON'S BEHAVIOR, INTEGRITY, CANDOR, AND DISPOSITION TOWARD CRIMINAL ACTIONS.   IT IS ALSO AGAINST SBA'S POLICY TO PROVIDE ASSISTANCE NOT IN THE BEST INTEREST OF THE UNITED STATES; FOR EXAMPLE, IF THERE IS REASON TO BELIEVE THE EFFECT OF SUCH ASSISTANCE WILL BE TO ENCOURAGE OR SUPPORT, DIRECTLY OR INDIRECTLY, ACTIVITIES HARMFUL TO THE SECURITY OF THE UNITED STATES.

THEREFORE, IT IS IMPORTANT THAT THE NEXT THREE QUESTIONS BE ANSWERED TRUTHFULLY AND COMPLETELY. AN ARREST OR CONVICTION RECORD WILL NOT NECESSARILY DISQUALIFY YOU; HOWEVER, AN UNTRUTHFUL A NSWER WILL CAUSE YOUR APPLICATION TO BE DENIED.

IF YOU ANSWER "YES" TO 6, 7, OR 8, FURNISH DETAILS IN A SEPARATE EXHIBIT. INCL UDE DATES, LOCATION, FINES, SENTENCES, WHETHER MISDEMEANOR OR FELONY, DATES OF PAROLE/PROBATION, UNPAID FINES OR PENALTIES, NA ME(S) UNDER WHICH CHARGED, AND ANY OTHER PERTINENT INFORMATION.

6. Are you presently under indictment, on parole or probation?
☐ Yes   ☐ No   (If yes, indicate date parole or probation is to expire.)

7. Have you ever been charged with and or arrested for any criminal offense other than a minor motor vehicle violation? Include offenses which have been dismissed, discharged, or not prosecuted (All arrests and charges must be disclosed and explained on an attached sheet.)
☐ Yes   ☐ No

8. Have you ever been convicted, placed on pretrial diversion, or placed on any form of probation, including adjudication withheld pending probation, for any criminal offense other than a minor vehicle violation?
☐ Yes   ☐ No

9. I authorize the Small Business Administration Office of Inspector General to request criminal record information about me from criminal justice agencies for the purpose of determining my eligibility for programs authorized by the Small Business Act, as amended.

CAUTION: Knowingly making a false statement on this form is a violation of Federal law and could result in criminal prosecution, significant civil penalties, and a denial of your loan, surety bond, or other program participation. A false statement is punishable under 18 USC 1001 by imprisonment of not more than five years and/or a fine of not more than $10,000; under 15 USC 645 by imprisonment of not more than two years and/or a fine of not more than $5,000; and, if submitted to a Federally insured institution, under 18 USC 1014 by imprisonment of not more than twenty years and/or a fine of not more than $1,000,000.

Signature   Title   Date

Agency Use Only

10. ☐ Fingerprints Waived
Date   Approving Authority

☐ Fingerprints Required
Date Sent to OIG   Date   Approving Authority

11. ☐ Cleared for Processing
Date   Approving Authority

☐ Request a Character Evaluation
Date   Approving Authority

Please Note: The estimated burden for completing this form is 15 minutes per response. You will not be required to respond to this information if a valid OMB approval number is not displayed. If you have questions or comments concerning this estimate or other aspects of this information collection, please contact the U.S. Small Business Administration, Chief, Administrative Information Branch, Washington, D.C. 20416 and/or Office of Management and Budget, Clearance Officer, Paperwork Reduction Project.

SBA FORM 912

ILLUSTRATION 3-J

	SBA LOAN NO.

COMPENSATION AGREEMENT FOR SERVICES IN CONNECTION WITH APPLICATION AND LOAN FROM (OR IN PARTICIPATION WITH) SMALL BUSINESS ADMINISTRATION

The undersigned representative (attorney, accountant, engineer, appraiser, etc.) hereby agrees that the undersigned has not and will not, directly or indirectly, charge or receive any payment in connection with the application for or the making of the loan except for services actually performed on behalf of the Applicant. The undersigned further agrees that the amount of payment for such services shall not exceed an amount deemed reasonable by SBA (and, if it is a participation loan, by the participating lending institution), and to refund any amount in excess of that deemed reasonable by SBA (and the participating institution). This agreement shall supersede any other agreement covering payment for such services.

A general description of the services performed, or to be performed, by the undersigned and the compensation paid or to be paid are set forth below. If the total compensation in any case exceeds $1,000 (or $300 for: (1) regular business loans of $15,000 or less; or (2) all disaster home loans) or if SBA should otherwise require, the services must be itemized on a schedule attached showing each date services were performed, time spent each day, and description of service rendered on each day listed.

The undersigned Applicant and representative hereby certify that no other fees have been charged or will be charged by the representative in connection with this loan, unless provided for in the loan authorization specifically approved by SBA.

GENERAL DESCRIPTION OF SERVICES

Paid Previously	$ _____
Additional Amount to be Paid	$ _____
Total Compensation	$ _____

(Section 13 of the Small Business Act (15 USC 642) requires disclosures concerning fees. Parts 103, 108, and 120 of Title 13 of the Code of Federal Regulations contain provisions covering appearances and compensation of persons representing SBA applicants. Section 103.13-5 authorizes the suspension or revocation of the privilege of any such person to appear before SBA for charging a fee deemed unreasonable by SBA for services actually performed, charging of unreasonable expenses, or violation of this agreement. Whoever commits any fraud, by false or misleading statement or representation, or by conspiracy, shall be subject to the penalty of any applicable Federal or State statute.)

Dated _____, 19 _____

_____
(Representative)

By _____

The Applicant hereby certifies to SBA that the above representations, description of services and amounts are correct and satisfactory to the Applicant

Dated _____, 19 _____

_____
(Applicant)

By _____

The participating lending institution hereby certifies that the above representations of service rendered and amounts charged are reasonable and satisfactory to it.

Dated _____, 19 _____

_____
(Lender)

By _____

NOTE: Foregoing certification must be executed, if by a corporation, in corporate name by duly authorized officer and duly attested; if by a partnership, in the firm name, together with signature of a general partner.

PLEASE NOTE: The estimated burden hours for the completion of this form of SBA Form 147, 148, 159, 160, 160A, 529B, 928, and 1059 is 6 hours per response. You will not be required to respond to this information collection if a valid OMB approval number is not displayed. If you have any questions or comments concerning this estimate or other aspects of this information collection, please contact the U.S. Small Business Administration, Chief, Administrative Information Branch, Washington D.C. 20416 and/or Office of Management and Budget, Clearance Officer, Paperwork Reduction Project (3245-0201), Washington, D.C. 20503.

SBA FORM 159

ILLUSTRATION 3-K

U.S. SMALL BUSINESS ADMINISTRATION
ASSURANCE OF COMPLIANCE FOR NONDISCRIMINATION

_____ Applicant/Licensee/Recipient/Subrecipient, (hereinafter referred to as applicant) in consideration of Federal financial assistance from the Small Business Administration, herewith agrees that it will comply with the nondiscrimination requirements of 13 CFR parts 112, 113, and 117, of the Regulations issued by the Small Business Administration (SBA).

13 CFR Parts 112, 113 and 117 require that no person shall on the grounds of age, color, handicap, marital status, national origin, race, religion or sex, be excluded from participation in, be denied the benefits of or otherwise be subjected to discrimination under any program or activity for which the applicant received Federal financial assistance from SBA.

Applicant agrees to comply with the record keeping requirements of 13 CFR 112.9, 113.5, and 117.9 as set forth in SBA Form 793, "Notice to New SBA Borrowers", to permit effective enforcement of 13 CFR 112, 113 and 117. Such record keeping requirements have been approved under OMB Number 3245-0076. Applicant further agrees to obtain or require similar Assurance of Compliance for Nondiscrimination from subrecipients, contractors/subcontractors, successors, transferees and assignees as long as it/they receive or retain possession of any Federal financial assistance from SBA. In the event the applicant fails to comply with any provision or requirements of 13 CFR Parts 112, 113 and 117, SBA may call, cancel, terminate, accelerate repayment or suspend any or all Federal financial assistance provided by SBA.

Executed the _____ day of _____ 19 _____

_____
Name Address & Phone No. of Applicant

By _____
Typed Name & Title of Authorized Official

Corporate Seal

_____
Signature of Authorized Official

_____
Name Address & Phone No. of Subrecipient

By _____
Typed Name & Title of Authorized Official

Corporate Seal

_____
Signature of Authorized Official

SBA FORM 652

ILLUSTRATION 3-L

**Certification Regarding
Debarment, Suspension, Ineligibility and Voluntary Exclusion
Lower Tier Covered Transactions**

This certification is required by the regulations implementing Executive Order 12549, Debarment and Suspension, 13 CFR Part 145. The regulations were published as Part VII of the May 26, 1988 *Federal Register* (pages 19160-19211). Copies of the regulations may be obtained by contacting the person to which this proposal is submitted.

(BEFORE COMPLETING CERTIFICATION, READ INSTRUCTIONS ON REVERSE)

(1) The prospective lower tier participant certifies, by submission of this proposal, that neither it nor its principals are presently debarred, suspended, proposed for disbarment, declared ineligible, or voluntarily excluded from participation in this transaction by any Federal department or agency.

(2) Where the prospective lower tier participant is unable to certify to any of the statements in this certification, such prospective participant shall attach an explanation to this proposal.

Business Name _____

Date _____   By _____
                                            Name and Title of Authorized Representative

                                         _____
                                         Signature of Authorized Representative

SBA FORM 1624

ILLUSTRATION 3-M

the SBA based on age, color, handicap, marital status, national origin, race, religion, or sex. A copy of this form can be found in Illustration 3-L.

✧ *Form 1624: Certification regarding debarment*—This document is required to attest that the borrower, the individual, and the business entity have not been debarred from doing business with the federal government due to any administrative, disciplinary, or other action specifically restricting the respective party. A copy of this form can be found in Illustration 3-M.

✧ *IRS Form 4506: Request for copy or transcript of tax form*—This document permits the SBA to obtain a copy of the borrower's income tax return for verification comparison to the income tax returns submitted by the borrower in the loan application. A copy of this form can be found in Illustration 3-E.

✧ *Justification*—The lender (and therefore the borrower) has to provide justification for why the SBA guaranty should be provided for the proposed transaction. There is no regulation form on which to submit this information.

There are several reasons why SBA-guaranteed loans are superior to conventional financing in the lending marketplace. These reasons include:

Terms—The SBA term limits allow the small business concern to borrow money for longer terms, which mean lower debt service and better cash flow for companies in their earlier years.

Interest rates—In some instances, the interest rate caps on SBA-guaranteed loans represent a lower rate than many small businesses would qualify for otherwise.

Qualification—Traditional lending sources avoid certain industries because of the inherent risks of lending money on special use assets, such as bowling allies or day care centers. The guaranty provides incentives for lenders to extend funds into these industries.

In addition, the SBA is sensitive to two particular uses of loan proceeds, both of which must be explained in order to justify the loan:

❝ SBA loans offer superior terms to conventional loans:

- *Longer repayment period*
- *Competitive interest rate*
- *Financing available to specialized industries. ❞*

PART 2

1. *Change of ownership.* The lender must demonstrate that the borrower is purchasing an entity not as an investment, but rather as a business to be personally operated by the borrower. Further, the lender has to prove that the buyer and seller are not related, and that there is not better alternative financing available.

2. *Refinancing debt.* The lender must demonstrate that there is a clear advantage to the borrower to refinance any debt with an SBA loan and that the previous loans have performed as agreed. The SBA will examine transcripts of the lender's previous loan to confirm that the lender is not unloading a bad loan on the agency.

There are a few additional SBA documents required with the loan application that must be prepared by the lender. These include Form 4-I (the Lender's Application for Guaranty) containing the Lender's Analysis, and Form 1846, the Statement Regarding Lobbying.

All documentation required by the lender to render a credit decision and to qualify for the SBA guaranty must be compiled by the lender and then submitted to the SBA. The lender must have approved the loan and be prepared to make it, subject to the SBA guaranty, before the SBA will review it.

While the list of data contained in this chapter may seem staggering, it is mostly information that is routinely available to and used by business owners. Government regulations increase the size of this list often just to comply with unrelated legislation. Neither the lender nor the SBA can reduce or relax federal rules, but must find ways to ensure compliance without interfering with transactions.

The SBA and the lender have a responsibility to administer and abide by the law. To modify some of the more irrelevant, burdensome requirements of this process will require business owners to seek reform in Congress to alleviate some of the regulatory interference and costs of borrowing capital for small businesses.

Another important assertion needed in the borrower's justification statement is confirmation that the borrower cannot locate reasonable financing elsewhere. Lack of funds available on similar repayment terms or a lower interest rate permits the borrower to offer this statement to assure the SBA that government funds are not unnecessarily supplementing the borrower's financing when alternatives are available.

CHAPTER 4

Explaining Circumstances

Sometimes things happen. More than ever before, lenders seem to be open to work with borrowers who have suffered through events in the past that devastated credit records. Learn:

- ✧ How to deal with a tough track record
- ✧ How to offer an explanation
- ✧ Getting over bad times
- ✧ It happens

Some borrowers have faced special circumstances that weaken their position for a loan proposal or dampen the lender's enthusiasm for considering a borrower's request. Because these situations require greater preparation, the borrower's determination is tested to get business financing.

These circumstances can vary, ranging from the indiscretions of youth to medical catastrophes. Often these circumstances have nothing to do with the borrower's past business performance, moral obligation to repay debts, or prospects for succeeding in the future. It is important for the borrower to be meticulously honest with the lender in discussing these situations. Was the borrower at fault? Was the borrower a victim? Can the borrower rehabilitate this financial condition?

The lender must evaluate if, based on this information, the borrower presents a greater risk and should therefore not be considered. This question is automatically answered affirmatively unless the borrower can convince the lender to investigate the previous problems in perspective.

The following suggestions are intended to assist borrowers in overcoming special conditions under which a personal credit record was tarnished through events beyond anyone's control. These events need not prevent the borrower from advancing to the next opportunity in life. This discussion is not intended to instruct anyone how to develop excuses to perpetuate a record of failure, deceit, or fraud. By following these important steps in explaining the particular situation, borrowers can develop thorough documentation to support explanations required in these matters.

Bankruptcy

Bankruptcy is a fact of life. Since bankruptcy protection statutes were liberalized in the 1980s, the number of businesses and individuals seeking protection has increased dramatically. From a business stand-point, bankruptcy is often a legitimate strategy. It is a method to deal with overwhelming liabilities or a dire situation. Although sometimes bankruptcy is abused, at times it can be the debtor's best logical decision.

But bankruptcy is not always a good strategy and can be very costly. Many businesses receive poor advice and seek bankruptcy prematurely, without recognition of the consequences. Once that decision is made, the debtor will live with it for many years.

Many lenders have a knee-jerk reaction to parties who have sought protection under bankruptcy laws. In fact, many lenders treat bank-ruptcy as the ultimate violation of the borrower's morality. Legitimate bankruptcy cases do not involve morals—they are about money. Bankruptcy is usually not about an unwillingness to repay money, but rather the inability to repay money. Because many lenders do not know enough about bankruptcy, it is a challenge to obtain financing once it is part of the borrower's track record.

Bankruptcy cases are under the jurisdiction of a federal court to pro-tect individuals or companies from creditors in circumstances where the debtor's liabilities exceed their assets. This protection is intended to pre-vent a particular creditor from unfairly collecting a debt at the expense of other creditors, violating the debtor's legal rights, or beyond the debtor's realistic ability to pay. Bankruptcy can help debtors by providing time to reorganize financial affairs in order to pay off debts without undue inter-ference from creditors.

There are three classes of bankruptcy:

Chapter 7—This class of bankruptcy is for liquidation of the debtor's estate to settle claims against it. The proceeds are distributed against claims prioritized by the court.

Skeleton in the closet?

✦ Be forthright with all the facts

✦ Present a comprehensive explanation

✦ Be prepared for tough examination of the facts

Chapter 11—This class of bankruptcy is for the reorganization of businesses (or high net worth individuals) in which debtors are permitted to restructure their financial affairs in order to pay all debts while containing the operation of the business.

Chapter 13—This class of bankruptcy is for individuals (with assets less than $350,000) to restructure or renegotiate the repayment terms of all liabilities with creditors. Regular payments are made through a court-appointed trustee until all debts are repaid.

There are countless circumstances that lead parties to seek the protection of a bankruptcy court. Without doubt, many parties are forced to choose this strategy due to events beyond anyone's control. In some cases, borrowers will have the chance to overcome the stigma of bankruptcy and to obtain new financing for starting over. Chances are better if the bankruptcy was an individual case rather than a business case.

Consider the following true-life examples of justifiable bankruptcies:

The first example involved a mother who delivered a premature baby. In receiving the best available medical treatment, the baby stayed in the hospital for six months. Thirty days after the child was released from the hospital, the parents were expected to pay a $300,000 invoice.

During the pregnancy term, the father was laid off from an international airline that had filed for bankruptcy protection. The airline abruptly (and illegally) stopped paying medical insurance premiums for its employees. With neither insurance coverage nor a job, the father could not produce $300,000 on short notice.

Filing bankruptcy was the only way for this family to protect itself from claims made by the hospital and doctors. It was not indicative of how well these people had previously managed financial affairs, nor should it have cast hardworking, productive people into financial purgatory.

How could anyone recreate a positive financial record without additional credit being extended? Fortunately an understanding lender listened, worked a little harder, and provided financing for a new business that put this family on the way to rebuilding a life.

A second example involved an ambitious chiropractor who started a practice six weeks after graduation without a sufficient number of patients. After obtaining a high interest loan and easy but short-term credit to buy start-up equipment, there were still not enough patients to earn money for the payments.

Bankruptcy was the only way that one creditor was stopped from literally walking out with the doctor's medical equipment during the treat-

❝ Bankruptcy is a business strategy to deal with a severe imbalance of assets and liabilities. ❞

PART 2

" Legitimate

bankruptcy cases do not

involve morals—they are

about money. "

ment of a patient. Should the misjudgment of an aggressive young doctor be a lifelong impediment to moving on to financial success?

While employed by another clinic for four years, this doctor got affairs in order. A loan was secured to finance the purchase and improvement of a building to house a growing practice. Now that doctor employs eight people and pays a lot of taxes because a practical lender listened and responded to that loan application.

The third example is one of the most famous corporate bankruptcy cases involving a publicly owned manufacturing company known as Johns-Manville Corporation. This company had a comfortable position in the marketplace, selling a variety of building insulation materials.

One of the company's most successful products was an asbestos-based insulation material. Asbestos was used for generations and the company sold millions of dollars' worth of insulation products that were later determined to be a hazardous material. Asbestos, it turns out, is a carcinogen. Johns-Manville quickly discontinued production of this material but the damage was done.

This information led to a flood of lawsuits against the company from thousands of persons who had come into contact with this insulation and later developed cancer. Johns-Manville was faced with a catastrophic liability that would have continued to grow until it consumed the company. But a pre-emptive filing for protection in bankruptcy court enabled the company to manage these undefined liabilities while continuing to operate. This action ensured its ability to survive and pay all eventual claims, which were filed through a trust established in 1988 for victims of its products.

This strategy was a bold move that changed how bankruptcy is viewed. Using bankruptcy as an offensive strategy permitted the company to settle its liabilities, which would have never been accomplished without court protection. And it permitted the company to survive and pay later claimants, who would not even know of future losses at the time that the company was under attack.

Obviously, bankruptcy can be abused, but recognition must be given to its legitimate use in circumstances that threaten individuals and businesses. Some lenders are shortsighted to adjudge that parties seeking bankruptcy protection do not have adequate moral standards. Each case must be evaluated according to its own particular circumstances.

The loan officer cannot assume that a borrower has a character flaw just because the borrower is involved in a bankruptcy case. There are many cases where overzealous or unreasonable creditors have forced bankruptcies rather than seeking more prudent remedies to deal with problem loans. Lenders must recognize that another lender's inflexibility can lead to mistakes that cause some borrowers to be unjustly penalized.

Lenders must consider the circumstances surrounding any borrower who has been involved in a bankruptcy case. Sometimes a better test of character is watching how the borrower manages to emerge after a bankruptcy case.

Borrowers involved in a previous bankruptcy may actually be a lower risk for lenders. These borrowers have a wealth of experience in dealing with difficult situations, better preparing them for the economic risks associated with operating a small business. Surviving these tough circumstances adds to the borrower's management and financial education.

Federal bankruptcy statutes restrict how soon individuals with previous involvement in a bankruptcy case can access protection again. This limitation protects subsequent lenders who deal with these borrowers.

If the borrower has been involved in a bankruptcy case (personal or business), the lender will discover this fact very early in the application process. It is better for the borrower to disclose the facts before the lender reads this information in a credit report.

Before referring to the bankruptcy, borrowers should have the loan officer interested in the transaction. If the loan officer is not comfortable with the attributes of the deal before learning about the bankruptcy, the borrower will never get the lender's full attention on the application.

Credit reports include information about prior connections with any bankruptcy. In addition to personal bankruptcy cases, the credit report records any business in which the borrower was an owner, shareholder, or partner. Even if borrowers have no control over the events leading to a business bankruptcy, they must be prepared to explain the circumstances of the case.

Because the proceedings of a bankruptcy case are a matter of public record, the lender is able to obtain a copy of the borrower's case file to verify the dates, creditors, debts, and final results of the case. In other words, a borrower's fictional account of the bankruptcy case could permanently destroy credibility with the lender.

In addition to telling the loan officer the bankruptcy story, the borrower should provide a written version for review purposes. Because the loan officer will probably have to relay the information in writing, it is better for the borrower to transcribe a detailed account as the basis for the lender's report.

" The three primary classes of bankruptcy protection are:

Chapter 7 - Liquidation

Chapter 11 - Business reorganization

Chapter 13 - Personal debt restructuring "

PART 2

❝ How borrowers handle their affairs after bankruptcy determines a lender's interest in giving them a second chance. ❞

The borrower should document the circumstances thoroughly and substantiate any difficulties that led to seeking bankruptcy protection. If debtors were not at fault, they should prove it by using affidavits from other parties, accident reports, medical records, pictures, newspaper articles, and any other information available to support these claims.

Former bankrupt debtors should prepare a detailed summary of how the case was resolved and what they did after the case was dismissed. This brief needs to be supported with documents verifying the borrower's personal involvement in the situation, court filings, financial reports, and trustee's report. How have the borrower's affairs changed since the bankruptcy? What has been accomplished to put the borrower's financial affairs in order?

If the bankruptcy experience was due to imprudent management rather than tragic circumstances, the truth is equally as important. Depending on how much time has lapsed, how much money was lost by the creditors, and how the borrower has managed in the post-petition period, the lender may still consider the loan application.

Litigation

Living in the most litigious society in the world can give a new meaning to the term "liability." Because over 75% of the world's lawyers are in the United States, American citizens have higher odds of being sued over a dispute. This exposure is increased for small business owners. People can spend considerable sums and suffer severe financial damage even when the only circumstance is merely being accused.

When the borrower's financial statement is scarred with the extraordinary costs of defending a suit, or when the borrower has settled a suit to limit these costs, the loan officer is entitled to a detailed explanation. By putting the matter in context and perspective, the loan officer can understand the impact of the litigation to the company's finances. This explanation helps the borrower move the application process beyond the legal situation, allowing the positive aspects of the loan proposal to be considered and emphasized.

The lender should receive copies of the lawsuit and the borrower's answer. In justifying the defensive side of the dispute, the borrower can provide the lender with copies of invoices, receipts, and other documents to show how the business was affected. If the borrower's attorney has detailed a favorable opinion of the borrower's situation, the lender should be given copies of this correspondence. At least the loan officer will understand the borrower's situation after this disclosure and not fear the risk of unknown parameters. But even if sympathetic, the loan officer retains the responsibility of underwriting the loan request. The loan officer will have to take the result of the litigation on the business into account, regardless of whether or not the borrower was at fault.

Most lenders will not proceed with a loan request if there is a material lawsuit pending at the time of the application. Routine matters that occur in the normal course of business, and that do not threaten the borrower's financial condition, should not interfere with the loan application. But if there is a matter of any substance against the company that is unresolved or on appeal, the lender will probably wait until final judgment has been rendered before proceeding.

Any judgment against the borrower could significantly change the financial condition. If the borrower were forced into a large settlement, or if the other party were enabled to lien the borrower's assets, the lender could suddenly have a problem loan. The collateral assets securing the loan could possibly have more claims outstanding than value.

If the situation has already cleared the judicial process and the borrower is faced with a judgment, the lender will be interested in how the matter is handled. If the borrower loses in court, the judgment must be honored. The lender will be interested in how the borrower reacts, because it may be indicative of how the borrower would react in a similar dispute with the lender at some future date.

Divorce

Divorce can be disastrous for a small business owner. Because the process can be strenuous for the individuals involved, months of underperformance in business responsibilities may elapse. In addition, the financial settlement can be somewhat disruptive if the borrower is forced to buy out or share the business ownership interests with the spouse.

If the business owner has recently completed the divorce process, it is important to provide an explanation to the lender about any impact the divorce had on the business or the owner's personal financial condition. The borrower should document this explanation with copies of bank records, financial statements, and a copy of the final divorce settlement. Disclosing personal (that is, emotional rather than financial)

❝ With over 75% of the world's lawyers in the U.S., citizens face much higher odds of being sued. ❞

PART 2

❝ Borrowers should disclose the financial, not emotional effects of a divorce.❞

aspects of the divorce should be avoided, as they are not only irrelevant but also potentially detrimental to the loan application.

Because of the stressful issues in divorce cases, the vengeful actions of one party may create liabilities for the other party. Alternatively, one party may refuse to pay legitimately allocated liabilities that are in the joint names of both parties. Divorce can become a disaster to the borrower's credit history and ability to borrower money.

These circumstances need to be carefully documented in order to demonstrate the borrower's innocence in such a situation. Divorce is probably the most abused excuse used by persons with bad credit. To earn credibility, the borrower has to show how the bad credit was created through the irresponsible actions of others.

The best defense is to pay off any unpaid accounts whether individually or jointly held. The borrower should try to protect a good credit history when possible, later pursuing the other party for recovery of these sums. To limit exposure, the borrower should close the joint credit accounts when the divorce process first begins and notify creditors that the borrower will not be responsible for future liabilities created on a joint account. While the borrower cannot escape joint and several liability on existing balances, a notice can prevent a creditor from holding the borrower liable for subsequent charges.

After discovering negative credit report information as a result of the divorce, the borrower should contact the credit bureau and provide a statement detailing the situation. The credit bureau is obligated to include this explanation in all future inquiries.

If the divorce is not yet finalized, the borrower should consider waiting until the process is over before making a business loan application. When the owner is resolving the complicated and emotional issues of divorce, the anxiety of seeking credit is compounded. The borrower benefits by focusing on the business at hand—one major negotiation at a time.

Bad Decisions

To err is human, but some mistakes are more costly than others. In a dynamic economy, strategic decisions must be made on a regular basis. Because small business owners are constantly making decisions with long-term implications, errors will sometimes be made.

In a changing world, small business owners often perform as the chief executive officer, chief financial officer, chief operating officer, advertising agent, transportation specialist, tax expert, and computer prodigy; then they go home to be a compassionate parent, loving spouse, and supportive partner! These roles are defined by a constant stream of ideas from newspapers, magazines, cable features, sitcoms, talk shows, books, videos, MTV, C-SPAN, pay-per-view, e-mail, and the Internet. So how can anyone make mistakes?

It is an age overrun with ideas and communication. Today's eighth wonder of the world is tomorrow's dinosaur. More decisions are demanded than ever before, but humans are still limited to one brain.

This explanation is given in order to offer universal forgiveness for making occasional bad business decisions. As long as the decision is based on the best option at the time, it should not be reconsidered. When the borrower documents an error for the lender, this page should be submitted with the loan request to provide some perspective to the loan officer.

When the loan officer is told about errors, the borrower's candor is factored into an assessment of the actions taken to overcome the mistake. If the borrower qualifies under the other criteria necessary to obtain financing, previous errors should not prevent the borrower from getting a loan.

> *"To err is human."*
>
> —*Alexander Pope*

Bad Health

Consider what would happen to the economic status of a borrower who becomes ill for an extended period. There are many possible consequences and most of them include serious financial damage. Should that mean that the borrower can never qualify for business credit? What if the borrower had a spotless track record before the illness? It hardly seems fair that after battling to survive, the borrower should also have to battle for the survival of the business. Once the borrower recovers, there remains the hard work of helping the business to recover.

The answer is to provide documentation to communicate and confirm the medical situation to the lender. The loan officer wants to know how the illness affected the borrower personally and how that impacted the operation of the business. Borrowers can expect compassion for these situations but should accept the burden of proof. Rather than telling the loan officer all of the details of the medical treatment and procedures, a generic description of the medical condition will provide enough personal information. After satisfying the general situation questions, the borrower should emphasize economic health and focus on the financial details.

Bad Credit

A poor credit history can result from many causes other than an irresponsible borrower. To clean up a tarnished track record:

✧ Pay off debts as quickly as possible, eliminating any numerous small debts first.

✧ Be sure to repay every creditor that lists the debt as charged off.

✧ After reducing the remaining liabilities to those with higher balances, target the ones with higher interest rates to be paid off next.

✧ Talk to creditors about situation and get a payment holiday that may convert past due payments to current status. Work out a realistic, but aggressive payment schedule. If you perform as agreed, ask the creditor for a written commendation for working out of a negative position.

Compounding several of the problems mentioned above is the trickle-down effect each has on the borrower's personal credit history. If the borrower's cash flow is interrupted for any reason and cash reserves are exhausted, payments to creditors will slow down accordingly. This problem must eventually be dealt with, since slow credit payments are one of the most troublesome problems in the eyes of the lender.

It is important to manage personal credit closely to keep one's payment history clean and avoid perpetuating negative entries into a credit record. Lenders focus on a number of aspects in the credit report, including the total amount of credit outstanding, payment history, and any public records that indicate the unsatisfactory conduct of personal affairs.

Understanding how to manage this process cannot repair one's previous poor credit record. But modifying current and future performance can improve a borrower's situation and end the poor performance reflected in the recent credit report. Borrowers should begin by using the following strategies:

✧ Pay off as much credit as possible by using savings, having a yard sale, taking back recently purchased merchandise, liquidating assets, borrowing money from the business, collecting outstanding debts, or even drawing down the cash surrender value of a life insurance policy. Cash should be obtained (without borrowing more) to pay off these accounts as fast as possible. Rather than reducing all the accounts, the ones with the lower balances should be paid off. It is better to have five past due accounts than ten past due accounts.

✧ After the small debts are cleared, borrowers should prioritize by paying off debt with higher payments or higher interest rates first. Paying off these accounts first gives the borrower more flexibility in the future.

✧ Payments should be managed so as not to exceed thirty days past due if possible, even if it means hand-delivering the payment. Payments less than thirty days late are not reported to the credit bureau.

✧ If cash shortage is temporary, the borrower should arrange to limit the number of creditors who will receive late payments. Rather than making one $500 payment on time and being late on four payments of $125, it is better to pay the four accounts on time and be late only on the one $500 payment.

✧ The credit bureau does not receive reports of late payments from such liabilities as public utilities, telephone companies, long distance suppliers, cable operators, merchandise buying clubs, and private note holders. Slowing payments to these accounts will not affect a public credit record and may help keep it clean. Getting too far behind on utility bills, however, will risk disconnection of that service, resulting in a deposit to be paid on restoration of service.

If the borrower has bad credit, the lender should be told why. Often bad credit is not the result of poor management or lack of responsibility, but rather circumstances that affect the borrower's ability to meet those responsibilities consistently. To earn the lender's confidence, the borrower must demonstrate that those circumstances have been improved to a degree that will not interfere with the borrower's ability to make payments on the loan being requested.

PART 2

✧ Contact the credit bureau to ensure all information on the credit report is accurate. If there are any errors, be persistent in following up to get them corrected—it takes time but the credit bureau is obligated by law to correct any errors and eliminate stale information.

✧ Don't pay for sham credit repair operations—no one can legally give you a new credit history, and trying to create one is illegal. If there are serious errors on the credit report that can't be fixed, contact an attorney.

CHAPTER 5

Improving the Odds of Loan Approval

There are many subtle ways to get a better deal. Entrepreneurs are creative, persevering types who will try whatever it takes to get the deal done. Learn:

- ✧ The power of an organized, positive approach
- ✧ Dealing direct with the whole story
- ✧ How to finesse the finer points

Complete and Organized Information

The easiest strategy to get a loan proposal approved is to provide the lender with the necessary information in an organized manner. Too many borrowers are needlessly rejected or delayed because they do not take the time to provide adequate documentation.

The lender has to completely understand the borrower's operation (its history and future) and the loan request. All of this information should be documented in order to provide a complete picture of the business, including the facts and figures necessary to approve the proposed loan. Without sufficient data to answer all of the questions, the lender will either have to ask for more information or take the easy way out by saying no to the proposal.

Often, the borrower will have the lender's complete attention at the first meeting when the loan proposal is submitted. The lender may be ready to get started on the request immediately after this meeting. If the process is delayed by the borrower's failure to provide sufficient information or promptly respond to the lender's inquiries, the lender may lose any momentum created for the deal.

The borrower should be on the offensive with information and answers about the business while the lender is interested and attentive to the loan proposal. Stretching the process out over weeks, which can easily become months, makes the loan more difficult to approve. The lender will either lose focus on it or will be less enthusiastic about assisting the borrower.

Anticipating what data will be needed and which questions will be asked should not be difficult for an experienced businessperson. Preparing this information in advance will make a positive impression about the borrower's management capabilities and competence.

Based on the information listed in Chapter 3, the borrower should assemble any data that might possibly be relevant to the loan request. By providing information in the initial meeting, the borrower increases the lender's responsibility to respond without delayed consideration. Because each borrower's situation is unique, it is impossible to anticipate every item the lender will need to evaluate the loan request. But the borrower should be prepared to respond quickly and thoroughly.

Positive Thinking

However strong or weak the borrower's proposal is, it will sound better if presented in a confident, enthusiastic tone. The positive demeanor of the borrower can be effective in gaining the lender's favorable impression of the proposal. Enthusiasm is important to demonstrate that the borrower is confident about the purpose and goals of the business. This confidence will carry over into the lender's review, assisting the lender in approving the transaction.

By accentuating the positive, the borrower concentrates on the successes and not on the failures. Even if the business has suffered its share of losses, the emphasis should be on the wins—the upbeat stories that reinforce the reasons for lending money to this company.

The Only Way to Get an Answer Is to Ask

Business people often hear horror stories from other small businesses about the condition of the lending market. Innuendoes, rumors, and negative tales convince many borrowers that there are no funds available. But what the borrower hears is only one side of the story. Just because someone else gets turned down for a loan does not mean the time is bad

Increase the odds of hearing "YES!"

✧ Organize a thorough set of information before applying for a loan.
✧ Be prepared to respond quickly to any information request.
✧ Dedicate the time required up front rather than allowing the process to drag over several months.

to apply for a loan. As described throughout this book, there are many parameters on which a loan request is judged, any one of which can lead a lender to deny someone's request for financing.

The borrower should concentrate on getting the loan approved on its own merits, without being discouraged by the failures of others. Even if there are flaws that will concern the lender, the worst thing that can happen is that the lender will say no. If the borrower does not ask, the lender cannot say yes.

Convincing the lender to provide financing is much like selling the borrower's services or products. The borrower has to identify prospects, qualify them, make the pitch, and close the deal. Getting the lender to make a loan requires the same steps.

After researching the market, the borrower can determine which lenders are prospects to handle the transaction. Which lender is best suited to provide the services to the borrower? Which lender is interested in the market in which this business is conducted? Which lender wants the borrower's business? Which lender is willing to invest the time, confidence, and funding to help the borrower succeed?

Does this lender understand the borrower's business? Is the lender interested in what the borrower is trying to accomplish? Does the lender feel comfortable with small businesses at the borrower's stage of growth? Is the lender qualified and experienced in lending with the SBA loan guaranty program? Can the lender feel comfortable with the borrower's strategy? Does the lender recognize how the borrower addresses the risks involved?

If the lender passes these qualifications, the borrower should lay out the proposal and ask for the loan. Presenting the loan request confidently, the borrower should have an organized, complete package of information—concise, clearly stated, convincing, and supported by the borrower's assumptions.

In addition, the borrower should prepare for the lender's objections. Questions need to be answered with direct, documented information that satisfies the lender's concern. Rather than assuming that the reply is sufficient, the borrower should ask the lender if the question has been fully answered.

It is easier to answer a question before it is asked. By anticipating questions, the answers can be included in the loan application. In that manner, the borrower benefits by controlling the slant and specifics of the information.

Don't let the failure of other loan proposals discourage the effort to get a loan.

PART 2

If the borrower is not sure how to answer a specific question, it is best to call the lender back as soon as practical to provide the response. The phone call should be followed with a letter to reiterate the answer.

In concluding the meeting, the borrower should summarize the business strategy, restate the deal, and review the answered objections. The goal is to make it easy and logical for the lender to give a positive reply to the loan request.

Dealing Directly about Negative Information

✧ Think positive!
✧ Unasked questions won't be answered.
✧ Carefully select targeted lenders.
✧ Fully inform the lender about business proposal in concise terms.

If part of the borrower's history includes a horror tale, such as one of the situations described in Chapter 4, it should not be hidden. As suggested in other sections of the book, the borrower should make sure the lender is interested in the positive attributes of the proposition before venturing into life's tragedies. But after becoming serious about the proposal, the lender should be led gently through the negative part of the story of the special circumstances.

In Chapter 4 there are suggestions about how to discuss several sensitive situations that the borrower may have experienced. By not apologizing for these events, the borrower acknowledges that they are an integral part of past experiences. It is unlikely that the borrower purposely intended to encounter these situations.

The lender is not likely to be particularly sympathetic or concerned. The borrower should not expect the lender to be forgiving. What the borrower needs is the lender's open-minded recognition that these past events do not necessarily predict the borrower's future events and that they should not preclude the borrower's getting a business loan.

Understanding the lender's perspective of these circumstances will help the borrower predict the lender's reaction and will therefore help the borrower prepare for this disclosure. The key objectives are to not alarm the lender and to provide assurances that the borrower does not have a pertinent character flaw, has a bright future, and represents an acceptable business risk.

Documentation about the event is important. How have these events affected the borrower? How has the borrower tried to minimize these effects for the benefit of family and creditors (in that order of importance)? What has transpired since the event, and how has the borrower diligently and capably recovered? Honesty is the best policy, even if it hurts. The more direct the information from the borrower, the better equipped the borrower is to get another chance.

Meeting at the Borrower's Office

As simple as it sounds, meeting on the borrower's turf can provide an advantage when presenting a loan proposal. When lenders are away from their desks, they are more likely to listen to borrowers without the defenses normally provided to them in their own office.

The lender cannot be distracted or interrupted in the borrower's office. There are no phone calls, letters to sign, or memos of review. Meeting at the borrower's place of business makes any additional information the lender may request accessible, and permits the lender to view the borrower's management and leadership firsthand.

The most important advantage is that the lender can see, hear, smell, and touch the borrower's business: customers, the store, busy employees, and the loading docks accepting and shipping inventory. Because the level of activity (if relevant) can also have a positive effect on the lender, the lender's visit should be scheduled during busier hours, when there are a lot of customers, employees, machines, or other activity involved. Translating the vision of the operation from the loan proposal to other decision makers will be easier for the lender if it can be described from a first-person recollection.

Be straightforward about negative events after the lender is interested in the deal.

Not Enough Collateral?

Most denied loan proposals are due to insufficient collateral. Borrowers cannot always reduce the amount of funds needed, and the lender is usually not able or willing to extend beyond the normal collateral coverage requirements. Sometimes there are minor ways to enhance or stretch the values of collateral assets to provide the lender with sufficient coverage, or at least to get the borrower close enough to convince the lender to give consideration.

Examining the Lender's Valuation Method

The borrower should make sure the lender is using accurate, reliable information when determining the value of the borrower's collateral. This suggestion may require the borrower to invest in a second opinion with another appraiser. If that second opinion convinces the lender to increase the loan, it is worth the time and cost.

If the collateral includes real estate, the borrower should be aware that increased scrutiny of real estate lending in the past several years has resulted in myriad new regulations and requirements of appraisers. The effect of these changes has been a general depression of real estate valuations, due to the appraisal industry's fear of future challenges of its assessments.

An appraisal is an estimate of value, based on three distinct valuation approaches: market, replacement cost, and income approach. Most full appraisals assess a valuation using each of the three approaches to determine a final statement of value based on a weighted average of the three, depending on the specifics of the property. In general terms, the three approaches are defined as follows:

1. *Market value.* This approach measures the likely value of a property based on recent, comparable sales ("comps") of similar properties in the general area. The appraiser attempts to find other, nearby, sales of properties of the same size and scale of improvement.
2. *Replacement cost.* This approach measures the likely cost of rebuilding the improvements on a particular property, plus the current value of the land based on comparable sales.
3. *Income approach.* When applicable, the appraiser examines the income being generated by a property, or the likely income generated from similar properties in the same area, based on prevailing market rents.

The borrower should be aware that appraisers have varying degrees of familiarity with the immediate geographic area and the type of improvement the borrower owns. The borrower should cooperate fully with the appraiser when the property is examined. It is a good idea to be on hand and to be prepared to provide any information the appraiser requests. The more information the appraiser has, the more accurate valuation the borrower will receive.

If the collateral includes furniture, fixtures, and equipment (FF&E), the borrower should examine the method under which the lender values this collateral. Most lenders will routinely discount these assets 50%, but the borrower should notice whether that valuation is based on the book value or the cost value. The borrower should encourage the lender to use the cost of the asset, since depreciation on most of these assets does not really affect their liquidation value.

If the FF&E is a major portion of the collateral assets, the borrower may even decide to request an appraisal. In doing so, risks can be reduced if the borrower carefully guides the lender to a capable appraiser.

Too often, lenders use liquidation companies and auctioneers for appraisals of FF&E assets. The liquidation value is based on liquidation-type sales and is therefore going to be substantially less than the true value of the asset. Liquidation value assumes that the asset is sold on a distressed basis. If sold over a reasonable time period, the asset would carry a much higher value.

Many lenders have a knee-jerk reaction to collateral liquidation, due to an unpleasant past experience. The borrower has to counteract that attitude with assurance about how the lender could reasonably expect to recover the loan when collateral is liquidated correctly. Lenders are apt to want to liquidate the collateral too fast, which depresses sale prices.

It's no secret that buyers scent blood when they watch a nervous lender pacing around an equipment auction, wondering how much of a loss is going to be taken. A better sale method would be to place the FF&E on consignment with a used equipment or furniture dealer, letting them sell the assets over a reasonable time frame when market demand will pay a higher price. These are the same dealers who are only too glad to buy the FF&E for ten cents on the dollar at the lender's auction.

The borrower should know the value of the assets on a liquidation basis, after understanding how to liquidate those assets on a reasonable basis. This information will permit the borrower to negotiate stronger collateral valuations with the lender, and ensure that the lender gives the borrower adequate credit for the collateral assets.

Offering the Lender Other Assets

If collateral assets are short, the borrower can offer to pledge other assets to the lender so that the loan will meet the lender's requirements. Other assets can sometimes cover a small margin needed by the lender as an alternative to lowering the loan amount.

When using this methodology, the borrower should be prepared to be generous in supplying whatever is available. If lenders do not ask for a particular asset in the beginning, then they probably do not place much value on it.

"Rope Theory: Financial projections can help 'swing' the deal, or if not plausible, 'hang' the deal."

PART 2

"Convincing lenders to secure long-term loans with short-term 'current' assets is a very difficult task."

These other assets may have marginal value, but if totaled, could provide the lender with a substantial contribution toward eliminating any existing collateral shortfall. These assets may include the borrower's FF&E, automobiles, rolling stock, accounts receivable, inventory, cash surrender value of insurance policies, notes receivable, and other miscellaneous assets on the borrower's business or personal balance sheet.

Maximizing the Valuation of Current Assets

Small business lenders usually do not attach much value to the accounts receivable and inventory assets of a borrower. This failure to recognize the value of these assets is prudent, since both can disappear in days unless the lender could control them.

Borrowers are often frustrated at the difficulty of leveraging current asset strength, unless they are willing to pay 25% to 30% for factored loans from asset-based lenders. The margin of adequate financing is sometimes tied up in the current assets of a business, seemingly untouchable at a reasonable cost to the borrower.

One method to increase the leverage of these current assets is to request that the lender include them in the borrower's collateral pool as contribution toward the collateral requirements of the borrower's term loan. The borrower can enhance the value of these assets by offering to permit the lender to monitor the assets and by being willing to pay related service fees to the lender for the cost of such monitoring.

In other words, if the lender would give the borrower credit for a lower-than-average advance percentage on current assets (for example, a 50% advance on sixty-day receivables and a 35% advance on inventory), this credit would provide the borrower with the margin of collateral needed to get the loan proposal approved. In exchange for the lender approving a long-term loan with short-term collateral, the borrower would allow the lender to monitor these assets to ensure adequate coverage continues.

The borrower would be required to provide the lender with a regular statement of asset values, on perhaps a weekly or monthly basis. This statement would detail the changes of accounts receivable and inventory, along with defining the components that comprise these asset totals. The borrower would also have to be willing to pay the lender the extra cost of reviewing these statements each period, recognizing the legitimate effort required over the term of the loan. These fees may equate to 1% to 2% of the loan balance each year.

This option is infrequently employed and is suited only for established businesses with a long track record of successful operations and good management systems. As a creative option, it may make the difference in qualifying for a loan. After the loan has been serviced for a couple of years, and the principal balance has been paid down below the normal margin required of the main collateral assets, the borrower may negotiate a release of the current asset collateral in order to lower costs and reporting requirements.

The Rope Theory—Projecting Performance

Borrowers are always required to provide the lender with projections of the company's financial performance for at least two years. These estimates are intended to give the lender confidence that the borrower can service the debt with cash flow from operations.

These projections are more difficult to estimate for start-up businesses or for businesses intending to use the loan proceeds for making major changes in their operations. It is incumbent on the borrower to use caution and salesmanship when developing these projections, since these numbers are a very important component of ultimate loan approval.

Financial projections can be described as a "Rope Theory." The borrower has the opportunity to *swing* or *hang*, depending on the success and accuracy of the projections.

The borrower can swing by using the projections persuasively, convincing the lender that the loan proceeds will enable the borrower either to increase profitable revenues or reduce specific costs in order to provide the monies to make future loan payments. The "rope" enables the borrower to obtain the funds needed to accomplish this success.

But if the projections do not come to fruition, then the borrower will hang. Loan default is certain, caused by an inadequate cash flow available to service the debt. This situation will lead to liquidation of the collateral assets, as well as a possible lawsuit against the borrower and any loan guarantors.

Any persuasive presentation to promote the borrower's ability to perform has to be reinforced with actual performance. In this sense, financial projections can be a powerful tool for the borrower to use in convincing the lender of the prudence of the proposed loan. But these same projections can smother the borrower with an untenable situation that could lead to the company's demise.

Inadequate collateral?

◆ Challenge the lender's valuation of collateral assets.
◆ Supplement collateral with other assets.
◆ Offer monitored receivables and inventory assets to shore up weak coverage.

Companion Loans

Most lenders and borrowers have allowed the legal limitations of the SBA guaranty to serve as an actual limitation on the loan size of an SBA-guaranteed loan. This limitation does not exist, however, and the perception of it has prevented many businesses and lenders from negotiating many good loans.

The program regulations provide for loan guaranty limits, based on the term and size of the loan. These regulations determine that the guaranty may not exceed a particular percentage of the loan (for example, 75% or 80%), but they do not require the guaranty to equate to that level. That is, the regulations that permit the lender to extend a 75% guaranteed loan do not prevent the lender from extending a 65% or 45% guaranteed loan.

Often lenders will set an artificial maximum loan limit for borrowers in order to achieve the maximum SBA guaranty on each loan. But if the borrower has the financial capacity and an eligible need for a higher loan amount, there is no SBA restriction on the lender's ability to make a larger loan. Characteristic of their conservative nature, some lenders are merely hesitant to fall below the maximum guaranteed leverage limit.

One method employed by many lenders to make larger guaranteed loans without taking on more exposure, has been the use of a senior companion loan. For example, a borrower may want $1,300,000 to finance the purchase of a motel. Many SBA lenders would limit their offer to a $1,000,000 loan since this loan would carry the maximum SBA guaranty of 75% or $750,000.

However, a more creative lender could actually solicit another lender to make a $300,000 first mortgage loan with the subject lender offering a $1,000,000 second mortgage loan backed with the 75% SBA guaranty. The first lender's senior loan is not guaranteed, but is effectively protected by the subordinated SBA loan, which requires the subject lender to repay the senior financing in case of a liquidation scenario.

This companion loan method enables the marketplace to bridge the gap between the program's fiscal restrictions and the true needs of the borrowing business sector. These situations highlight the fact that Congress has not updated the size limitations on SBA-guaranteed loans to meet the realities faced by small businesses.

> There is no limit to the size of a 7(a) loan. Lenders are limited to a maximum guaranty of $750,000 or 75% of the loan, whichever is less.

Start-Up Businesses

Regardless of the borrower's industry or business, the toughest loan for a lender to consider is to a start-up business. In almost all circumstances, this phase of a business is the most difficult for the borrower, and certainly the most risky for the lender.

In focusing on the risks faced by the lender in this situation, the borrower needs to overcome the skepticism that accompanies the lender's desire to help. The lender has to be assured that the borrower can effectively marshal available resources to generate profitable revenues quickly enough to survive and repay the loan as scheduled. For a start-up business loan, there is greater emphasis on equity capital, because the lender wants the borrower to have enough cash reserve to meet unexpected expenses or unanticipated slowness in sales.

If the borrower is a start-up business, the following items required in the loan application (discussed in Chapter 3) need special emphasis to overcome the lender's aversion to this stage of business lending:

Borrower's equity. The lender will be adamant about requiring a strong capital contribution from the borrower in the form of operating cash. There is no substitute for operating funds to ensure that the borrower can weather the start-up phase of the business, which always produces many unforeseen expenses.

The borrower's revenue expectations, if over- or underestimated, can also play havoc with the cash requirements of the start-up period. The borrower should have a readily available source of short-term working capital to manage these requirements in the likely event that the financial projections are inaccurate.

Financial projections. The borrower's financial projections are going to be scrutinized very carefully, because start-up borrowers do not have a previous track record against which to compare the reasonableness of these numbers. Every figure will be questioned when the projections are presented to the lender.

Income and expense projections should be constructed realistically. The borrower cannot perform too much research on these figures. What kind of marketing efforts are required to produce sales? What fixed expenses are involved in opening the business? What variable costs are incurred at the level of sales projected?

Borrowers should consult with noncompetitors in similar markets to determine whether or not the projections are attainable. Experienced

> *Lenders are inclined to be skeptical of new ideas.*

PART 2

business owners who will not be affected can quickly evaluate the forecasts to ensure that the borrower has not missed something significant that could lead to disaster.

Feasibility. The borrower should make an effort to demonstrate to the lender that the new business idea is feasible and that the borrower can, in fact, succeed with the plan. In identifying the demand for the product or service, the borrower must show the experience or ability to meet that demand.

The country is littered with the skeletons of great business ideas that were not thought out far enough. One former professional football player started a local chain of necktie stores to capitalize on his popularity and the attention his stylish and colorful neckties had received. Unfortunately, he lived in Miami, Florida, where much of the local business community does not frequently wear neckties, because of the tropical climate.

Marketing plan. Borrowers must demonstrate to the lender that they have identified the target audience and have ascertained the most effective method of attracting that audience to the business. Good businesses must have a lot of paying customers to become great businesses.

Borrowers should consult with advertising consultants who not only place advertising but who develop ideas for communicating to the consumer group most likely to buy the borrower's products or services. Most start-up businesses do not have enough money to determine marketing through trial and error.

If the borrower is a franchised company, much of this function will be purchased as part of the package. In addition, it is wise to consult with a specialist in the market area to test the franchiser's assumptions about how to advertise the business locally.

Start-up businesses should expect to have a more difficult job getting a loan approved. But emphasis on these items will assist in giving the lender confidence in the most important factors of the business: cash flow and revenue generation.

CHAPTER 6

Getting the Loan Closed

Some loans can be easy to get committed, but the devil from which to really get any money. Getting approval is only the halfway mark—it's never a deal till the money is in your hand. Learn:

- ✧ The details of getting the deal closed
- ✧ How to make things go faster
- ✧ Slowing down the expensive closing fees

Now What Happens?

Once the loan has been approved by the lender and the SBA, the lender is responsible for setting the activities in motion to have the loan transaction executed (commonly referred to as "closed") and funded. This process is somewhat involved in itself, despite all the work that has been expended getting the application assembled and the loan approved.

The loan closing phase requires the borrower to produce additional documentation, specific to the collateral assets. The lender's attorney is charged with preparing the loan and security documents according to the SBA Loan Authorization and Agreement and with ensuring that all parties are in compliance with the terms described therein. The lender may or may not take an active role in the process.

Borrowers frequently get frustrated at the time required to move from SBA approval to the actual fund of the loan. It is typically not until this stage that myriad professional consultants become involved: appraisers, engineers, surveyors, and attorneys. The borrower is usually hesitant to spend money on the due diligence required before having the loan formally approved. There is much work to be done, and, usually, the borrower is in line with several other borrowers for the services that are needed.

The first activity required is for the lender and the lender's attorney to review the SBA Loan Authorization and Agreement, ensuring that it accurately reflects the lender's understanding of and intent for the transaction. If not, changes have to be addressed with the SBA in writing, which may delay further closing activity. Once the lender has confirmed this information, the parties are ready to start working toward a closing.

Next, the lender or closing attorney will engage in a series of activities for which the borrower will be obligated to pay—whether or not the loan is ever closed. Depending on the borrower's collateral, the lender will order a title and lien search, an appraisal, an environmental report, and a survey. The results of these reports are needed to confirm the assumptions the lender is depending on to go forward with the loan.

Should any of these reports come back with different results than expected, or with newly identified problems, there may be additional time delays, a modification of the loan terms, or even withdrawal of the lender's commitment. It is important for the borrower to understand the dynamics of this stage of the closing, to ensure that the lender does not overreact to unexpected results. This information is discussed further in this chapter.

The borrower should remember that the closing attorney is not an arbitrary participant in the closing process. The closing attorney represents only the lender. One attorney cannot represent two parties in the same transaction. Whether the borrower should be represented by an attorney is a different question and is addressed in Chapter 7.

Borrowers should also be aware of a growing trend among major SBA participating lenders that have begun preparing their own closing documents for SBA loans. Closing costs have become a new competitive tool in recent years with lenders utilizing software to produce legal forms to document loans in every state.

This chapter will discuss the activities that are common for loan closings, why these activities are needed, and what the associated costs are likely to be. Further, this chapter describes ways the borrower can shorten the time necessary to get the loan closed, and maybe even reduce some of the associated costs.

> Some lenders prepare their own loan closing documents. Attorney's participation with these lenders is reduced to title searches and escrow responsibilities, which drastically reduce fees for the borrowers by $2,000+. Find out which lenders provide this feature before you commit to a loan.

The SBA Authorization and Loan Agreement

The first step toward closing the loan is when the lender obtains the SBA Authorization and Loan Agreement ("Authorization") from the SBA.

This document contains the terms and conditions under which the SBA will provide the loan guaranty to the lender. The lender must comply with the provisions of this document to the letter or risk having the SBA guaranty canceled.

Typically fourteen to sixteen pages in length, the Authorization describes the loan transaction, its term, the required collateral, the guarantors, and the other negotiated conditions. The lender's attorney uses the Authorization to develop the specific set of closing documents needed to comply with the loan agreement.

The Authorization is delivered to the lender along with the promissory note, security agreement, guaranty agreements, and settlement sheets required by the SBA to document the loan. Presented in a standard SBA format, the Authorization is informally organized into six parts: declarations, documentation, precedents, terms, conditions and covenants, and executions.

Declarations. The first section declares the SBA's authorization and agreement to guaranty the lender's loan as specified, identifying the borrower, the amount of the loan, and the extent of the guaranty.

Documentation. The second section defines which SBA documents are required by the agency to enact this guaranteed transaction:

- ✧ *SBA Note: Form 147*—The SBA requires the lender to use this form as the promissory note governing the transaction. A conformed copy of the note is sent back to the SBA along with the guaranty fee, which is defined in this section.
- ✧ *SBA settlement sheet: Form 1050*—The SBA requires the lender to report each disbursement of loan proceeds on this form, which identifies to whom the loan proceeds are paid. This requirement ensures that the loan is disbursed in consistence with the SBA approval of the loan.
- ✧ *Compensation agreements: Form 159*—The SBA requires the lender to submit this form for each party who received a professional fee for work related to the subject loan.
- ✧ *Authorization*—The SBA requires the lender to obtain the borrower's signature on the Authorization and retain the original in the loan file.

Precedents. The third section usually defines four conditions that the lender must affirm and comply with in order to ensure the SBA participation:

❝ The SBA Authorization describes the terms of the loan guaranty as agreed to between the lender and SBA. These terms will define how the lender structures the transaction with the borrower. ❞

PART 3

❝ Borrowers should request a copy of the SBA Authorization as soon as it is available to ensure that its terms are consistent with the transaction agreed to with the lender. ❞

1. The lender must acknowledge that the guaranty is subject to the provisions of the Guaranty Agreement between the SBA and the lender.

2. The lender must acknowledge and agree to disburse the loan within a specified time frame, unless the SBA consents to extending that period.

3. The lender must affirm that it has not received any evidence of unsatisfied adverse changes in the borrower's financial condition or status since the loan approval that would warrant withholding further disbursement of the loan.

4. The lender affirms that the Authorization is subject to the representations made by the borrower, representations made by the lender, conditions set forth by the lender in its application for the guaranty, and conditions set forth in the Authorization.

Terms. The fourth section defines the specific terms under which the contemplated loan is to be enacted in order to qualify for the guaranty.

✧ *Repayment terms*—The Authorization defines the exact repayment terms under which the loan is extended, including the following information:

> *Repayment period*—The repayment term of the loan is defined, including the number of years in which repayment is to occur and the number of installments expected in that period. The first payment date is also specified.
>
> *Interest rate*—The interest rate of the loan is defined. If the rate is variable, the index by which the rate may be adjusted is explained, along with the time period in which such an adjustment may occur. Disclosure is made that, if the SBA repurchases its guaranteed portion of the loan in the event of default, the interest rate will be permanently fixed at the then current interest rate.
>
> *Maturity*—The maturity of the loan is defined as the length of time it takes for the loan to be paid in full. There are several variables that determine the maturity. For example, the lender is permitted to apply installment payments first to any outstanding interest and then to the principal. This provision can significantly impact the repayment

of the loan in a situation where the borrower is frequently late in submitting payments.

The Authorization states that any unpaid principal and interest will be due at the date of the last scheduled installment, regardless of the amount of a normal install-ment. The borrower will also be liable for reimbursing the lender for any extraordinary costs incurred in adminis-trating, collecting, or liquidating the loan at the time of the final payment.

A "due on sale" provision is contained in this section; it states that if the borrower transfers or encumbers any asset used as collateral for the loan without permission from the lender and the SBA, the maturity of the loan may be accelerated.

The lender is permitted to assess the borrower with a late penalty of 5% of the payment amount for any installment received more than ten days after that payment was due.

◆ *Use of proceeds limitations*—The Authorization specifies the exact allocation of loan proceeds as approved by the lender and the SBA, with the following provisions governing these distributions:

1. The lender is to distribute the funds whenever possible with joint payee checks issued to the borrower and the ultimate recipient of the proceeds.
2. The borrower must usually present documentation to sub-stantiate the allocations, such as a contract, bill of sale, price quote, or invoice. If the borrower has been approved for working capital financing, the lender will expect an updated budget of where the proceeds will be allocated. These funds will be distributed directly to the borrower. If the borrower is refinancing another loan, the other lender will have to fur-nish a written payoff as of the date of closing.
3. Up to 10% of the loan amount, to a maximum of $10,000, may be disbursed directly to the borrower as working capital if the final budgeted allocation of loan proceeds and closing costs do not use the entire loan.

◆ *Collateral requirements*—The Authorization will specify the exact assets that are to be used to secure the loan, and will detail the conditions under which their encumbrance is expected. A variety

Most lenders accept a boilerplate SBA Authorization with no effort to customize the restrictions on the borrower.

PART 3

“ Read the loan agreement and all covenants carefully. Understand all of the restrictions implied and consider how they will impact the business. ”

of SBA security documents may be referred to, depending on the specific collateral offered by the borrower:

Form 1059: Security Agreement—The borrower is required to execute this form to encumber personal property assets, and the Authorization should specify in which lien position the lender should be. If the lender is to be subordinated to a senior lender, the Authorization will note the name of the lender and the amount of the outstanding senior loan.

The Authorization will also refer to use of the UCC-1 Financing Statement, which is a standard document for recording public notice of the lender's lien on the borrower's personal property assets. The lender will attach a detailed list of these assets (with serial numbers, if available) to the UCC-1 and will record this statement in the county where the property is located.

RO IV 147: Deed to Secure Debt—The borrower is required to execute this form to encumber real property assets, and the Authorization should specify in which lien position the lender should be. If the lender is to be subordinated to a senior lender, the Authorization will note the name of the lender and the amount of the outstanding senior loan.

Form 148: Guaranty—The borrower (or the individuals who own the borrowing entity) are required to execute this form, which provides for a joint and several personal guaranty of the loan. Provisions describing this requirement may or may not describe collateral, depending on the agreement the borrower has reached with the lender during negotiations.

RO IV Form 82: Assignment of Life Insurance—The borrower (or the individuals who own the borrowing entity) are required to execute this form if there is a requirement to provide life insurance to secure the loan. A comparable form provided by the ensurer may be substituted.

Lease Agreement—The borrower is required to submit a copy of the Lease Agreement (if the borrower occupied leased premises) to confirm that the remaining term of the lease is extended to a minimum of the length of the loan repayment period.

RO IV Form 77: Lessor's Agreement—The borrower is required to obtain the execution of this agreement with the lessor. The Lessor's Agreement protects the lender from a landlord attempting to assert any interest in the borrower's personal assets or other assets in which the lender encumbers to secure the loan and that may be situated in the landlord's premises.

RO IV Form 79: Collateral Assignment of Lease—If the borrower has been approved for financing using the Alter Ego Concept, this form is required to provide the lender with an assignment of the lease on the business premises to the Alter Ego. The Alter Ego Concept is employed when assets are purchased in the name of the business owner and leased to the business entity, which also guarantees the loan.

✧ Additional real estate requirements—There are an additional set of covenants and documents required if the lender is encumbering real estate collateral. These include:

Single property deed to secure debt—The lender is required to file a separate deed to secure debt for each parcel of real property taken as collateral.

RO IV Form 26: Agreement as to Additional Advances— When the lender is taking a subordinate position on the borrower's real property, the lender will require the senior lender to execute this document. This form protects the lender from losing collateral coverage if a senior lender were to advance additional proceeds to the borrower under the senior loan agreement.

Title insurance—The lender is required to obtain title insurance without any survey exceptions on real property parcels where the lender is to have a first priority lien. This requirement includes a current survey of the subject property to ensure that there are no property encroachments or boundary errors.

RO IV Form 37: Attorney's Certificate of Title—The lender is permitted to use a guaranteed title search for parcels where the lender is to be in a subordinated lien position.

"SBA loans always carry a 'due on sale' clause. Loans cannot be automatically assumed by a subsequent buyer."

PART 3

❝ The SBA permits lenders to assess up to a 5% penalty on payments more than ten days late.❞

Separate guaranty—Each owner of title on a particular parcel of real property will be required to execute a separate guaranty, even if the title holder does not have a direct interest in the borrower.

Appraisal—The borrower is required to provide the lender with an appraisal that is not more than six months old that supports the specific valuation used to obtain approval of the loan. If the appraisal determines that the property has a lower value, the borrower will have to provide additional equity or additional collateral, or the lender may reduce the loan.

Survey—The borrower is required to provide the lender with a current survey that shows the existing boundaries and improvements.

Minimum occupancy—For existing buildings, the borrower is required to occupy at least 50% of the premises.

✦ *Additional personal property requirements*—There are an additional set of covenants and documents required if the lender is encumbering personal property collateral. These include:

Schedule A—The lender will require that the borrower provide a detailed list of the personal property assets securing the loan. This list will be attached to the UCC-1 and the Security Agreement, both of which will contain language specifying that the property pledged will include but will not be limited to the items on Schedule A. Where applicable, all assets on Schedule A should be described with the manufacturer's name and the model and serial numbers.

Lien search—The lender is required to conduct a lien search to evidence that the requisite lien position is acquired.

On-site inspection—The lender must certify to the SBA that an on-site inspection of the personal property asset was conducted prior to the first disbursements of the loan proceeds.

There may be other documentation required to perfect the borrower's collateral, depending on the exact nature, ownership, and location of the collateral assets.

Conditions and covenants. The fifth section sets forth several conditions that the borrower must agree to comply with during the term of the loan.

✦ *Execution*—The borrower must agree to execute all of the documents required, which are mentioned previously in this chapter.

✦ *Reimbursable expenses*—The borrower agrees to reimburse the lender on demand for all expenses incurred for the borrower's application and the making and administration of the loan. Most of these expenses will be charged to the borrower at the loan closing.

✦ *Books, records, and reports*—The borrower agrees to maintain records of business activities (including financial reports) and to provide them to the lender upon request. Further, the borrower agrees that the lender may inspect the financial records or appraise any asset of the business at any time. The borrower also authorizes any municipal, state, or federal government authority to provide the lender or SBA with copies of information that may be on file about the borrower.

✦ *Management consultants*—The borrower agrees not to engage the services of a management consultant without prior approval of the lender and the SBA.

✦ *Distributions and compensation*—The borrower agrees to not make distributions of capital or assets, retire stock or partnership interests, consolidate or merge with another company, or make preferential arrangements with affiliated companies during the term of the loan. Further, the borrower will not provide any bonuses, distributions, gifts, or loans to any owner, director, officer, or employee in any manner other than reasonable compensation for services during the term of the loan.

✦ *Hazard insurance*—The borrower agrees to maintain hazard insurance on the fixed assets that are used to secure the loan. All insurance policies will name the lender as loss payee and/or mortgagor, as appropriate. The borrower's furniture, fixtures, and equipment must be insured to at least 90% of replacement cost.

Policies insuring buildings must include a mortgagor's clause indicating that the interest of the mortgagor shall not be invalidated by the neglect of the owner, and that the mortgagor will be given thirty days notice prior to cancellation. This clause is commonly referred to as the New York Standard Mortgage Clause.

> ❝ *The proceeds from an SBA loan must be disbursed in accordance to representations made to the SBA, or their prior approval is required to make any changes.* ❞

PART 3

❝ Borrowers occupying leased premises should expect the lender to require a waiver to be executed by the landlord subordinating any interests in the borrower's tangible assets. These waivers can be difficult to negotiate with landlords a mid-term of the lease.❞

✧ *Federal taxes*—The borrower must ensure that all federal withholding taxes are paid up to date and that there are no outstanding tax liens against the borrower.

✧ *Change of ownership*—The borrower must agree not to change the ownership, control of the business, the business name, or the form of business organization, without the approval of the lender and the SBA.

✧ *Receipt of SBA forms*—The borrower must execute the following SBA forms in compliance with federal regulations governing guaranteed loans:

> *Form 1624: Certification Regarding Debarment*—This document is required to attest that the borrower, the individual, and the business entity have not been debarred from doing business with the federal government due to any administrative, disciplinary, or other action specifically restricting the respective parties.

> *Form 652: Assurance of Compliance For Nondiscrimination*—This document is required to attest that the borrower and any subsequent recipients of the SBA-guaranteed loan proceeds agree to comply with SBA regulations pertaining to discrimination. These regulations require that no person be excluded from participation in, or be denied the benefits of, any federal financial assistance from the SBA based on age, color, handicap, marital status, national origin, race, religion, or sex.

✧ *Business licenses*—The borrower is required to provide the lender with a copy of business licenses and any special operating permits or licenses required by the State.

✧ *Negative pledge covenant*—The borrower agrees not to encumber or convey any asset or ownership of the business without prior approval of the lender and the SBA.

✧ *ADO Form 20: Opinion of Counsel*—The lender's attorney is required to provide an opinion regarding the loan transaction.

✧ *Other insurance*—Depending on the nature of the collateral provided by the borrower, additional insurance may be required:

> *Flood insurance.* If the business or collateral is located in a special hazard area subject to flooding, mud slides, or ero-

sion, the borrower must agree to maintain Federal Flood Insurance in the maximum amount available.

Automobile insurance. If motor vehicles are used as collateral, the borrower must agree to maintain collision and liability in an amount satisfactory to the lender, with the lender named as the loss payee.

✧ *Borrower's equity*—Prior to the first disbursement of the loan, the borrower must provide satisfactory evidence of the requisite equity injection, as represented in the loan application.

✧ *Form 155: Standby Agreement*—Any subordinate creditors of the borrower must execute a Standby Agreement to subordinate the lien rights and other general rights in favor of the SBA lender.

✧ *Organizational authority*—The borrower must substantiate its authority to enter into the loan by producing organizational documents providing such information:

If the borrower is a corporation, it must provide:
    Corporate Resolution—Form 160
    Certificate of Good Standing
    Articles of Incorporation
    Qualification of foreign corporation to do business in the resident state, if applicable

If the borrower is a partnership, it must provide:
    Partnership Agreement
    Certificate as to Partners—Form 160A
    Certificate of Limited Partnership, if applicable
    Certificate of Existence

✧ *Bulk-sales notice*—If applicable, the borrower must provide the lender with evidence of compliance with any applicable state or federal bulk-sales laws.

✧ *Building compliance*—The borrower must provide evidence that any commercial buildings used as collateral conform to all applicable building, zoning, and sanitation codes, as well as the Americans With Disabilities Act of 1990, as amended.

✧ *Fixed asset limit*—If included, the borrower may agree to limit the acquisition of fixed assets to a particular level, subject to approval from the lender and the SBA.

" Lenders require title insurance on all real property priority mortgages. Savvy borrowers extend that coverage for the entire property value. "

PART 3

> ❝ *Multiple business owners are required to give a 'joint and several' personal guaranty to secure an SBA loan. Effectively a lender could single out one guarantor to pursue for repayment in lieu of default.* ❞

✧ *Franchise agreement*—The borrower must provide the lender with a copy of any franchise agreement to which it is a party.

✧ *Alien registration*—If applicable, the borrower must provide the lender with a copy of the alien registration of any owners who are not U.S. citizens.

✧ *Environmental assessment conditions*—If the borrower is securing the loan with commercial property, the lender and the SBA will require that an environmental assessment of the property be obtained. The following conditions will be included in the Authorization:

> *Option to modify or cancel.* The lender and SBA reserve the right to modify or cancel the loan if environmental contamination is discovered on the property.
>
> *Environmental assessment.* The lender and the SBA will require an Environmental Disclosure Form, an Environmental Questionnaire (ADO For 001), or a Phase 1 Environmental Audit. The determination of which assessment is used is based on the historic use of the property and development in the immediate area.
>
> *UST requirements.* If the property contains underground storage tanks (USTs), the borrower is required to comply with all federal and state regulations for USTs. The borrower must also provide the lender with evidence on an annual basis of compliance with these regulations, including the EPA financial responsibility regulations.

✧ *Alter Ego concept*—If using an Alter Ego loan, the borrower must agree that the respective ownership in collateral assets and in the business entity will remain identical and in the same proportion until the loan is repaid, unless the lender and the SBA consent to any change.

✧ *Construction loan conditions*—If the borrower is using any portion of the loan proceeds to build a new structure or make improvements on an existing structure, the following provisions shall be in the Authorization:

> *Construction documentation.* The borrower will be required to provide the lender with the following documentation related to construction:

Building plans and specifications

Evidence of builder's risk insurance and workers compensation insurance carried by the contractor

Evidence that the contractor has furnished a performance bond for 100% of labor and materials, with the borrower and lender named as the obligees

Agreement of Compliance: Form 601

Construction contract

Borrower's equity. Evidence of the borrower's equity contribution toward the construction project must be provided, since the borrower's funds will be used before any loan proceeds will be advanced.

Survey. The borrower must furnish an as-built survey prior to any advances of the construction funds in order to show existing boundaries and improvements.

Earthquake standards. For new buildings, the borrower must provide evidence that the project will meet the requirements of the "National Earthquake Hazards Reduction Program Recommended Provisions for the Development of Seismic Regulations for New Buildings." A certificate may be obtained from the project architect to fulfill this requirement.

Interim inspections. As the borrower requests loan advances, the lender will conduct interim inspections of the project to verify that construction conforms to plans and specifications.

Retainage. The lender will withhold 10% of the construction contract proceeds until the project is completed.

Lien waivers. The lender will require all contractors, subcontractors, and suppliers to sign a lien waiver prior to each loan disbursement.

Cost overruns. If the borrower's project experiences cost overruns, the borrower or the lender must provide additional funds to complete the project.

Minimum occupancy. For newly constructed buildings, the borrower is required to occupy at least 67% of the premises.

✧ *American-made products*—To the extent possible, the borrower agrees to purchase American-made equipment and products with the proceeds of the loan.

✧ *Lottery income restriction*—The borrower must acknowledge that the Authorization restricts the borrower to no more than 33% of

❝ One common pre-condition is that the borrower agree to execute anything required by the lender to perfect a collateral assignment.❞

annual gross revenue being generated from commissions on official state lottery sales.

Execution. The sixth section confirms the general legal conditions of the Authorization that the SBA and lender acknowledge and execute in this section.

How Can the Borrower Close the Loan Faster?

Most borrowers are ready to close the loan within a week of the final loan approval, but it is rare that the lender can be prepared in this time frame. There is a lot of work to prepare for a loan closing.

Rather than sit frustrated on the sidelines, the borrower can assist the lender and closing attorney with many tasks. This help will make a difference in the time required to complete the transaction.

Start closing before the loan is approved. Much of the due diligence required before closing, such as appraisals, surveys, and environmental assessments, is not conducted until after final approval of the loan. This delay is due to the unwillingness of most borrowers to risk spending thousands of dollars on these studies without having the assurance that the loan will be approved.

One method to shorten the time gap between SBA loan approval and loan closing is to initiate these time-consuming activities earlier in the process. While this does jeopardize the borrower's funds, in many situations the risk is low because of the borrower's clear financial qualification and SBA eligibility. The lender should be able to express some degree of confidence as to whether the borrower should take this risk.

If the borrower has the appraisal, survey, environmental assessment, life insurance, and even a title opinion and lien search in hand when the loan is approved, the loan could be closed in a matter of days.

Review the authorization. The borrower should obtain a copy of the Authorization from the lender or the SBA as soon as possible and carefully review it. The borrower should determine that the document accurately reflects the transaction negotiated between the borrower and the lender.

The borrower should ensure that it is capable of complying with the terms of the Authorization and should inquire up front about any items that are not understood. If any modifications are needed, the borrower should bring these items to the attention of the lender immediately, since changes may require several weeks for approval.

Get life insurance! If the Authorization requires the borrower to furnish life insurance on any of the individual owners or managers, application for these insurance policies should begin immediately. A $1 million life insurance policy can no longer be obtained over the telephone.

With the greater incidence of life-threatening infections related to HIV, insurers are much more selective about issuing large policies, and most will require a blood test for even a $100,000 policy. Blood work requires time, and the underwriting of the insurer may also include financial qualification in order to justify the policy.

To evidence compliance with the insurance requirement, the borrower may be required to furnish an actual policy at the loan closing. The life insurance policy may take four to six weeks to issue. It is wise to apply for life insurance coverage as soon as possible during the loan closing stage.

Get the lender's attention. A borrower can help the lender and closing attorney by providing additional information or performing some assigned tasks. A borrower who communicates directly, regularly, and constructively can shorten the time required to close.

Supply additional documentation. The borrower may be required to produce additional material for the lender's attorney, primarily to document specific conditions and to provide further information about the collateral.

Even though some of this information may have been provided previously to the lender, it is easier for the borrower to reproduce it for the closing attorney. The attorney will be particularly concerned about preparation of the security documents and ensuring compliance with the terms of the Authorization. The Authorization may involve documentation that was not required during the application stage. The borrower will need to produce this additional information for the closing attorney.

Monitor the professionals. Borrowers using real estate as collateral will be required to obtain assistance from professionals for preparation of an appraisal, survey, environmental assessment, and other information required by the lender's due diligence. These professionals may be efficient in producing their reports, or they may hold up the entire closing. The borrower should get involved in this part of the process to ensure that it moves as swiftly as possible.

The borrower should coordinate the work with these professionals as closely as possible. After determining who the lender has engaged for these matters, the borrower should contact them independently of the lender to schedule an appointment.

To close the loan faster:

✧ If confident of approval, order independent reports before loan commitment from lender-approved consultants.

✧ Study and understand an SBA authorization and loan agreement to ensure compliance.

✧ If required to buy life insurance, start the process early. New insurance can take up to eight weeks to approve!

✧ Manage the lender and attorney effectively by staying in contact regularly and being accessible.

✧ Be ready to produce additional information upon request.

✧ Allow time for unexpected problems to be resolved.

PART 3

"Anticipate problems by monitoring progress of the lender, attorney, and other professionals regularly."

The borrower should make an effort to be present when the professional inspects the property. Often, the professional will have questions about the site or structure and, if no one is available, assumptions may be substituted for facts. The borrower's presence can enhance the report by supplying updated information that is usually more accurate and more detailed than would otherwise be available to the professional.

Put out the fires. Problems frequently arise during the due diligence performed in preparation for loan closing. Maybe the borrower's appraisal came in too low, or some environmental contamination was discovered on the real property. Maybe an old, unsatisfied mortgage is found to be outstanding from a lender paid off ten years ago, and the property has been subsequently sold three times.

Often, the lender or the lender's attorney will react to these problems as if the deal is off, as if the borrower is out of luck. But, the problem can usually be resolved and the transaction is far from dead. Of greater concern is getting the parties focused on resolving the problem without any unnecessary delay in closing the loan.

It is important for the borrower to determine as quickly as possible the exact nature of the problem and the remedy for solving it. The borrower should not rely strictly on the lender's attorney to define the resolution, because the lender's best solution is not always optimum for the borrower. The borrower should obtain the appropriate professional assistance in managing the resolution of the particular problem.

No one will make solving the problem a greater priority than the borrower. Instead of waiting for someone else to initiate the resolution, the borrower must manage the situation personally to make sure the loan closing is postponed for weeks instead of months.

If the problem is rather minor, the borrower may be able to continue with the closing on schedule by setting aside enough money in escrow to cover the maximum exposure to the problem. For example, if there is an outstanding mortgage for $3,000 that the seller asserts has been satisfied, but the holder cannot be located immediately, the borrower can put $3,000 in escrow at closing to assure the lender that the mortgage will be satisfied.

How Can the Closing Costs Be Reduced?

One of the most frequent complaints about SBA loans is the total cost involved to close the loan. Borrowers obtaining long-term real estate financing can expect to pay as much as 6% of the total loan to close. In reality, many of these costs are simply inherent to the deal and cannot be avoided.

Accepting these closing expenses is a combination of putting the costs in perspective and determining which costs can be reduced or eliminated. The borrower can influence these costs in certain circumstances. The following paragraphs describe some of the common costs associated with closing an SBA loan and how the borrower might lower them in certain instances.

SBA Guaranty Fee

The lender must pay and usually requires the borrower's reimbursement of a fee to the SBA for the loan guaranty. This fee was raised in FY 1996 to the following scale:

GUARANTEED PORTION OF LOAN	GUARANTY FEE
$0–$80,000	2%
$80,001–$250,000	3%
$250,001–$500,000	3.5%
$500,001–$750,000	3.875%

If the loan carries a 75% guaranty, the fee is calculated by multiplying the guaranteed portion of the loan by the appropriate fee. This fee is essentially the insurance premium to fund the agency's bad loan losses from its collective portfolio of guaranteed loans.

The only way to reduce this fee is to be fortunate enough to be in a competitive situation between two lenders. If both lenders want to make the business loan, the borrower could negotiate to have one of the lenders absorb all or part of the SBA guaranty fee. This option is available only to the strongest borrowers who are highly qualified financially.

Attorney's Fees

The SBA loan is always closed by an attorney due to the complexities involved in complying with the Authorization. Lenders would simply invite too much exposure not to involve a professional for this task. And, of course, the cost of the attorneys will be passed on to the borrower.

Depending on the dynamics of the transaction, attorneys will have varying degrees of involvement. If there is real property included, the

The SBA guaranty fee is akin to a credit insurance premium paid to cause the lender to make the loan. It substitutes for the fee charged by most lenders for conventional loans.

PART 3

" There are a wide

range of charges imputed

by attorneys, depending

on the responsibilities

assigned by the

lender. "

attorneys will have more responsibilities in the closing and the costs will be proportionately greater.

Attorney's fees will vary greatly depending on the locale, the local market, the size of the firm, and the firm's familiarity with SBA loans. These fees may range from a flat $1,500 up to roughly 1% of the transaction plus title insurance.

The borrower can reduce the attorney's fees in several ways:

✧ The borrower can ask the lender to select a firm with lower costs. Understanding that the borrower is sensitive to the closing costs, the lender may have some latitude to influence the firm selection and to request a lower fee.

✧ The borrower can ask the lender to select an attorney who has previously worked for the borrower. If the attorney does not have a conflict of interest, the familiarity with the borrower may reduce the costs of the transaction, even though the attorney will now represent the lender.

✧ The borrower can ask the attorney for a written fee estimate. This way, the borrower can discuss the level of the estimate with the lender and the attorney before any work begins. Attorneys, like other professionals, find it easier to charge higher fees once the work has been performed. When seeking the business, they seem to be a little more reasonable on fees, particularly when required to provide a quote up front.

✧ If certain legal work has been done in the past couple of years that relates to the loan or the collateral, such as title examinations, the borrower can provide this information to the attorney. If the borrower's real property has title insurance, the attorney may be able to renew the old title policy and conduct a shorter title search. This combination should significantly reduce a portion of the legal fees involved.

✧ The borrower may be able to provide some of the clerical work for the attorney, thereby reducing the add-on cost associated with a loan closing. For example, because the attorney must assemble several closing packages, the borrower saves money by providing several copies of the necessary documents. The borrower can reproduce them less expensively than the attorney.

Other Professional Fees

The borrower will have to bear the costs of several professionals involved in the due diligence phase of closing the loan. Such specialists as an appraiser, environmental engineer, surveyor, and construction inspector may be involved to provide independent opinions for the specific transaction.

Fees for these specialists may range from $750 to $4,000 each, depending on the situation, the specific nature of their engagement, and the local market in which they work. The best way to manage these fees are as follows:

✧ The borrower can ask the lender to select a professional with lower costs. Understanding that the borrower is sensitive to these costs, the lender may have some latitude to influence firm selection and to request that the professional negotiate a lower fee.

✧ The borrower can ask the lender to select a professional who has previously worked for the borrower. If these professionals are familiar with the borrower or the borrower's assets, this fact may reduce the costs of the transaction, even though they are now representing the lender. In the case of a surveyor, appraiser, or environmental engineer, the lender should be able to accept an update of the previous work performed.

✧ The borrower can ask the professional for a written fee estimate. This way, the borrower can discuss the level of the estimate with the lender and the professional before any work begins. Specialists find it easier to charge higher fees once the work has been performed. When seeking the engagement, they seem to be a little more reasonable on fees, particularly when required to provide a quote up front.

✧ If certain work has been done in the past couple of years for the borrower that relates to the collateral, such as appraisals or environmental reports, the borrower can provide this information to the specialist. This information could significantly reduce the professional fees involved.

✧ If appropriate, the borrower can ask the lender to limit the scope of the professional's engagement to the exact information

---

Reduce closing costs:

✧ Find lender which prepares its own closing documents.

✧ If lender uses attorneys, discuss their fees to find the most reasonable one.

✧ Discuss fees with the consultants preparing the due diligence reports. All of these fees are subject to reasonableness, according to SBA regulations.

✧ Close the loan as near as possible to the end of the month to avoid prepaid interest charges.

required by the Authorization. Often, the professional's report includes information not requested or required, which can lead to higher fees for the borrower.

Recording Costs and Taxes

Many counties and states assess fees for the recording of certain documents required to perfect the lender's lien on the borrower's collateral assets, such as mortgages and UCC-1s. These fees vary greatly from state to state, but usually must be considered the cost of doing business. They are certainly not negotiable, and the lender will typically not absorb them.

Prepaid Interest

Depending on when the loan is closed, the borrower will be responsible for a varying sum of prepaid interest. SBA loans are placed on a standardized repayment schedule, which calls for the first loan payment to be due on the first day of the second month after the loan closes.

For example, if a loan closes on the fifteenth day of January, the first payment will be due on March 1. However, since interest is billed in arrears (payable for the period preceding the payment), the interest collected on the March 1 payment would be for the period February 1 through March 1. Therefore, at the loan closing, the lender would collect a prepaid interest charge for the period from January 15 through January 31. This prepaid interest is in lieu of a payment being due on February 1—on larger loans, the prepaid interest can significantly alter the cash disbursed at the loan closing. Borrowers can lower this sum by closing the loan as close as possible to the last day of the month.

It is important for the borrower to put the costs of closing a loan in perspective. In reality, these costs are a necessary part of borrowing money and simply cannot be avoided. The borrower should view the costs over the life of the loan, rather than simply in the period in which they are incurred. If the borrower is obtaining a $1,000,000 real estate loan for twenty-five years, the $40,000 in closing costs equate to only $1,600 per year.

CHAPTER 7

Other Borrower Issues

There are many other considerations to decide on before applying for a loan. How much help do you want? Is there a good investment to assure the best deal? Learn:

- ✦ Professional assistance: cost and benefit
- ✦ Not to be worried about the SBA
- ✦ How affiliates can kill your deal

Should the Borrower Use a Loan Packager?

Many small business owners seeking financing have recognized the value of using professional advice. But just as many business people have become victims of unscrupulous or inept loan brokers—loan brokers who either waste valuable time conducting a hopeless search for capital or who collect fees that they never earned.

Loan consultants play an important role in today's banking environment. With the consolidation of thousands of banks and the introduction of many new financing venues, entrepreneurs cannot be expected to keep track of the constantly changing financial marketplace.

Fortunately, there are many consultants whose primary efforts are focused on the SBA loan market. These consultants, often referred to as "packagers," are positioned to provide small businesses with the expertise of how and where to access SBA financing. The value of these services is generally in proportion to what they cost.

Any consultant willing to work on behalf of the borrower for several months without a retainer, purely on a contingency basis, is usually worth everything paid to them—nothing. Because borrowers can be

Be wary of fees charged up front by packagers unless you have a written agreement which details when they have earned a fee.

fickle, seasoned consultants will not make large time investments without tangible commitments on the part of clients in form of monetary deposits. These consultants have successfully raised many millions of dollars in loans for borrowers who changed their minds, resulting in no compensation for the considerable effort.

Before writing a check to engage these consultants, the borrower should take the time to validate their capabilities in successfully obtaining loans. Does their track record match their confidence about how well they will accomplish their mission? This short exercise could save the borrower from an expensive and frustrating exercise in futility.

First, the borrower should request a list of references from the consultant. In contacting these businesses that engaged the services of this consultant, the borrower can determine how well the consultant performed. Did the business obtain the financing it needed? If not, why? If so, was the time frame reasonable? Did the consultant communicate with the business on a regular and informed basis? Did the consultant have a firm grasp of the company's objectives, and were those objectives met due to the efforts of the consultant?

The borrower can then ask the consultant for references in the lending community. Obviously, the consultant will not permit the borrower to contact any potential lender that may be the target of the loan proposal. But the borrower can speak with other lenders, outside the scope of the proposed deal, to which the consultant has referred transactions.

What was the lender's attitude toward the consultant? Does the lender rely on the consultant merely for referrals, or does the lender express confidence in the consultant's ability to analyze potential deals? In other words, does the consultant's opinion count, or is the consultant only throwing darts at the wall with the borrower's deal.

Finally, the borrower should determine whether the consultant is a member of any trade associations such as the chamber of commerce, the National Federation of Independent Businesses, the National Association of Government Guaranteed Lenders or other groups that support small businesses. These memberships are not necessarily a qualification, but they can be indicative of the success and standing of the consultant in the industry. These groups rarely provide references, but the borrower can verify the claimed membership status of the consultant.

The borrower should remember that the consultant is not the decision maker for the loan request. Rather the consultant prepares the application and helps structure the transaction. But after selecting the lender and presenting the case, the consultant loses control of the timing and decision involved.

Most lenders commonly disregard the time constraints of their customers. If the loan needs to be reviewed by a government guarantor, such as the SBA, the lender also loses control of the deal. Everyone is in a hurry. As long as the consultant demonstrates diligence in performing specific responsibilities, the consultant should not be blamed for the actions of others.

These consultants are businesspeople, too. It is not unreasonable, therefore, for consultants to request the borrower to engage their services with a written agreement and to require a retainer as an expression of commitment on the borrower's part. Services and advice cannot be repossessed, and the consultant should not be penalized for changes in the borrower's situation or strategy that render those services and advice useless.

To be cautious, the borrower should understand and agree to the compensation expectations of the consultant before work begins on the borrower's behalf. The consultant's willingness to work on a contingency may sound like a good arrangement for the borrower, but it also may indicate that the borrower is employing an inexperienced party to work on the loan application. Borrowers should beware of people who can make a living collecting $250 application fees.

A reasonable consultant will not ask for a retainer unless confident about successfully completing the borrower's deal. The prospects of obtaining a loan cannot be reliably predicted without a thorough review of the borrower's financial statements and other pertinent data.

Loan consultants can easily create value for a business; they allow the borrower to concentrate on the company rather that hopping through twenty banks, leaving a track record on the owner's credit report for every lender that turned down the deal. But borrowers should be willing to pay for quality services and should know who is engaged for this important assignment.

How Should the Borrower Us an Attorney?

Many borrowers utilize legal counsel for a variety of business affairs, and naturally want them involved in closing the SBA loan. Although there is nothing wrong with this procedure, it may prove to be an expensive duplication of efforts.

Selecting a packager:

✧ Get borrower and lender references and check them out!

✧ Determine any trade association memberships and call them.

✧ Get fee arrangement in writing.

PART 3

What the borrower's attorney can provide to the process is to review the documents the borrower is required to execute in order to obtain the loan and to fulfill the requirements of the lender and the SBA. That review can ensure that someone representing the borrower's interest interprets these documents and understands the obligations.

What the borrower's attorney has very little chance of doing is to make many meaningful changes in the documentation for the borrower's benefit. The principal documentation used for SBA-guaranteed loans is provided by the SBA and cannot be altered. These guaranteed loans are similar to federally insured housing loans. The standardization of documentation is necessary since these loans are eligible to be sold in a secondary market by the lender.

The borrowers attorney can function effectively by reviewing the Loan Authorization and Agreement. This document sets forth the terms under which the loan is being extended, and refers to the other documentation that is necessary. From this information, the borrower's attorney can determine the nature of the deal, clarify what is being required of the borrower in terms of repayment and collateral, and describe the consequences of default.

Dispelling Common Myths about the SBA

Thousands of businesses have avoided seeking assistance from the SBA due to a number of misconceptions about the agency. Professionals serving the market often spend time convincing qualified borrowers that participation is worth the effort, and that nothing terrible would happen to the business if the SBA guaranteed the debt. Of course, the paperwork is at times overwhelming, but so is the paperwork for a conventional loan. This section addresses many of the most common and misleading myths.

The SBA program is primarily for women and minorities. This is not true. The SBA guaranty programs are available for participation by all persons, regardless of race, color, creed, age, or ethnicity. In FY 1994, 65% of all SBA loan guarantees were made for white males.

The agency does employ a relatively new initiative to encourage women and minority borrowers to utilize the program. These borrower categories are permitted to be preapproved for loan guarantees before a lender has formally approved their loan requests. However, the agency does not provide any special funding allocations for these categories. Nor

> SBA regulations governing independent loan agents specify that no one can charge fees determined solely as a percentage of the loan amount, or "points" in connection with an SBA-guaranteed loan. Any third party assistance can only be provided with charges detailed on an invoice itemizing hours spent on various tasks and the hourly rate charged. Further, all such fees must be disclosed to the lender and the SBA on SBA form 159 (found in Illustration 3-K).

do women or minority participants receive any special consideration or credit-scoring that would provide agency assistance in a situation in which other borrowers would be denied.

Anybody can get an SBA loan. There are limits. Participation with the SBA guaranty program is restricted to borrowers who qualify under certain conditions relating to the size of the small business concern (in terms of revenues, net income, net worth, or number of employees; depending on the type of loan guaranty and the industry involved) and the nature of the business activity.

Borrowers seeking to benefit under the 7(a) guaranty program are restricted by either gross revenues of $5.0 million (with some exceptions based on the industry of the borrower) or limited by 500 employees in some specific industries that are labor intensive, such as manufacturing. Questions of eligibility can be directed to the agency for clarification about specific situations.

Borrowers seeking to get assistance under the 504 Development Program are restricted by their average net income over the past three years (no more than $2.0 million annually, including affiliates) and net worth (no more than $6.0 million, including affiliates).

Businesses involved in real estate development, lending activities, gambling, and illegal activities are prohibited from receiving assistance from the loan guaranty program.

The government will monitor the business. Fears of "Big Brother" cause many small businesses to hesitate about the SBA guaranty program. Participation with the SBA includes no monitoring of the borrower's business activities, no government audits, and no interagency communications about the business operations.

The SBA does not have the interest, personnel, or mandate to provide any extraordinary supervision of the business unless the borrower is in default of the loan. When the borrower is in default, the SBA's interest will be strictly focused on working with the lender to recover the loan.

Obtaining SBA assistance does not increase the borrower's chances of being audited by the IRS or being examined by OSHA, the EPA, the Corps of Engineers, or any other government agency that regulates the operations of business and industry.

The lender does not care how good or bad the business is. This is totally false. Lenders participating with the SBA guaranty programs are responsible for making good loans. The SBA guaranty is intended to enhance a loan, not subsidize the lender to build a bad loan portfolio.

❝ The SBA program is not a grant program for social engineering of the business sector. It provides a public impetus to assist small businesses overcome capital constraints in order to finance essential enterprises that are in demand, but avoided by regulated banking sources due to inherent risks. ❞

PART 3

An unguaranteed portion of every loan will expose the lender to the full risk of the credit, and that portion is likely to increase in the next few years as funding for this program is restricted. Collecting bad loans can be very expensive in terms of time and money.

Do Affiliated Companies Affect the Application?

Affiliated companies affect the borrower's participation in the SBA loan guaranty programs by enlarging the parameters by which the lender has to determine eligibility for participation. Affiliates are defined as any other business entity in which at least a 20% interest is owned by the borrower, or any owner of at least 20% of the borrower. The affiliated companies are considered collectively with the enterprise for which the borrower is seeking finance, for purposes of determining whether the subject company seeking financing is eligible under the program limitations.

That is, any and all business interests in which the borrower and any owners of the borrower, individually or collectively, own at least a 20% stake, are considered together with the entity seeking to borrow money. This composite is used to calculate the total sales, number of employees, net income, or net worth in determining the eligibility limitations for obtaining a loan guaranty.

The lender is required to confirm the borrower's eligibility if any affiliated companies exist. The borrower, therefore, should be prepared to provide the lender with financial information about the affiliated entities in order to allow assessment of eligibility. This financial documentation has to be provided to the SBA as well.

The Value of Relationship Banking

If the lender is a bank, the borrower should be sensitive to the fact that the bank is in the business of providing many more services than commercial loans. In fact, banks are currently seeking to expand their list of services beyond the traditional services of cash management and handling currency and to enter into securities and insurance.

Banks need deposits with which to make loans. It is not important where they get these deposits, or even whether they are time or demand deposits. Each day, banks need millions of dollars on deposit to meet their demands for cash to cover loans and withdrawals. Recognizing this aspect of the banking business, the borrower should be prepared to be confronted with a request or requirement to utilize the bank's depository services if the business loan is extended.

Relationship banking can have many positive features, and it is important to know the dynamics so that the borrower receives every advantage available. While the lending personnel are traditionally recognized as the bankers with significant influence in the business, the borrower should be aware that there are many other persons who are worthwhile to know.

In measuring a banking relationship, there are many services that a business may purchase:

✧ *Demand deposit account (DDA)*—Virtually every person and certainly every commercial business maintains a demand deposit account or checking account. These are funds that the depositor places into an account to avoid having to manage large or frequent sums of cash. These funds are withdrawn upon the depositor's "demand," a directive issued in the form of a written check.

✧ *Time deposits (TD)*—These accounts are placed on deposit with a bank for a definite or indefinite amount of time. The bank pays the depositor interest on these funds, the amount of which varies according to how long the depositor agrees to leave the funds in the account. There are a variety of time deposit accounts, including savings accounts and certificates of deposit, all of which have specific features and benefits.

✧ *Safe deposit boxes*—Banks provide safe deposit boxes within their vault for storage of a depositor's valuable assets or documents.

✧ *Merchant credit services*—Every retail business that accepts MasterCard, Visa, American Express, or Discover cards has to have a merchant account through which to clear these charges. These accounts are provided on a qualified basis, dependent on confirmation of the merchant's business operation and financial stability.

✧ *Credit*—The best-known service provided by banks is credit. There are more types of loans available than ever before, with banks using a variety of credit products to deliver funds to con-

❝ While banks can't legally 'tie' customers with conditioned lending/deposit arrangements, using a relationship commitment will allow a business to negotiate better interest rates and an enhanced level of service. ❞

PART 3

«Larger banks are more difficult to forge relationships with due to impersonal approach to small business and high turnover.»

sumers for short-, intermediate-, and long-term reasons. Many banks make car loans, issue credit cards, and handle home loans.

The point of discussing these other services is to suggest that business borrowers should use their demand for these services as an attribute when requesting a commercial loan. If the borrower can demonstrate to the lender that the accommodation of credit will also provide the bank with a substantive customer for other services, the lender may be persuaded to stretch in some ways to approve the loan request or grant more favorable terms. A combination of a few of these accounts can mean thousands of dollars in fee income to the bank, and can provide a new source of inexpensive deposits for them.

Considering all of the services used, personally and in business, the borrower represents an impressive opportunity for the bank. Other shareholders, partners, and even senior managers can be included when the borrower compiles a list of potential business available to the bank.

The prospect of these other relationship accounts will not make a bad loan proposal good, but it can certainly enhance a questionable deal—and provide the lender with incentives to give the borrower a chance. If the borrower does not need this kind of assistance for loan approval, the relationship accounts may help improve the interest rate or other terms offered on the loan by the bank.

CHAPTER 8

What If the Lender Says No?

Sometimes there just isn't a deal in the cards. Sometimes the lender errs due to poor listening skills or a misunderstanding. Why the word "no" is used is important. Learn:

- ✦ How to understand rejection
- ✦ How to respond to a loan denial
- ✦ How to move on to the next deal

How to Handle Rejection

Sometimes the lender says no—maybe even without conditions, exceptions, or encouragement; maybe even without a phone call or a letter. Regardless of how positive the discussions have been, how upbeat the loan officer is about the borrower's prospects, and how much the lender wants to say yes, the borrower's application is subject to denial.

Many lending personnel expose their distance from the decision-making process, or their own inexperience, by continually encouraging the borrower about the prospects of approval up through the last minute. But when the committee says no, the loan officer can find all sorts of things that are wrong with the proposed deal. This scenario goes back to the weaknesses in the loan approval process discussed earlier.

No is one half of the possible replies available to the lender in responding to a loan request. The borrower should listen carefully to the no to understand the different ways it may have been said. An astute borrower will listen carefully to the explanation spoken by the lender after the word "because."

❝ What part of 'no' don't you understand?

Ask.❞

The lender makes a decision based on business, not on personality. The lender is responsible for making a decision based on qualifying the loan request within the parameters that must be maintained.

The borrower should not: get mad, become defensive, be hurt, feel betrayed, or say anything that may irreparably damage future opportunities to obtain financing from this lender. Perhaps the loan officer has a difficult time being blunt; perhaps the loan officer is matter-of-fact about the unwillingness of the institution to provide the loan; or perhaps the loan officer feels uneasy about communicating the disappointing news.

No matter how well or how badly the lender delivers the answer to the borrower, and regardless of how well or how badly the borrower handles the news, it is important for the borrower to keep a positive demeanor and be very cordial. The borrower needs the loan officer's assistance to understand the reasoning behind the lender's rejection. That assistance will not be forthcoming if the borrower creates an uncomfortable situation after being turned down.

How Did the Loan Officer Say No?

There are many ways in which a lender can say no. Listening to and analyzing the negative reply to the loan request is the next step in the loan application process. It is what the loan officer says that is important: the explanation, the details, the analysis of the borrower's position. How does the lender say no?

"No, but . . . ," Perhaps the lender is providing the borrower with ways to change the request in order to provide the lender with a way to say yes. Often, borrowers hear only the word "no" and miss the lender's request to hear the word "please."

"No, unless . . . ," Maybe the lender gave the borrower a conditional no, which could be changed if the borrower were to meet specified conditions or agree to more restrictive terms.

"I cannot say yes because . . . ," Sometimes the lender does not say no at all, but also does not say yes. Listening can sometimes tell the borrower how to overcome the lender's specific reservations in order to get the final yes.

"Not yet . . . ," Maybe the borrower has submitted the request too early. Is the lender not yet comfortable with the level of success of the business? Is it too early for substantive trends to justify the borrower's ambition to expand? Sometimes the lender is actually saying wait.

"No, because the borrower . . . ," Maybe lenders turn down requests because of specific objections or reservations that they cannot overcome. Identifying these problems will assist the borrower in refocusing the loan request at a later date or submitting it to another lender.

"No, because the lender . . . ," Sometimes the restrictions of the institution will not allow a lender to say yes. Maybe the request is outside the lender's market area, or greater than the lending limit. If the lender's answer to the loan request is no because of what they cannot or will not do, the borrower can be encouraged that the request is valid. The borrower can probably find another lender to agree with the request.

"Hell no . . . ," Sometimes a blunt no should cause the borrower to reflect inward as to the validity of the proposal. Is it realistic that any lender will be able to extend the financing? Negative replies without explanations sometimes indicate fundamental weaknesses in the proposal. The borrower can use a negative response constructively for redesigning the business plan.

There are as many variations of saying no as there are people and situations. It is not the answer the borrower is seeking, but neither is it invaluable or irreversible. Listening to the loan rejection is the key to learning how to get the proposal approved.

What Is the Next Step?

There are many ways to respond to a loan denial. Selecting the correct response will be integral to getting approval the next time the borrower presents the proposal. Determining the next step requires that the borrower fully understand how and why the lender turned the application down.

As mentioned earlier, it is imperative for the borrower to listen to the lender's explanation without allowing an emotional response to cloud understanding. Without putting the lender on the defensive, the borrower should ask questions. Respectful inquiries and specific answers will benefit the borrower in making the proposal succeed at a later date.

Several days later, the borrower can call the lender to request an appointment for additional information about why the loan was rejected. The purpose of this meeting is for the borrower to learn by seeking answers from someone with a degree of expertise. These discussions are not intended to change the lender's mind about the proposed transaction, but rather to prepare the borrower for the next lender.

Handling rejection:

◇ Listen carefully to the lender's rejection.
◇ Determine whether there are errors in the lender's reasoning beyond a difference of opinion.
◇ Don't get angry or take rejection personally—its business.
◇ Ask questions and learn more about the weaknesses in the proposal.
◇ Address the weaknesses and try, try again.

PART 3

Listen carefully to the words following 'no.' There is usually a door through which to come.

In preparing for this interview, the borrower should focus on business issues rather than personal reactions. By encouraging the lender to respond with directness, the borrower can create an opportunity for instructive commentary.

From the lender's perspective, what factors about the business were not acceptable: the industry, location, products, employees, capitalization, track record, deal, or even management? What weaknesses need to be addressed in the business for the next loan proposal?

Was the negative reply due to the lender? Often, lenders steer away from particular loans because of a previous bad experience in the industry or because of the type of loan. Maybe the lender's loan policies, market area, or lending limits restrict participation in the borrower's request. Often, lenders do not think in terms of what can be done, but rather in terms of what cannot be done. The burden of asking the right question is usually left with the borrower, who must determine on what basis the loan officer will respond affirmatively.

Was the lender's rejection intended to be permanent, or can conditions or specific benchmarks change the response? Will the lender ever consider this financing? If so, exactly what changes or conditions are required? Where is the lender's level of comfort, and can the borrower attain it? This information will give the borrower more parameters in which to react and make future choices.

Maybe the lender is telling the borrower to move on to the next lender. In this case, this lender can make recommendations about where else to apply. The borrower can ask why the proposal may be acceptable somewhere else; the answer will help the borrower know how the next lender should be approached.

Responding to the Lender's Objections

Identifying the qualifications, exceptions, alterations, and finality of the lender's rejection helps the borrower to determine why the lender said no. The following list includes some of the most common reasons for rejecting a loan request and some logical responses for the borrower:

Objection 1: The business is undercapitalized.

Lenders want the borrower to have either contributed or earned a substantive portion of the net worth of the business. In comparing the total debt to the total equity, there should be some measurable part of the company's financing provided from a source other than the lender.

Response: The borrower can take a number of measures to increase equity in the business:

⬧ The borrower can inject more money into the company from such sources as savings, a second mortgage on an owner's home, liquidated investments, and the cash surrender value of a life insurance policy.

⬧ The borrower can convert any subordinated debt or notes payable to the company to equity. Although this act may have consequences if and when the holders want to withdraw the money, it may be necessary to convince the lender of the borrower's commitment to the success of the business.

⬧ The borrower can reduce any other liabilities of the company to a reasonable extent, at a discount if possible. Lowering the debt leverage can permit lenders to have a stronger position, without other liabilities distracting from their ability to be repaid.

⬧ If the borrower does not have additional capital to contribute, maybe relatives, friends, employees, or suppliers would be willing to invest in the business. This additional capital could be structured to ensure their priority in redemption as soon as the business accumulated additional capital to satisfy the requirements of the lender.

Objection 2: The business has not earned money yet.

Lenders expect that the borrower can support the business strategy with a track record of business success. If the company has perpetually lost money, most lenders may reason that additional financing will compound those losses and the borrower will be unable to repay the borrowed funds.

Response: The borrower's explanation of the financial history of the business (suggested earlier in the book) was not sufficient or was not reasonable. If the business has failed to profit, it is important to demonstrate why and to explain how the borrower will correct the problem.

Sometimes the borrower's strategy to earn profits is as simple as acquiring more efficient assets to achieve profitability. Lenders can usually accept this strategy if the borrower can prove that increases in productivity will indeed provide profits.

> *Find a way to get the lender to say YES, then find a way to live with all of the conditions.*

PART 3

❝ Realize that everyone has a different perspective of risk. Sometimes those willing to take the most risks have nothing to lose.❞

Sometimes, however, the strategy may be as vague as projecting additional expenditures on advertising and marketing. Lenders are less comfortable about financing this strategy since there are so many undefined and poorly understood variables that can cause failure.

The borrower should provide candid and detailed documentation explaining the periods in which a profit was not earned. In comparing those loss periods to periods in which the business did earn profits, the borrower can explain how the operations may have been different. Then the borrower should explain how the loan proceeds will be used to position the enterprise in a manner that can return or deliver profits to the business.

Objection 3: The proposed loan is too much money.

Lenders try to minimize loan requests by either reducing the marginal funds or trying to force the borrower to spend less in a particular part of the proposal. Their intent is to control their exposure and perhaps get the loan balance down as a percentage of the collateral.

Response: Only the borrower can decide if the business strategy can be achieved with a lower amount of funding. And, typically, only the borrower will know how much extra financial padding, incorporated into the request, can be lowered and not affect the business.

The borrower's response has to be based on how much money is actually needed and how an expenditure can be reduced without having a negative impact on the business plans. Alternatively, offering to provide additional collateral may cause the lender to reconsider the restriction, since the borrower has reduced the lender's perceived risk in the transaction.

Objection 4: The business strategy is not sound.

Loan officers will test the borrower's ideas against their collective experience (or inexperience) to evaluate whether the business has a reasonable chance of succeeding. If lenders have strong reservations about the borrower's prospects, they will not provide financing.

Response: Lenders are not always correct—and they are almost always conservative. Maybe the borrower did not explain the business concept sufficiently to the lender, or maybe the loan officer has an incorrect or incomplete understanding of exactly what the borrower plans to accomplish.

The borrower should review the business strategy carefully, making sure that it fully describes each detail of the concept. These ideas can be supported with the articles, surveys, marketing studies, and demographics that influenced, inspired, or convinced the borrower to undertake this strategy.

It is a good idea to have a strategy of how to accomplish your goals on fewer dollars.

Objection 5: The business is too risky.

Lenders exclude some industries from their lending market because the real or perceived risks inherent in those businesses are beyond the acceptable parameters of the lender. These exclusions may apply only to the local lender, or they may be fairly common among most lenders, depending on the industry within which the borrower operates.

Response: Perhaps the borrower has not effectively communicated how some of the risks can be counterbalanced. Depending on the locale and nature of the industry, the lender that may not want to finance the business may be the only lender that can.

Therefore, the borrower has to convince the lender that the risks can be eliminated or limited. For example, by accepting tighter terms or providing sufficient collateral, the borrower can structure the transaction to protect the lender from exposure to costly servicing or potential loan losses.

Objection 6: There is not enough collateral.

This objection is probably the one most often used by lenders to turn down a loan. The lender wants a minimum of 1:1 collateral coverage, based on a discounted valuation of that collateral. Usually lenders will use their leverage to encumber virtually every asset the borrower has, even if those additional assets contribute little or no value as collateral to secure the loan.

The quantity and sufficiency of the collateral can overcome many objections, because lenders are usually too glad to rent the borrower its own money, even when that money may be tied up in other assets that can be encumbered for liquidation should the loan not be repaid.

Response: The borrower's response should be based on an honest recognition of the true value of the collateral. How much would it be worth in liquidation? Lenders are inclined to sell off repossessed assets grossly under market, seeking merely to recover their loan balance rather than getting the full value of the assets.

❝ Learn from the lenders rejection—it will be a useful lesson on managing future loan requests. ❞

The borrower must learn about the market for selling assets similar to those offered as collateral. For example, a ten-year-old lathe that cost $5,000 has a discounted value for the lender. The borrower should pay for an appraisal from a used equipment dealer or equipment auctioneer. The dealer can quickly assess what the equipment would bring in a timely sale or in an auction. This information is germane to determining the leverage the lender will give the borrower on those assets.

Real estate assets also have to be valued, based on appraisals. The lender will typically advance a standard amount of the market value, thereby providing a margin for the lender to cover the time and associated cost of selling the property.

If the lender has not valued the collateral adequately, the borrower can provide additional information to prove the value. The borrower can challenge the lender's assessments only when a different value can be documented. When asked to review their reasoning, lenders can at least recognize a compromise value based on the evidence produced by the borrower.

If the assets are insufficient, the borrowers should offer to provide more collateral. Sometimes there are creative solutions to obtaining collateral value from assets that cannot be pledged. The borrower should review personal and business financial statements carefully, searching for a way to assign values to the lender.

In the absence of such collateral, the borrower can seek assistance from relatives, friends, associates, or investors who might be willing to hypothecate personal assets to the lender in order to secure the loan. In effect, these third parties would be providing a limited guaranty for the loan, only to the extent of their ownership in the assets they would agree to use as collateral for the loan.

Objection 7: The financial projections are unreliable.

Lenders will pay particular attention to the financial projections of the proposal to determine exactly how the borrower intends to repay the loan. Based on contributing factors, the lender does not always agree with the conclusions about revenue production or the cost of operations. If the lender does not accept the projections, the borrower's ability to service the debt becomes questionable.

Response: The borrower should examine the projections carefully and ensure that the expectations have been adequately communicated. Reviewing the data or historical figures on which these projections have been based, the borrower should ensure that this evidence is documented in the footnotes of the pro forma.

The borrower may need to make modifications to correct an error discovered by the lender or to revise the calculations. When comparing the new numbers against the debt service to pay back the loan, the borrower can determine if the deal is still feasible.

When confident with the numbers, the borrower should present them again with a line-by-line discussion (as necessary) to convince the lender of the soundness of these expectations. Determining the basis of the lender's questions or doubts, the borrower can attempt to validate those specific entries thoroughly.

Responding to any of these objections does not guaranty that the lender will change the decision, but it is the logical step to take after the loan has initially been rejected. Since considerable effort has been invested in educating this lender about the company, the borrower should try to address these concerns before completely starting over with a new proposal to a new lender.

❝ Some lenders will announce their loan decision and not be open to further discussion.

Move on. ❞

Keep Improving the Proposal

The burden to convince lenders to change the decision is on the borrower. Lenders are responsible only for evaluating the information put before them. In fact, after a decision has been made, it can be more difficult to persuade someone to change it. But if the loan officer is candid about what influenced the decision, the borrower may be able to challenge and overcome these objections. The loan could be approved quicker on reconsideration than if the borrower started over with a new lender, not understanding why the first lender denied the loan.

While the borrower is pursuing financing, it is important to continue updating the proposal with fresh information as it is available or as it is acquired. The company is completing a financial period every thirty days, and the financial information provided to the lender must be constantly updated to include the latest information.

If the borrower comes across pertinent information about the business, industry, or strategy to support the thesis of the proposal, the application should be updated with this information. Even if the proposal has already been submitted to the lender, the borrower should send the additional information for review.

Continue to build on your proposal with fresh information and data as it becomes available.

Every sixty to ninety days (if the search for financing lasts for such a period), the borrower should review the entire plan from beginning to end. The proposal needs to be edited for updated information, corrections, and consistency. During the review process, the borrower can take advantage of any information or ideas obtained from a lender that turned down the request. By constantly polishing the proposal, the borrower can improve the chances of success.

There Are Other Lenders

Borrowers often lose sight that there are literally thousands of lenders. Given the commodity nature of SBA lending, the borrower has access not only to the local banks but also to several nonbank lenders making SBA loans into any state.

Within these thousands of lenders, there are even more loan officers. Many of them will be less experienced in business than the borrower, and will be making decisions based on a limited career. Just because a lender reaches a certain conclusion does not mean it is correct. If the borrower feels confident about the merits of the loan proposal, one lender's negative reply should not prevent the plan from being presented to another lender.

Different lenders have different loan appetites, different expertise, even different levels of acceptable risk. The borrower should keep searching until the right lender, which understands the business and feels comfortable with the management, is found. These lenders are out there; they are sometimes just harder to find.

Sometimes the Borrower Will Not Qualify

The final answer may be that the business does not qualify for the loan it seeks—not only with the lender that rejected the loan but with any lender. If the loan is turned down more than three times, there may be an inherent weakness preventing approval from any source. If this is the case, the borrower may need assistance from someone who can objectively evaluate the situation and the financing. Whether turning to a business consultant, CPA, or lender, the borrower should be able to rely on their direct experience and meaningful advice.

Sometimes there are other ways to accomplish the borrower's objectives than with a loan. Financing is not restricted to borrowing money but can include such diverse options as selling part of the business, franchising, or bartering. All of these are other ways to exchange value owned for value needed.

Sometimes the borrower can reduce the loan by financing part of the transaction in another way. Although there are many possibilities, most of them may be more difficult, more expensive, and more time-consuming. But if the borrower wants the financing, it may have to be taken in the manner in which it is available.

Maybe the borrower has tried to obtain financing prematurely. Perhaps another six, twelve, or eighteen months would improve the chances of approval by demonstrating the validity of the business strategy or other measurements of financial success.

The borrower should recognize that time is a good investment and can be healthy for the business. It may not satisfy ambition, but it may allow the borrower to obtain the financing from a position of strength. The established and stable record of a business decreases the lender's exposure, as well as the risk to the borrower.

PART 3

Appendix

Web site Resources

U.S. Small Business Administration (national resource Web sites)
http://www.sba.gov
http://www.onlinewbc.org
http://www.smallbizpartners.com/
http://www.nys.sbdc.org

Small Business Development Center (national Web site)
http://www.sbdcnet.utsa.edu

General Business Assistance Web sites
http://www.businessadviser.com
http://www.toolkit.com/
http://www.homeofficemag.com/
http://www.entrepreneurmag.com
http://www.palo-alto.com/

SBA District Offices Addresses

U.S. Small Business Administration
District Office
222 W. 8th Ave., Rm. 67
Anchorage, AK 99501
907-271-4022

U.S. Small Business Administration
District Office
2121 8th Ave. N., Ste. 200
Birmingham , AL 35203-2398
205-731-1344

U.S. Small Business Administration
District Office
320 W. Capitol Ave., Rm. 601
Little Rock, AR 72201
501-378-5871

U.S. Small Business Administration
District Office
2005 N. Central Ave., 5th Fl.
Phoenix, AZ 85004
602-379-3737

U.S. Small Business Administration
District Office
2719 N. Air Fresno Dr.
Fresno, CA 93727-1547
209-487-5189

U.S. Small Business Administration
District Office
330 N. Grand Blvd.
Glendale, CA 91203
213-894-2956

U.S. Small Business Administration
District Office
901 W. Civic Ctr. Dr., Rm. 160
Santa Ana, CA 92703
714-836-2494

U.S. Small Business Administration
District Office
880 Front St., Ste. 4-S-29
San Diego, CA 92188
619-557-5440

U.S. Small Business Administration
District Office
211 Main St., 4th Fl.
San Francisco, CA 94105-1988
415-974-0649

U.S. Small Business Administration
District Office
721 19th St., Rm. 407
Denver, CO 80202-2599
303-844-2607

U.S. Small Business Administration
District Office
330 Main St., 2nd Fl.
Hartford, CT 06106
860-240-4700

U.S. Small Business Administration
District Office
1111 18th St., NW 6th Fl.
Washington, DC 20036
202-634-1500

U.S. Small Business Administration
District Office
1320 S. Dixie Highway, Ste. 501
Coral Gables, FL 33146
305-536-5521

U.S. Small Business Administration
District Office
7825 Baymeadows Way, Ste. 100B
Jacksonville, FL 32256-7504
904-443-1950

U.S. Small Business Administration
District Office
1720 Peachtree Rd. NW, 6th Fl.
Atlanta, GA 30309
404-347-4326

U.S. Small Business Administration
District Office
300 Ala Moana Blvd., Rm. 2213
Honolulu, HI 96850
808-541-2990

U.S. Small Business Administration
District Office
373 Collins Rd. NE, Rm. 100
Cedar Rapids, IA 52402-3118
319-399-2571

U.S. Small Business Administration
District Office
210 Walnut St., Rm. 749
Des Moines, IA 50309
515-284-4422

U.S. Small Business Administration
District Office
1020 Main St., Ste. 209
Boise, ID 83702
208-334-1696

U.S. Small Business Administration
District Office
219 S. Dearborn St., Rm. 437
Chicago, IL 60604-1779
312-353-4528

U.S. Small Business Administration
District Office
575 N. Pennsylvania St., Rm. 578
Indianapolis, IN 46204-1584
317-226-7272

U.S. Small Business Administration
District Office
110 E. Waterman St., 1st Fl.
Wichita, KS 67202
316-269-6571

U.S. Small Business Administration
District Office
600 M.L. King, Jr. Pl., Rm. 188
Louisville, KY 40202
502-582-5976

U.S. Small Business Administration
District Office
1661 Canal St., Ste. 2000
New Orleans, LA 70112
504-589-6685

U.S. Small Business Administration
District Office
10 Causeway St., Rm. 265
Boston, MA 02222-1093
617-565-5590

U.S. Small Business Administration
District Office
10 N. Calvert St., 3rd Fl.
Baltimore, MD 21202
301-962-4392

U.S. Small Business Administration
District Office
40 Western Ave., Rm. 512
Augusta, ME 04330
207-622-8378

U.S. Small Business Administration
District Office
477 Michigan Ave., Rm. 515
Detroit, MI 48226
313-226-6075

U.S. Small Business Administration
District Office
100 N. 6th St., Ste. 610
Minneapolis, MN 55403-1563
612-370-2324

U.S. Small Business Administration
District Office
1103 Grand Ave., 6th Fl.
Kansas City, MO 64106
816-374-3419

U.S. Small Business Administration
District Office
815 Olive Street, Rm. 242
St. Louis, MO 63101
314-539-6600

U.S. Small Business Administration
District Office
101 W. Capitol St., Ste. 322
Jackson, MS 39269-0396
601-965-4378

U.S. Small Business Administration
District Office
301 S. Park, Rm. 528
Helena, MT 59626
406-449-5381

U.S. Small Business Administration
District Office
222 S. Church St., Rm. 300
Charlotte, NC 28202
704-371-6563

U.S. Small Business Administration
District Office
657 2nd Ave., N. Rm. 218
Fargo, ND 58108-3086
701-239-5131

U.S. Small Business Administration
District Office
11145 Mill Valley Rd.
Omaha, NE 68154
402-221-4691

U.S. Small Business Administration
District Office
60 Park Place, 4th Fl.
Newark, NJ 07102
201-645-2434

U.S. Small Business Administration
District Office
5000 Marble Ave., NE Rm. 320
Albuquerque, NM 87100
505-262-6171

U.S. Small Business Administration
District Office
301 E. Stewart St., Rm. 301
Las Vegas, NV 89125
702-388-6611

U.S. Small Business Administration
District Office
26 Federal Plaza, Rm. 3100
New York, NY 10278
212-264-4355

U.S. Small Business Administration
District Office
100 S. Clinton St., Rm. 1071
Syracuse, NY 13260
315-423-5383

U.S. Small Business Administration
District Office
1240 E. 9th St., Rm. 317
Cleveland, OH 44199
216-522-4180

U.S. Small Business Administration
District Office
85 Marconi Blvd., Rm. 512
Columbus, OH 43215
614-469-6860

U.S. Small Business Administration
District Office
200 NW 5th St., Ste. 670
Oklahoma City, OK 73102
405-231-4301

U.S. Small Business Administration
District Office
222 SW Columbia, Ste. 500
Portland, OR 97201-6605
503-326-2682

U.S. Small Business Administration
District Office
475 Allendale Rd., Ste. 210
King of Prussia, PA 19406
215-962-3846

U.S. Small Business Administration
District Office
960 Penn Ave., 5th Fl.
Pittsburgh, PA 15222
412-644-2780

U.S. Small Business Administration
District Office
Carlos Chardon Ave., Rm. 691
Hato Rey, PR 00918
809-753-4002

U.S. Small Business Administration
District Office
380 Westminster Mall, 5th Fl.
Providence, RI 02903
401-528-4561

U.S. Small Business Administration
District Office
1835 Assembly St., Rm. 358
Columbia, SC 29202
803-765-5376

U.S. Small Business Administration
District Office
101 S. Main Ave., Ste. 101
Sioux Falls, SD 57102-0527
605-336-4231

U.S. Small Business Administration
District Office
50 Vantage Way, 2nd Fl.
Nashville, TN 37228-1500
615-736-5850

U.S. Small Business Administration
District Office
1100 Commerce St., Rm. 3C-36
Dallas, TX 75242
214-767-0605

U.S. Small Business Administration
District Office
10737 Gateway W., Ste. 320
El Paso, TX 79902
915-541-7586

U.S. Small Business Administration
District Office
2525 Murworth, Ste. 112
Houston, TX 77054
713-660-4401

U.S. Small Business Administration
District Office
7400 Blanco Road, Ste. 200
San Antonio, TX 78216
512-229-4535

U.S. Small Business Administration
District Office
125 S. State St., Rm. 2237
Salt Lake City, UT 84138-1195
801-524-5800

U.S. Small Business Administration
District Office
400 N. 8th St., Rm. 3015
Richmond, VA 23240
804-771-2617

U.S. Small Business Administration
District Office
87 State St., Rm. 205
Montpelier, VT 05602
802-828-4474

U.S. Small Business Administration
District Office
915 Second Ave., Rm. 1792
Seattle, WA 98174-1088
206-442-5534

U.S. Small Business Administration
District Office
W. 601 First Ave., 10th Fl.
Spokane, WA 99204
509-353-2807

U.S. Small Business Administration
District Office
212 E. Washington Ave., Rm. 213
Madison, WI 53703
608-264-5261

U.S. Small Business Administration
District Office
168 W. Main St., 5th Fl.
Clarksburg, WV 26301
304-623-5631

U.S. Small Business Administration
District Office
100 East B. St., Rm. 4001
Casper, WY 82602-2839
307-261-5761

SBA ELIGIBILITY CRITERIA ACCORDING TO THE STANDARD INDUSTRIAL CODE

SIC (* = NEW SIC CODE IN 1987 NOT USED IN 1972)	DESCRIPTION (N.E.C. = NOT ELSEWHERE CLASSIFIED)	SIZE STANDARDS IN NUMBER OF EMPLOYEES OR MILLIONS OF DOLLARS

For all industries not specifically listed in this table, except for those in Divisions I and J
of the SIC System, the size standard is $5.0 million in annual receipts.

DIVISION A - AGRICLUTURE

MAJOR GROUP 01-AGRICULTURAL PRODUCTION-CROPS

SIC	Description	Size
111	Wheat	$ 500,000
112	Rice	$ 500,000
115	Corn	$ 500,000
116	Soybeans	$ 500,000
119	Cash Grains, N.E.C.	$ 500,000
131	Cotton	$ 500,000
132	Tobacco	$ 500,000
134	Sugarcane and Sugar Beets	$ 500,000
139	Irish Potatoes	$ 500,000
161	Field Crops, Except Cash Grains, N.E.C.	$ 500,000
171	Vegetables and Melons	$ 500,000
172	Grapes	$ 500,000
173	Tree Nuts	$ 500,000
174	Citrus fruits	$ 500,000
175	Deciduous Tree Fruits	$ 500,000
179	Fruits and Tree Nuts, N.E.C.	$ 500,000
181	Ornamental Floriculture Nursery Products	$ 500,000
182	Food Crops Grown Under Cover	$ 500,000
191	General Farms, Primarily Crop	$ 500,000

MAJOR GROUP 02-LIVESTOCK AND ANIMAL SPECIALTIES

SIC	Description	Size
211	Beef Cattle Feedlots (Custom)	$ 1,500,000
212	Beef Cattle, Except Feedlots	$ 500,000
213	Hogs	$ 500,000
214	Sheep and Goats	$ 500,000
219	General Livestock, Except Dairy and Poultry	$ 500,000
241	Dairy Farms	$ 500,000
251	Broiler, Fryer, and Roaster Chickens	$ 500,000
252	Chicken Eggs	$ 900,000
253	Turkeys and Turkey Eggs	$ 500,000
254	Poultry Hatcheries	$ 500,000
259	Poultry and Eggs, N.E.C.	$ 500,000
271	Fur-Bearing Animals and Rabbits	$ 500,000
272	Horses and Other Equines	$ 500,000
273	Animal Aquaculture	$ 500,000
279	Animal Specialties, N.E.C.	$ 500,000
291	General Farms, Primarily Livestock and Animal Specialties	$ 500,000

MAJOR GROUP 07 - AGRICULTURAL SERVICES

711	Soil Preparation Services	$	5,000,000
721	Crop Planting, Cultivating, and Protecting	$	5,000,000
722	Crop Harvesting, Primarily by Machine	$	5,000,000
723	Crop Preparation Service for Market, Except Cotton Ginning	$	5,000,000
724	Cotton Ginning	$	5,000,000
741	Veterinary Services for Livestock	$	5,000,000
742	Veterinary Services for Animal Specialties	$	5,000,000
751	Livestock Services, Except Veterinary	$	5,000,000
752	Animal Specialty Services, Except Veterinary	$	5,000,000
761	Farm Labor Contractors and Crew Leaders	$	5,000,000
762	Farm Management Services	$	5,000,000
781	Landscape Counseling and Planning	$	5,000,000
782	Lawn and Garden Services	$	5,000,000
783	Ornamental Shrub and Tree Services	$	5,000,000

MAJOR GROUP 08 - FORESTRY

811	Timber Tracts	$	5,000,000
831	Forest Nurseries and Gathering of Forest Products	$	5,000,000
851	Forestry Services	$	5,000,000

MAJOR GROUP 09 - FISHING, HUNTING, AND TRAPPING

912	Finfish	$	3,000,000
913	Shellfish	$	3,000,000
919	Miscellaneous Marine Products	$	3,000,000
921	Fish Hatcheries and Preserves	$	3,000,000
971	Hunting and Trapping, and Game Propagation	$	3,000,000

DIVISION B - MINING

MAJOR GROUP 10 - METAL MINING

1011	Iron Ores		500
1021	Copper Ores		500
1031	Lead and Zinc Ores		500
1041	Gold Ores		500
1044	Silver Ores		500
1061	Ferroalloy Ores, Except Vanadium		500
1081	Metal Mining Services	$	5,000,000
1094	Uranium-Radium-Vanadium Ores		500
1099	Miscellaneous Metal Ores, N.E.C.		500

MAJOR GROUP 12 - COAL MINING

1221*	Bituminous Coal and Lignite Surface Mining		500
1222*	Bituminous Coal Underground Mining		500
1231*	Anthracite Mining		500
1241*	Coal Mining Services	$	5,000,000

MAJOR GROUP 13 - OIL AND GAS EXTRACTION

1311	Crude Petroleum and Natural Gas		500
1321	Natural Gas Liquids		500
1381	Drilling Oil and Gas Wells		500
1382	Oil and Gas Field Exploration Services	$	5,000,000
1389	Oil and Gas Field Services, N.E.C.	$	5,000,000

MAJOR GROUP 14 - MINING AND QUARRYING OF NONMETALLIC

MINERALS, EXCEPT FUELS

1411	Dimension Stone		500
1422	Crushed and Broken Limestone		500
1423	Crushed and Broken Granite		500
1429	Crushed and Broken Stone, N.E.C.		500
1442	Construction Sand and Gravel		500
1446	Industrial Sand		500
1455	Kaolin and Ball Clay		500
1459	Clay, Ceramic, and Refractory Minerals, N.E.C.		500
1474	Potash, Soda, and Borate Minerals		500
1475	Phosphate Rock		500
1479	Chemical and Fertilizer Mineral Mining, N.E.C.		500
1481	Nonmetalic Minerals Services, Except Fuels	$	5,000,000
1499	Miscellaneous Nonmetallic Minerals, Except Fuels		500

DIVISION C - CONSTRUCTION

MAJOR GROUP 15 - BUILDING CONSTRUCTION - GENERAL CONTRACTORS

AND OPERATIVE BUILDERS

1521	General Contractors -- Single-Family Houses	$	17,000,000
1522	General Contractors -- Residential Buildings,		
	Other Than Single-Family	$	17,000,000
1531	Operative Builders	$	17,000,000
1541	General Contractors -- Industrial Buildings and		
	Warehouses	$	17,000,000
1542	General Contractors - Nonresidential Buildings,		
	Other Than Industrial Buildings and Warehouses	$	17,000,000

MAJOR 16 - HEAVY CONSTRUCTION OTHER THAN

BUILDING CONSTRUCTION-CONTRACTORS

1611	Highway and Street Construction, Except		
	Elevated Highways	$	17,000,000
1622	Bridge, Tunnel, and Elevated Highway Construction	$	17,000,000
1623	Water, Sewer, Pipeline, and Communications		
	and Power Line Construction	$	17,000,000
1629	Heavy Construction, Except Dredging, N.E.C.	$	17,000,000
1629	Dredging and Surface Cleanup Activities	$	13,500,000

MAJOR GROUP 17 - CONSTRUCTION-SPECIAL TRADE CONTRACTORS

1721	Painting and Paper Hanging	$	7.0
1731	Electrical Work	$	7.0
1741	Masonry, Stone Setting, and Other Stone Work		
1742	Plastering, Drywall, Acoustical and Insulation Work	$	7.0
		$	7.0
1751	Carpentry Work	$	7.0
1752	Floor Laying and Other Floor Work, N.E.C.	$	7.0
1761	Roofing, Siding, and Sheet Metal Work	$	7.0
1771	Concrete Work	$	7.0
1781	Water Well Drilling	$	7.0
1791	Structural Steel Erection	$	7.0
1793	Glass and Glazing Work	$	7.0
1794	Escavation Work	$	7.0
1795	Wrecking and Demolition Work	$	7.0
1796	Installation or Erection of Building Equipment, N.E.C.		
1799	Special Trade Contractors N.E.C.	$	7.0
....	Base Housing Maintenance	$	7.0

DIVISION D - MANUFACTURING

MAJOR GROUP 20 - FOOD AND KINDRED PRODUCTS

2011	Meat Packing Plants	500
2013	Sausages and Other Prepared Meat Products	500
2015*	Poultry Slaughtering and Processing	500
2021	Creamery Butter	500
2022	Natural, Processed, and Imitation Cheese	500
2023	Dry, Condensed, and Evaporated Dairy Products	500
2024	Ice Cream and Frozen Desserts	500
2026	Fluid Milk	500
2032	Canned Specialties	1,000
2033	Canned Fruits, Vegetables, Preserves, Jams, and Jellies	500
2034	Dried and Dehydrated Fruits, Vegetables, and Soup Mixes	500
2035	Pickled Fruits and Vegetables, Vegetable Sauces	500
	and Seasonings, and Salad Dressings	500
2037	Frozen Fruits, Fruit Juices, and Vegetables	500
2038	Frozen Specialties, N.E.C.	500
2041	Flur and Other Grain Mill Products	500
2043	Cereal Breakfast Foods	1,000
2044	Rice Milling	500
2045	Prepared Flour Mixes and Doughs	500
2046	Wet Corn Milling	750
2047	Dog and Cat Food	500
2048	Prepared Feeds and Feed Ingredients for Animals and	
	Fowls, Except Dogs and Cats	500
2051	Bread and Other Bakery Products, Except Cookies and crackers	500
2052	Cookies and Crackers	750
2053*	Frozen Bakery Products, Except Bread	500
2061	Cane Sugar, Except Refining	500

MAJOR GROUP 20 (CONT.)

2062	Cane Sugar Refining	750
2063	Beet Sugar	750
2064*	Candy and Other Confectionery Products	500
2066	Chocolate and Cocoa Products	500
2067	Chewing Gum	500
2068*	Salted and Roasted Nuts and Seeds	500
2074	Cottonseed Oil Mills	500
2075	Soybean Oil Mills	500
2076	Vegetable Oil Mills, Except Corn, Cottonseed, and Soybean	1,000
2077	Animal and Marine Fats and Oils	500
2079	Shortening, Table Oils, Margarine, and Other Edible Fats and Oils, N.E.C.	750
2082	Malt Beverages	500
2083	Malt Beverages	500
2084	Wines, Brandy, and Brandy Spirits	500
2085	Distilled and Blended Liquors	750
2086	Bottled and Canned Soft Drinks and Carbonated Waters	
2087	Flavoring Extracts and Flavoring Syrups, N.E.C.	500
2091	Canned and Cured Fish and Seafoods	500
2092	Prepared Fresh or Frozen Fish and Seafoods	500
2095	Roasted Coffee	500
2096*	Potato Chips, Corn Chips, and Similar Snacks	500
2097	Manufactured Ice	500
2098	Macaroni, Spaghetti, Vermicelli, and Noodles	500
2099	Food Preparations, N.E.C.	500

MAJOR GROUP 21 - TOBACCO PRODUCTS

2111	Cigarettes	1,000
2121	Cigars	500
2131	Chewing and Smoking Tobacco and Snuff	500
2141	Tobacco Stemming and Redrying	500

MAJOR GROUP 22 - TEXTILE MILL PRODUCTS

2211	Broadwoven Fabric Mills, Cotton	1,000
2221	Broadwoven Fabric Mills, Manmade Fiber and Silk	500
2231	Broadwoven Fabric Mills, Wool (Including Dying and Finishing)	500
2241	Narrow Fabric and Other Smallwares Mills; Cotton, Wool, Silk and Manmade Fiber	500
2251	Women's Full-Length and Knee-Length Hosiery Except Socks	500
2252	Hosiery, N.E.C.	500
2253	Knit Outerwear Mills	500
2254	Knit Underwear and Nightwear Mills	500
2257	Weft Knit Fabric Mills	500
2258	Lace and Warp Knit Fabric Mills	500
2259	Knitting Mills, N.E.C.	500
2261	Finishers of Broadwoven Fabrics of Cotton	1,000
2262	Finishers of Broadwoven Fabrics of Manmade Fiber and Silk	500
2269	Finishers of Textiles, N.E.C.	500
2273*	Carpets and Rugs	500

MAJOR GROUP 22 - (CONT.)

2281	Yarn Spinning Mills	500
2282	Yarn Texturizing, Throwing Twisting, and	
	Winding Mills	500
2284	Thread Mills	500
2295	Coated Fabrics, Not Rubberized	1,000
2296	Tire Cord and Fabrics	1,000
2297	Nonwoven Fabrics	500
2298	Cordage and Twine	500
2299	Textile Goods, N.E.C.	500

MAJOR GROUP 23 - APPAREL AND OTHER FINISHED PRODUCTS

MADE FROM FABRICS AND SIMILAR MATERIALS

2311	Men's and Boys' Suits, Coats and Overcoats	500
2321	Men's and Boys' Shirts, Except Work Shirts	500
2322	Men's and Boys' Underwear and Nightwear	500
2323	Men's and Boys' Neckwear	500
2325*	Men's and Boys' Separate Trousers and Slacks	500
2326*	Men's and Boys' Work Clothing	500
2329	Men's and Boys' Clothing, N.E.C.	500
2331	Women's, Misses', and Juniors' Blouses and Skirts	500
2335	Women's, Misses', and Juniors' Dresses	500
2337	Women's, Misses', and Juniors' Suits, Skirts and Coats	500
		500
2339	Women's, Misses', and Juniors' Outerwear, N.E.C.	500
2341	Women's, Misses', Childrens', and Infants' Underwear	500
	and Nightwear	500
2342	Brassieres, Girdles, and Allied Garments	500
2353*	Hats, Caps, and Millinery	500
2361	Girls', Children's, and Infants' Dresses, Blouses, and Shirts	500
2369	Girls', Children's, and Infants' Outerwear, N.E.C.	500
2371	Fur Goods	500
2381	Dress and Work Gloves, Except Knit and All-Leather	500
2384	Robes and Dressing Gowns	500
2385	Waterproof Outerwear	500
2386	Leather and Sheep-Lined Clothing	500
2387	Apparel Belts	500
2389	Apparel and Accessories, N.E.C.	500
2391	Curtains and Draperies	500
2392	Housefurnishings, Except Curtains and Draperies	500
2393	Textile Bags	500
2394	Canvas and Related Products	500
2395	Pleating, Decorative and Novelty Stitching, and	500
	Tucking for the Trade	500
2396	Automotive Trimmings, Apparel Findings, and	500
	Related Products	500
2397	Schiffli Machine Embroideries	500
2399	Fabricated Textile Products, N.E.C.	500

MAJOR GROUP 24 - LUMBER AND WOOD PRODUCTS, EXCEPT FURNITURE

2411	Logging	500
2421	Sawmills and Planing Mills, General	500
2426	Hardwood Dimension and Flooring Mills	500
2429	Special Product Sawmills, N.E.C.	500
2431	Millwork	500
2434	Wood Kitchen Cabinets	500
2435	Hardwood Veneer and Plywood	500
2436	Softwood Veneer and Plywood	500
2439	Structural Wood Members, N.E.C.	500
2441	Nailed and Lock Corner Wood Boxes and Shook	500
2448	Wood Pallets and Skids	500
2449	Wood Containers, N.E.C.	500
2451	Mobile Homes	500
2452	Prefabricated Wood Buildings and Components	500
2491	Wood Preserving	500
2493*	Reconstituted Wood Products	500
2499	Wood Products, N.E.C.	500

MAJOR GROUP 25 - FURNITURE AND FIXTURES

2511	Wood Household Furniture, Except Upholstered	500
2512	Wood Household Furniture, Upholstered	500
2514	Metal Household Furniture	500
2515	Mattresses, Foundations, and Convertible Beds	500
2517	Wood Television, Radio, Phonograph, and Sewing Machine Cabinets	500
2519	Household Furniture, N.E.C.	500
521	Wood Office Furniture	500
522	Office Furniture, Except Wood	500
2531	Public Building and Related Furniture	500
2541	Wood Office and Store Fixtures, Partitions, Shelving and Lockers	500
2542	Office and Store Fixtures, Partitions, Shelving, and Lockers	
	Except Wood	500
2591	Drapery Hardware and Window Blinds and Shades	500
2599	Furniture and Fixtures, N.E.C.	500

MAJOR GROUP 26 - PAPER AND ALLIED PRODUCTS

2611	Pulp Mills	750
2621	Paper Mills	750
2631	Paperboard Mills	750
2652	Setup Paperboard Boxes	500
2653	Corrugated and Solid Fiber Boxes	500
2655	Fiber Cans, Tubes, Drums, and Similar Products	500
2656*	Sanitary Food Containers, Except Folding	750
2657*	Folding Paperboard Boxes, Including Sanitary	750
2671*	Packaging Paper and Plastics Film, Coated and Laminated	
2672*	Coated and Laminated Paper, N.E.C.	500
2673*	Plastics, Foil, and Coated Paper Bags	500
2674*	Uncoated Paper and Paperboard and Cardboard	500
2675*	Die-Cut Paper and Paperboard and Cardboard	500
2676*	Sanitary Paper Products	500

MAJOR GROUP 26 (CONT.)

2677*	Envelopes	500
2678*	Stationery, Tablets, and Related Products	500
2679*	Converted Paperboard Products, N.E.C.	500

MAJOR GROUP 27 - PRINTING, PUBLISHING, AND ALLIED INDUSTRIES

2711	Newspapers: Publishing, or Publishing and Printing	500
2721	Periodicals; Publishing, or Publishing and Printing	500
2731	Books: Publishing, or Publishing and Printing	500
2732	Book Printing	500
2741	Miscellaneous Publishing	500
2752	Commercial Printing, Lithographic	500
2754	Commercial Printing, Gravure	500
2759*	Commercial Printing, N.E.C.	500
2761	Manifold Business Forms	500
2771	Greeting Cards	500
2782	Blankbooks, Losseleaf Binders and Devices	500
2789	Bookbinding and Related Work	500
2791	Typesetting	500
2796*	Platemaking and Related Services	500

MAJOR GROUP 28 - CHEMICALS AND ALLIED PRODUCTS

2812	Alkalies and Chlorine	1,000
2813	Industrial Gases	1,000
2816	Inorganic Pigments	1,000
2819	Industrial Inorganic Chemicals, N.E.C.	1,000
2821	Plastics Materials, Synthetic Resins, and Nonvulcanizable Elastomers	750
2822	Synthetic Rubber (Vulcanizable Elastomers)	1,000
2823	Cellulosic Manmade Fibers	1,000
2824	Manmade Organic Fibers, Except Cellulosic	1,000
2833	Medicinal Chemicals and Botanical Products	750
2834	Pharmaceutical Preparations	750
2835*	In Vitro and In Vivo Diagnostic Substances	500
2836*	Biological Products, Except Diagnostic Substances	500
2841	Soap and Other Detergents, Except Specialty Cleaners	750
2842	Specialty Cleaning, Polishing, and Sanitation Preparations	500
2843	Surface Active Agents, Finishing Agents, Sulfonated Oils, and Assistants	500
2844	Perfumes, Cosmetics, and Other Toilet Preparations	500
2851	Paints, Varnishes, Lacquers, Enamels, and Allied Products	500
2861	Gum and Wood Chemicals	500
2865	Cyclic Organic Crudes and Intermediates, and Organic Dyes and Pigments	750
2869	Industrial Organic Chemicals, N.E.C.	1,000
2873	Nitrogenous Fertilizers	1,000
2874	Phosphatic Fertilizers	500
2875	Fertilizers, Mixing Only	500
2879	Pesticides and Agricultural Chemicals, N.E.C.	500
2891	Adhesives and Sealants	500
2892	Explosives	750

MAJOR GROUP 28 (CONT.)

2893	Printing Ink	500
2895	Carbon Black	500
2899	Chemicals and Chemical Preparations, N.E.C.	500

MAJOR GROUP 29 - PETROLEUM REFINING AND RELATED INDUSTRIES

2911	Petroleum Refining	1,500
2951	Asphalt Paving Mixtures and Blocks	500
2952	Asphalt Felts and Coatings	750
2992	Lubricating Oils and Greases	500
2999	Products of Petroleum and Coal, N.E.C.	500

MAJOR GROUP 30 - RUBBER AND MISCELLANEOUS PLASTICS PRODUCTS

3011		1,000
3021	Rubber and Plastics Footwear	1,000
3052*	Rubber and Plastics Hose and Belting	500
3053*	Gaskets, Packing, and Sealing Devices	500
3061*	Molded, Extruded, and Lathe-Cut Mechanical Rubber Goods	500
3069	Fabricated Rubber Products, N.E.C.	500
3081*	Unsupported Plastics Film and Sheet	500
3082*	Unsupported Plastics Profile Shapes	500
3083*	Laminated Plastics Plate, Sheet, and Profile Shapes	500
3084*	Plastics Pipe	500
3085*	Plastics Bottles	500
3086*	Plastics Foam Products	500
3087*	Custom Compounding of Purchased Plastics Resins	500
3088*	Plastics Plumbing Fixtures	500
3089*	Plastics Products, N.E.C.	500

MAJOR GROUP 31 - LEATHER AND LEATHER PRODUCTS

3111	Leather Tanning and Finishing	500
3131	Boot and Shoe Cut Stock and Findings	500
3142	House Slippers	500
3143	Men's Footwear, Except Athletic	500
3144	Women's Footwear, Except Athletic	500
3149	Footwear, Except Rubber, N.E.C.	500
3151	Leather Gloves and Mittens	500
3150	Luggage	500
3171	Women's Handbags and Purses	500
3172	Personal Leather Goods, Except Women's Handbags	500
3199	Leather Goods, N.E.C.	500

MAJOR GROUP 32 - STONE, CLAY, GLASS, AND CONCRETE PRODUCTS

3211	Flat Glass	1,000
3221	Glass Containers	750
3229	Pressed and Blown Glass and Glassware, N.E.C.	750
3231	Glass Products, Made of Purchased Glass	500
3241	Cement, Hydraulic	750
3251	Brick and Structural Clay Tile	500
3253	Ceramic Wall and Floor Tile	500
3255	Clay Refractories	500

MAJOR GROUP 32 (CONT.)

3259	Structural Clay Products, N.E.C.	500
3261	Vitreous China Plumbing Fixtures and China and Earthenware Fittings and Bathroom Accessories	750
3262	Vitreous China Table and Kitchen Articles	500
3263	Fine Earthenware (Whiteware) Table and Kitchen Articles	500
3264	Porcelain Electical Supplies	500
3269	Pottery Products, N.E.C.	500
3271	Concrete Block and Brick	500
3272	Concrete Products, Except Block and Brick	500
3273	Ready Mixed Concrete	500
3274	Lime	500
3275	Gypsum Products	1,000
3281	Cut Stone and Stone Products	500
3291	Abrasive Products	500
3292	Asbestos Products	750
3295	Minerals and Earths, Ground or Otherwise Treated	500
3296	Mineral Wool	750
3297	Nonclay Refractories	750
3299	Nonmetallic Mineral Products, N.E.C.	500

MAJOR GROUP 33 - PRIMARY METAL INDUSTRIES

3312	Steel Works, Blast Furnaces (Including Coke Ovens) and Rolling Mills	1,000
3313	Electrometallurgical Products, Except Steel	750
3315	Steel Wiredrawing and Steel Nails and Spike	1,000
3316	Cold-Rolled Steel Sheet, Strip, and Bars	1,000
3317	Steel Pipe and Tubes	1,000
3321	Gray and Ductile Iron Foundries	500
3322	Malleable Iron Foundries	500
3324	Steel Investment Foundries	500
3325	Steel Foundries, N.E.C.	500
3331	Primary Smelting and Refining of Copper	1,000
3334	Primary Production of Aluminum	1,000
3339	Primary Smelting and Refining of Nonferrous Metals, Except Copper and Aluminum	750
3341	Secondary Smelting and Refining of Nonferrous Metals	500
3351	Rolling, Drawing, and Extruding of Copper	750
3353	Aluminum Shet, Plate, and Foil	750
3354	Aluminum Extruded Products	750
3355	Aluminum Rolling and Drawing, N.E.C.	750
3356	Rolling, Drawing, and Extruding of Nonferrous Metals, Except Copper and Aluminum	750
3357	Drawing and Insulating of Nonferrous Wire	1,000
3363*	Aluminum Die-Castings	500
3364*	Nonferrous Die-Castings, Except Aluminum	500
3365*	Aluminum Foundries	500
3366*	Copper Foundries	500
3369	Nonferrous Foundries, Except Aluminum and Copper	500
3398	Metal Heat Treating	750
3399	Primary Metal Products, N.E.C.	750

MAJOR GROUP 34 - FABRICATED METAL PRODUCTS, EXCEPT

MACHINERY AND TRANSPORTATION EQUIPMENT

3411	Metal Cans	1000
3412	Metal Shipping Barrels, Drums, Kegs, and Pails	500
3421	Cutlery	500
3423	Hand and Edge Tools, Except Machine Tools	500
3425	Saw Blades and Handsaws	500
3429	Hardware, N.E.C.	500
3431	Enameled Iron and Metal Sanitary Ware	750
3432	Plumbing Fixture Fittings and Trim	500
3433	Heating Equipment, Except Electric and Warm Air Furnaces	500
3441	Fabricated Structural Metal	500
3442	Metal Doors, Sash, Frames, Molding, and Trim	500
3443	Fabricated Structural Metal	500
3444	Sheet Metal Work	500
3446	Architectural and Ornamental Metal Work	500
3448	Prefabricated Metal Buildings and Components	500
3449	Miscellaneous Structural Metal	500
3451	Screw Machine Products	500
3452	Bolts, Nuts, Screws, Rivets, and Washers	500
3462	Iron and Steel Forgings	500
3463	Nonferrous Forgings	500
3465	Automotive Stampings	500
3466	Crowns and Closures	500
3469	Metal Stampings, N.E.C.	500
3471	Electroplating, Plating, Polishing, Anodizing, and Coloring	500
3479	Coating, Engraving, and Allied Services, N.E.C.	500
3482	Small Arms Ammunition	1,000
3483	Ammunition, Except for Small Arms	1,500
3484	Small Arms Ammunition	1,000
3489	Ordnance and Accessories, N.E.C.	500
3491*	Industrial Valves	500
3492*	Fluid Power Valves and Hose Fittings	500
3493	Steel Springs, Except Wire	500
3494	Valves and Pipe Fittings, N.E.C.	500
3495	Wire Springs	500
3496	Miscellaneous Fabricated Wire Products	500
3497	Metal Foil and Leaf	500
3498	Fabricated Pipe and Pipe Fittings	500
3499	Fabricated Metal Products, N.E.C.	500

MAJOR GROUP 35 -- INDUSTRIAL AND COMMERCIAL MACHINERY

AND COMPUTER EQUIPMENT

3511	Steam, Gas, and Hydraulic Turbines, and	1,000
	Turbine Generator Set Units	
3519	Internal Combustion Engines, N.E.C.	1,000
3523	Farm Machinery and Equipment	500
3524	Lawn and Garden Tractors and Home Lawn and	
	Garden Equipment	500
3531	Construction Machinery and Equipment	750

MAJOR GROUP 35 (CONT.)

3532	Mining Machinery and Equipment, Except Oil	500
	and Gas Field Machinery and Equipment	500
3533	Oil and Gas Field Machinery and Equipment	500
3534	Elevators and Moving Stairways	500
3535	Conveyors and Conveying Equipment	500
3536	Overhead Traveling Cranes Hoists, and	500
	Monorail Systems	500
3537	Industrial Trucks, Tractors, Trailers and Stackers	750
3541	Machine Tools, Metal Cutting Types	500
3542	Machine Tools, Metal Forming Types	500
3543*	Industrial Patterns	500
3544	Special Dies and Tools, Die Sets, Jigs and Fixtures,	500
	and Industrial Molds	
3545	Cutting Tools, Machine Tool Accessories, and	500
	Machinists' Precision Measuring Devices	
3546	Power-Driven Handtools	500
3547	Rolling Mill Machinery and Equipment	500
3548*	Electric and Gas Welding and Soldering Equipment	500
3549	Metalworking Machinery, N.E.C.	500
3552	Textile Machinery	500
3553	Woodworking Machinery	500
3554	Paper Industries Machinery	500
3555	Printing Trades Machinery and Equipment	500
3556*	Food Products Machinery	500
3559	Special Industry Machinery, N.E.C.	500
3561	Pumps and Pumping Equipment	500
3562	Ball and Roller Bearings	500
3563	Air and Gas Compressors	500
3564	Industrial and Commercial Fans and Blowers	500
	and Air Purification Equipment	
3565*	Packaging Machinery	500
3566	Speed Changers, Industrial High-Speed Drives and Gears	500
3567	Industrial Process Furnaces and Ovens	500
3568	Mechanical Power Transmission Equipment, N.E.C.	500
3569	General Industrial Machinery and Equipment, N.E.C.	500
3571*	Electronic Computers	1,000
3572*	Computer Storage Devices	1,000
3575*	Computer Terminals	1,000
3577*	Computer Peripheral Equipment, N.E.C.	1,000
3578*	Calculating and Accounting Machines, Except	
	Electronic Computers	1,000
3579	Office Machines, N.E.C.	500
3581	Automatic Vending Machines	500
3582	Commercial Laundry, Drycleaning, and Pressing Machines	500
3585	Air-Conditioning and Warm Air Heating Equipment and Commercial	
	and Industrial Refrigeration Equipment	750
3586	Measuring and Dipensing Pumps	500
3589	Service Industry Machinery, N.E.C.	500
3592	Carburetors, Pistons, Piston Rings, and Valves	500
3593*	Industrial and Commerial Machinery and Equipment, N.E.C.	500

MAJOR GROUP 35 (CONT.)

3594*	Fluid Power Pumps and Motors	500
3596	Scales and Balances, Except Laboratory	500
3599	Industrial and Commercial Machinery and Equipment, N.E.C.	500

MAJOR GROUP 36 - ELECTRONIC AND OTHER ELECTRICAL EQUIPMENT AND COMPONENTS

EXCEPT COMPUTER EQUIPMENT

3612	Power, Distribution, and Specialty Transformers	750
3613	Switchgear and Switchboard Apparatus	750
3621	Motors and Generators	1,000
3624	Carbon and Graphite Products	750
3625*	Relays and Industria Contorls	750
3629	Electrical Industrial Apparatus, N.E.C.	500
3631	Household Cooking Equipment	500
3632	Household Refrigerators and Home and Farm Freezers	750
3633	Household Laundry Equipment	1,000
3634	Electric Housewares and Fans	1,000
3635	Household Vacuum Cleaners	750
3639	Household Appliances, N.E.C.	750
3641	Electric Lamp Bulbs and Tubes	1,000
3643	Current-Carrying Wiring Devices	500
3644	Noncurrent-Carrying Wiring Devices	500
3645	Residential Electic Lighting Fixtures	500
3646	Commercial, Industrial, and Institutional Electric Lighting Fixtures	500
3647	Vehicular Lighting Equipment	500
3648	Lighting Equipment, N.E.C.	500
3651	Household Audio and Video Equipment	750
3652	Phonograph Records and Prerecorded Audio Tapes and Disks	750
3661	Telephone and Teegraph Apparatus	750
3663*	Radio and Television Broadcasting and Communications Equipment	1,000
3669*	Communications Equipment, N.E.C.	750
3671	Electron Tubes	750
3672*	Printed Circuit Boards	500
3674	Semiconductors and Related Devices	500
3675	Electronic Connectors	500
3676	Electronic Resistors	500
3677	Electronic Coils, Transformers, and Other Inductors	500
3678	Electronic Connectors	500
3679	Electronic Components, N.E.C.	500
3691	Storage Batteries	500
3692	Primary Batteries, Dry and Wet	1,000
3694	Electrical Equipment for Internal Combustion Engines	750
3695	Magnetic and Optical Recording Media	1,000
3699	Electrical Machinery, Equipment, and Supplies, N.E.C.	750

MAJOR GROUP 37 - TRANSPORTATION EQUIPMENT

3711	Motor Vehicles and Passenger Car Bodies	1,000
3713	Truck and Bus Bodies	500
3714	Motor Vehicle Parts and Accessories	750
3715	Truck Trailers	500
3716	Motor Homes	1,000
3721	Aircraft	1,500
3724	Aircraft Engines and Engine Parts	1,000
3728	Aircraft Parts and Auxiliary Equipment	1,000
3731	Shipbuilding and Repair of Nuclear Propelled Ships	1,000
	Shipbuilding of Nonnuclear Propelled Ships and	
	Nonpropelled Ships	1,000
	Ship Repair (Including Overhauls and Conversions)	
	Performed on Nonnuclear Propelled and Nonpropelled	
	Ships East of the 108 Meridian	1,000
	Ship Repair (Including Overhauls and Conversions)	
	Performed on Nonnuclear Propelled and Nonpropelled	
	Ships West of the 108 Meridian	1,000
3732	Boat Building and Repairing	500
3743	Railroad Equipment	1,000
3751	Motorcycles, Bicycles, and Parts	500
3761	Guided Missiles and Space Vehicles	1,000
3764	Guided Missiles and Space Vehicle Propulsion	
	Units and Propulsion Unit Parts	1,000
3769	Guided Missile and Space Vehicle Parts and	
	Auxiliary Equipment, N.E.C.	1,000
3792	Travel Trailers and Campers	500
3795	Tanks and Tank Components	1,000
3799	Transportation Equipment, N.E.C.	500

MAJOR GROUP 38 - MEASURING, ANALYZING, AND CONTROLLING INSTRUMENTS
                PHOTOGRAPHIC, MEDICAL, AND OPTICAL GOODS; WATCHES
                AND CLOCKS

3812	Search, Detection, Navigation, Guidance,	
	Aeronautical, and Nautical Systems and Instruments	750
3821*	Laboratory Apparatus and Furniture	500
3822	Automatic Controls for Regulating Residential and Commercial	
	Environments and Appliances	500
3823	Industrial Instruments for Measurements, Display, and	
	Control of Process Variables; and Related Products	500
3824	Totalizing Fluid Meters and Counting Devices	500
3825	Instruments for Measuring and Testing of	500
	Electricity and Electrical Signals	500
3826	Laboratory Analytical Instruments	500
3827*	Optical Instruments and Lenses	500
3829	Measuring an Controlling Devices, N.E.C.	500
3841	Surgical and Medical Instruments and Apparatus	500
3842	Orthopedic, Prosthetic, and Surgical Appliances and Supplies	500
3843	Dental Equipment and Supplies	500
3844*	X-Ray Apparatus and Tubes and Related Irradiation Apparatus	500

MAJOR GROUP 38 (CONT.)

3845*	Electromedical and Eletrotherapeutic Apparatus	
3851	Ophthalmic Goods	
3861	Photographic Equipment and Supplies	
3873	Watches, Clocks, Clockwork Operated Devices, and Parts	

MAJOR GROUP 39 - MISCELLANEOUS MANUFACTURING INDUSTRIES

3911	Jewelry, Precious Metal	500
3914	Silverware, Plated Ware, and Stainless Steel Ware	500
3915	Jewelers' Findings and Materials, and Lapidary Work	500
3931	Musical Instruments	500
3942	Dolls and Stuffed Toys	500
3944	Games, Toys, and Children's Vehicles, Except	500
	Dolls and Bicycles	500
3949	Sporting and Athletic Goods, N.E.C.	500
3951	Pens, Mechanical Pencils, and Parts	500
3952	Lead Pencils, Crayons, and Artists' Materials	500
3953	Marking Devices	500
3955	Carbon Paper and Inked Ribbons	500
3961	Costume Jewelry and Costume Novelties, Except	500
	Precious Metal	500
3965*	Fasteners, Buttons, Needles, and Pins	500
3991	Brooms and Brushes	500
3993	Signs and Advertising Specialties	500
3995	Burial Caskets	500
3996	Linoleum, Asphalted-Felt-Base, and Other	750
	Hard Surface Floor Coverings, N.E.C.	
3999	Manufacturing Industries, N.E.C.	500

DIVISION E - TRANSPORTATION, COMMUNICATIONS ELECTRIC,
GAS AND SANITARY SERVICES

MAJOR GROUP 40 - RAILROAD TRANSPORTATION

4011	Railroads, Line-Haul Operating	1,500
4013	Railroad Switching and Terminal Establishments	500

MAJOR GROUP 41 - LOCAL AND SUBURBAN TRANSIT AND INTERURBAN
AND SANITARY SERVICES

4111	Local and Suburban Transit	$	5,000,000
4119	Local Passenger Transportation, N.E.C.	$	5,000,000
4121	Taxicabs	$	5,000,000
4131	Intercity and Rural Bus Transportation	$	5,000,000
4141	Local Bus Charter Service	$	5,000,000
4142	Bus Charter Sercice, Except Local	$	5,000,000
4151	School Buses	$	5,000,000
4173*	Terminal and Sercice Facilities for Motor		
	Vehicle Passenger Transportation	$	5,000,000

MAJOR GROUP 42 - MOTOR FREIGHT TRANSPORTATION AND WAREHOUSING

4212	Local Trucking Without Storage	$	18,500,000
4213	Trucking, Except Local	$	18,500,000
4214	Local Trucking With Storage	$	18,500,000

MAJOR GROUP 42 (CONT.)

4215*	Courier Services, Except by Air	$	18,500,000
4221	Farm Product Warehousing and Storage	$	18,500,000
4222	Refrigerated Warehousing and Storage	$	18,500,000
4225	General Warehousing and Storage	$	18,500,000
4226	Special Warehousing and Storage, N.E.C.	$	18,500,000
4231	Terminal and Joint Terminal Maintenance		
	Facilities for Motor Freight Transportation	$	5,000,000

MAJOR GROUP 44 - WATER TRANSPORTATION

4412	Deep Sea Foreign Transportation of Freight		500
4424*	Deep Sea Domestic Transportation of Freight		500
4432*	Freight Transportation on the Great Lakes--		500
	St. Lawrence Seaway		
4449*	Water Transportation of Freight, N.E.C.		500
4481*	Deep Sea Transportation of Passengers, Except		500
	by Ferry		
4482*	Ferries		500
4489*	Water Transportation of Passengers, N.E.C.		500
4491*	Marine Cargo Handling	$	18,500,000
4492*	Towing and Tugboat Services	$	5,000,000
4493*	Marinas	$	5,000,000
4499*	Water Transportation Services, N.E.C.	$	5,000,000

MAJOR GROUP 45 - TRANSPORTATION BY AIR

4512*	Air Transportation, Scheduled		1,500
4513*	Air Courier Services		1,500
4522*	Air Transportation, Nonscheduled		1,500
4581*	Airports, Flying fields, and Airport		
	Terminal Services	$	5,000,000

MAJOR GROUP 46 - PIPELINES, EXCEPT NATURAL GAS

4612	Crude Petroleum Pipelines		1,500
4613	Refined Petroleum Pipelines		1,500
4619	Pipelines, N.E.C.	$	25,000,000

MAJOR GROUP 47 - TRANSPORTATION SERVICES

4724*	Travel Agencies	$	1,000,000
4725*	Tour Operators	$	5,000,000
4729*	Arrangement of Passenger Transportation	$	5,000,000
4731*	Arrangement of Transportation of Freight and Cargo	$	18,500,000
4741*	Rental of Railroad Cars	$	5,000,000
4783	Packing and Crating	$	18,500,000
4785*	Fixed Facilities and Inspection and Weighing		
	Services for Motor Vehicle Transportation	$	5,000,000
4789	Transportation Services, N.E.C.	$	5,000,000

MAJOR GROUP 48 - COMMUNICATIONS

4812*	Radiotelephone Communications		1,500
4813	Telephone Communications, Except Radiotelephone		1,500
4822	Telegraph and Other Message Communications	$	5,000,000

MAJOR GROUP 48 (CONT.)

4832	Radio Broadcasting Stations	$	5,000,000
4833	Television Broadcasting Stations	$	10,500,000
4841*	Cable and Other Pay Television Services	$	11,000,000
4899	Communications Services, N.E.C.	$	11,000,000

MAJOR GROUP 49 - ELECTRIC, GAS, AND SANITARY SERVICES

4911	Electric Services	4 million megawatt hrs.	
4922	Natural Gas Transmission	$	5,000,000
4923	Gas Transmission and Distribution	$	5,000,000
4924	Natural Gas Distribution	$	500
4925	Mixed, Manufactured, or Liquefied Petroleum Gas Production and/or Distribution	$	5,000,000
4931	Electric and Other Services Combined	$	5,000,000
4932	Gas and Other Services Combined	$	5,000,000
4939	Combination Utilities, N.E.C.	$	5,000,000
4941	Water Supply	$	5,000,000
4952	Sewerage Systems	$	5,000,000
4953	Refuse Systems	$	6,000,000
4959	Sanitary Services, N.E.C.	$	5,000,000
4961	Steam and Air-Conditioning Supply	$	9,000,000
4971	Irrigation Systems	$	5,000,000

DIVISION F - WHOLESALE TRADE

(Not Applicable to Government procurement of supplies.
The nonmanufacturer size standard of 500 employees shall
be used of purposes of Government procurement of supplies.)

MAJOR GROUP 50 - WHOLESALE TRADE - DURABLE GOODS

5012	Automobiles and Other Motor Vehicles	100
5013	Motor Vehicle Supplies and New Parts	100
5014	Tires and Tubes	100
5015*	Motor Vehicle Parts, Used	100
5021	Furniture	100
5023	Homefurnishings	100
5031	Lumber, Plywood, Millwork, and Wood Panels	100
5032*	Brick, Stone, and Related Construction Materials	100
5033*	Roofing, Siding, and Insulation Materials	100
5039	Construction Materials, N.E.C.	100
5043	Photographic Equipment and Supplies	100
5044*	Office Equipment	100
5045*	Computers and Computer Peripheral Equipment and Software	100
5046*	Commercial Equipment, N.E.C.	100
5047*	Medical, Dental, and Hospital Equipment and Supplies	100
5048*	Ophthalmic Goods	100
5049*	Professional Equipment and Supplies, N.E.C.	100
5051	Metals Service Centers and Offices	100
5052	Coal and Other Minerals and Ores	100
5063	Electrical Apparatus and Equipment, Wiring Supplies, and Construction Materials	100
5064	Electrical Appliances, Television and Radio Sets	100

MAJOR GROUP 50 (CONT.)

5065	Electronic Parts and Equipment, N.E.C.	100
5072	Hardware	100
5074	Plumbing and Heating Equipment and Supplies (Hydronics)	100
5075	Warm Air Heating and Air-Conditioning Equipment and Supplies	100
5078	Refrigeration Equipment and Supplies	100
5082	Construction and Mining (Except Petroleum) Machinery and Equipment	100
5083	Farm and Garden Machinery and Equipment	100
5084	Industrial Machinery and Equipment	100
5085	Industrial Supplies	100
5087	Service Establishment Equipment and Supplies	100
5088	Transportation Equipment and Supplies, Except Motor Vehicles	100
5091*	Sporting and Recreational Goods and Supplies	100
5092*	Toys and Hobby Goods and Supplies	100
5093	Scrap and Waste Materials	100
5094	Jewelry, Watches, Precious Stones, and Precious Metals	100
5099	Durable Goods, N.E.C.	100

MAJOR GROUP 51 - WHOLESALE TRADE - NONDURABLE GOODS

5111	Printing and Writing Paper	100
5112	Stationery and Office Supplies	100
5113	Industrial and Personal Service Paper	100
5122	Drugs, Drug Proprietaries, and Druggists' Sundries	100
5131*	Piece Goods, Notions, and Other Dry Goods	100
5136	Men's and Boys' Clothing and Furnishings	100
5137	Women's, Children's, and Infants' Clothing and Accessories	100
5139	Footwear	100
5141	Groceries, General Line	100
5142	Packaged Frozen Foods	100
5143	Dairy Products, Except Dried or Canned	100
5144	Poultry and Poultry Products	100
5145	Confectionery	100
5146	Fish and Seafood	100
5147	Meats and Meat Products	100
5148	Fresh Fruits and Vegetables	100
5149	Groceries and Related Products, N.E.C.	100
5153	Grain and Field Beans	100
5154	Livestock	100
5159	Farm-Product Raw Materails, N.E.C.	100
5162*	Plastics Materials and Basic Forms and Shapes	100
5169*	Chemical and Allied Products, N.E.C.	100
5171	Petroleum Bulk Stations and Terminals	100
5172	Petroleum and Petroleum Products Wholesalers, Except Bulk Stations and Terminals	100
5181	Beer and Ale	100
5182	Wine and Distilled Alcoholic Beverages	100
5191	Farm Supplies	100
5192*	Books, Periodicals, and Newspapers	100

MAJOR GROUP 51 (CONT.)

5193	Flowers, Nursery Stock, and Florists'		100
5194	Tobacco and Tobacco Products		100
5198	Paints, Varnishes, and Supplies		100
5199	Nondurable Goods, N.E.C.		100

DIVISION G - RETAIL TRADE

(Not Applicable to Government procurement of supplies. The nonmanufacturer size standard of 500 employees shall be used for purposes of Government procurement of supplies.)

MAJOR GROUP 52 - BUILDING MATERIALS, HARDWARE, GARDEN
SUPPLY, AND MOBILE HOME DEALERS

5211	Lumber and Other Building Materials Dealers	$	5,000,000
5231	Paint, Glass, and Wallpaper Stores	$	5,000,000
5251	Hardware Stores	$	5,000,000
5261	Retail Nurseries, Lawn and Garden Supply Stores	$	5,000,000
5271	Mobile Home Dealers	$	95,000,000

MAJOR GROUP 53 - GENERAL MERCHANDISE STORES

5311	Department Stores	$	20,000,000
5331	Variety Stores	$	8,000,000
5399	Miscellaneous General Merchandise Stores	$	5,000,000

MAJOR GROUP 54 - FOOD STORES

5411	Grocery Stores		
5421*	Meat and Fish (Seafood) Markets, Including		
	Freezer Provisioners	$	5,000,000
5431	Fruit and Vegetable Markets	$	5,000,000
5441	Candy, Nut, and Confectioner Stores	$	5,000,000
5451	Dairy Products Stores	$	5,000,000
5461	Retail Bakeries	$	5,000,000
5499	Miscellaneous Food Stores	$	5,000,000

MAJOR GROUP 55 - AUTOMOTIVE DEALERS AND GASOLINE SERVICE STATIONS

5511	Motor Vehicle Dealers (New and Used)	$	21,000,000
5521	Motor Vehicle Dealers (Used Only)	$	17,000,000
5531	Auto and Home Supply Stores	$	5,000,000
5541	Gasoline Service Stations	$	65,000,000
5551	Boat Dealers	$	5,000,000
5561	Recreational Vehicle Dealers	$	5,000,000
5571	Motorcyle Dealers	$	5,000,000
5599	Automotive Dealers, N.E.C.	$	5,000,000

MAJOR GROUP 56 - APPAREL AND ACCESSORY STORES

5611	Men's and Boys' Clothing and Accessory Stores	$	65,000,000
5621	Women's Clothing Stores	$	65,000,000
5632*	Women's Accesory and Specialty Stores	$	5,000,000
5641	Children's and Infants' Wear Stores	$	5,000,000
5651	Family Clothing Stores	$	65,000,000
5661	Shoe Stores	$	65,000,000
5699	Miscellaneous Apparel and Accessory Stores	$	5,000,000

DIVISION H - FINANCE, INSURANCE, AND REAL ESTATE

MAJOR GROUP 60 - DEPOSITORY INSTITUTIONS

6021*	National Commercial Banks	$100 Million
6022	State Commercial Banks	$100 Million
6029*	Commercial Banks, N.E.C.	$100 Million
6035	Savings Institutions, Federally Chartered	$100 Million
6036*	Savings Institutions, Not Federally Chartered	$100 Million
6061	Credit Unions, Federally Chartered	$100 Million
6062	Credit Unions, Not Federally Chartered	$100 Million
6081	Branches and Agencies of Foreign Banks	$100 Million
6082	Foreign Trade and International Banks	$100 Million
6091	Nondeposit Trust Facilities	$ 5,000,000
6099	Functions Related to Depositor Banking, N.E.C.	$ 5,000,000

MAJOR GROUP 61 - NONDEPOSITORY INSTITUTION

6141	Personal Credit Institutions	$ 5,000,000
6153	Short-Term Business Credit Institutions, Except Agriculture	$ 5,000,000
6159	Miscellaneous Business Credit Institutions	$ 5,000,000
6162	Mortgage Bankers and Loan Correspondents	$ 5,000,000
6163	Loan Brokers	$ 5,000,000

MAJOR GROUP 62 - SECURITY AND COMMODITY BROKERS, DEALERS, EXCHANGES AND SERVICES

6211	Security Brokers, Dealers and Flotation Companies	$ 5,000,000
6221	Commodity Contracts Brokers and Dealers	$ 5,000,000
6231	Security and Commodity Exchanges	$ 5,000,000
6282	Investment Advice	$ 5,000,000
6289	Services Allied With the Exchange of Securities or Commodities, N.E.C.	$ 5,000,000

MAJOR GROUP 63 - INSURANCE CARRIERS

6311	Life Insurance	$ 5,000,000
6321	Accident and Health Insurance	$ 5,000,000
6324	Hospital and Medical Service Plans	$ 5,000,000
6331	Fire, Marine, and Casualty Insurance	$ 1,500
6351	Surety Insurance	$ 5,000,000
6361	Title Insurance	$ 5,000,000
6371	Pension, Health and Welfare Funds	$ 5,000,000
6399	Insurance Carriers, N.E.C.	$ 5,000,000

MAJOR GROUP 64 - INSURANCE AGENTS, BROKERS, AND SERVICE

6411	Insurance Agents, Brokers, and Service	$ 5,000,000

MAJOR GROUP 65 - REAL ESTATE

6512	Operators of Nonresidential Buildings	$	5,000,000
6513	Operators of Apartment Buildings	$	5,000,000
6514	Operators or Dwellings Other Than Apartment Buildings	$	5,000,000
6515	Operators of Residential Mobile Home Sites	$	5,000,000
	Leasing of Building Space to Federal Government by owners	$	15,000,000
6517	Lessors of Railroad Property	$	5,000,000
6519	Lessors of Real Property, N.E.C.	$	5,000,000
6531	Real Estate Agents and Managers	$	15,000,000
6541	Title Abstract Offices	$	5,000,000
6552	Land Subdividers and Developers, Except Cemeteries	$	5,000,000
6553	Cemetery Subdividers and Developers	$	5,000,000

MAJOR GROUP 67 - HOLDING AND OTHER INVESTMENT OFFICES

6712	Offices of Bank Holding Companies	$	5,000,000
6719	Offices of Holding Companies, N.E.C.	$	5,000,000
6722	Management Investment Offices, Open-End	$	5,000,000
6726	Unit Investment Trusts, Face-Amount Certificate	$	5,000,000
	Offices, and Closed-End Management Investment Offices		
6732	Educational, Religious, and Charitable Trusts	$	5,000,000
6733	Trusts, Except Educational, Religious, and Charitable	$	5,000,000
6792	Oil Royalty Traders	$	5,000,000
6794	Patent Owners and Lessors	$	5,000,000
6798	Real Estate Investment Trusts	$	5,000,000
6799	Investors, N.E.C.	$	5,000,000

DIVISION I - SERVICES

MAJOR GROUP 70 - HOTELS, ROOMING HOUSES, CAMPS, AND OTHER LODGING PLACES

7011	Hotels and Motels	$	5,000,000
7021	Rooming and Boarding Houses	$	5,000,000
7032	Sporting and Recreational Camps	$	5,000,000
7033	Recreational Vehicle Parks and Campsites	$	5,000,000
7041	Organization Hotels and Lodging Houses, on Membership Basis	$	5,000,000

MAJOR GROUP 72 - PERSONAL SERVICES

7211	Power Laundries, Family and Commercial	$	10,500,000
7212	Garment Pressing, and Agents for Laundries and Drycleaners	$	5,000,000
7213	Linen Supply	$	10,500,000
7215	Coin-Operated	$	5,000,000
7216	Drycleaning Plants, Except Rug Cleaning	$	35,000,000
7217	Carpet and Upholstery Cleaning	$	35,000,000
7218	Industrial Launderers	$	10,500,000
7219	Laundry and Garment Services, N.E.C.	$	5,000,000
7221	Photographic Studios, Portrait	$	5,000,000
7231	Beauty Shops	$	5,000,000
7241	Barber Shops	$	5,000,000
7251	Shoe Repair Shops and Shoeshine Parlors	$	5,000,000
7261	Funeral Service and Crematories	$	5,000,000
7291*	Tax Return Preparation Services	$	5,000,000
7299	Miscellaneous Personal Services, N.E.C.	$	5,000,000

MAJOR GROUP 73 - BUSINESS SERVICES

7311	Advertising Agencies	$	5,000,000
7312	Outdoor Advertising Services	$	5,000,000
7313	Radio, Television, and Publishers' Advertising	$	5,000,000
	Representatives	$	5,000,000
7319	Advertising, N.E.C.	$	5,000,000
7322*	Adjustment and Collection Services	$	5,000,000
7323*	Credit Reporting Services	$	5,000,000
7331	Direct Mail Advertising Services	$	5,000,000
7334*	Photocopying and Duplicating Services	$	5,000,000
7335*	Commercial Photography	$	5,000,000
7336*	Commercial Art and Graphic Design	$	5,000,000
7338*	Secretarial and Court Reporting Services	$	5,000,000
7342	Disinfecting and Pest Control Services	$	5,000,000
7349	Building Cleaning and Maintenance Services, N.E.C.	$	12,000,000
7352*	Medical Equipment Rental and Leasing	$	5,000,000
7353*	Heavy Construction Equipment Rental and Leasing	$	5,000,000
7359*	Equipment Rental and Leasing, N.E.C.	$	5,000,000
7361	Employment Agencies	$	5,000,000
7363*	Help Supply Services	$	5,000,000
7371*	Computer Programming Services	$	18,000,000
7372	Prepackaged Software	$	18,000,000
7373*	Computer Integrated Systems Design	$	18,000,000
7374	Computer Processing and Data Preparation and	$	18,000,000
	Processing Services	$	18,000,000
7375*	Information Retrieval Services	$	18,000,000
7376*	Computer Facilities Management Services	$	18,000,000
7377*	Computer Rental and Leasing	$	18,000,000
7378*	Computer Maintenance and Repair	$	18,000,000
7379	Computer Related Services, N.E.C.	$	18,000,000
7381*	Detective, Guard, and Armored Car Services	$	9,000,000
7382*	Security Systems Services	$	9,000,000
7383*	News Syndicates	$	5,000,000
7384	Photofinishing Laboratories	$	5,000,000
7389*	Business Services, N.E.C.	$	5,000,000

MAJOR GROUP 75 - AUTOMOTIVE REPAIR, SERVICES, AND PARKING

7513	Truck Rental and Leasing, Without Drivers	$	18,500,000
7514*	Passenger Car Rental	$	18,500,000
7515*	Passenger Car Leasing	$	18,500,000
7519	Utility Trialer and Recreational Vehicle Rental	$	5,000,000
7521*	Automoile Parking	$	5,000,000
7532*	Top, Body, and Upholstery Repair Shops and Paint Shops	$	5,000,000
7533*	Automotive Exhaust System Repair Shops	$	5,000,000
7534	Tire Retreading and Repair Shops	$	5,000,000
7536*	Automotive Glass Replacement Shops	$	10,500,000
7537*	Automotive Transmission Repair Shops	$	5,000,000
7538	General Automotive Repair Shops	$	5,000,000
7539	Automotive Repair Shops, N.E.C.	$	5,000,000
7542	Carwashes	$	5,000,000
7549	Automotive Services, Except Repair and Carwashes	$	5,000,000

MAJOR GROUP 76 - MISCELLANEOUS REPAIR SERVICES

7622	Radio and Television Repair Shops	$	5,000,000
7623	Refrigeration and Air-Conditioning Service and Repair Shops	$	5,000,000
7629	Electrical and Electronic Repair Shops, N.E.C.	$	5,000,000
7631	Watch, Clock, and Jewelry Repair	$	5,000,000
7641	Reupholstery and Furniture Repair	$	5,000,000
7692	Welding Repair	$	5,000,000
7694	Armature Rewinding Shops	$	5,000,000
7699	Repair Shops and Related Services, N.E.C.	$	5,000,000

MAJOR GROUP 78 - MOTION PICTURES

7812*	Motion Picture and Video Tape Production	$	21,500,000
7819	Services Allied to Motion Picture Production	$	21,500,000
7822*	Motion Picture and Video Tape Distribution	$	21,500,000
7829	Services Allied to Motion Picture Distribution	$	5,000,000
7832	Motion Picture Theaters, Except Drive-In	$	5,000,000
7833	Drive-In Motion Picture Theaters	$	5,000,000
7841*	Video Tape Rental	$	5,000,000

MAJOR GROUP 79 - AMUSEMENT AND RECREATION SERVICES

7911	Dance Studios, Schools, and Halls	$	5,000,000
7922	Theatrical Producers (Except Motion Picture) and Miscellaneous Theatrical Services	$	5,000,000
7929	Band, Orchestras, Actors, and Other Entertainers and Entertainment Groups	$	5,000,000
7933	Bowling Centers	$	5,000,000
7941	Professional Sports Clubs and Promoters	$	5,000,000
7991*	Physical Fitness Facilities	$	5,000,000
7993	Coin-Operated Amusement Devices	$	5,000,000
7996	Amusement Parks	$	5,000,000
7997	Membership Sports and Recreation Clubs	$	5,000,000
7999	Amusement and Recreation Services, N.E.C.	$	5,000,000

MAJOR GROUP 80 - HEALTH SERVICES

8011	Offices and Clinics of Doctors of Medicine	$	5,000,000
8021	Offices and Clinics of Dentists	$	5,000,000
8031	Offices and Clinics of Doctors of Osteopathy	$	5,000,000
8041	Offices and Clinics of Chiropractors	$	5,000,000
8042	Offices and Clinics of Optometrists	$	5,000,000
8043*	Offices and Clinics of Podiatrists	$	5,000,000
8049	Offices and Clinics of Health Practitioners, N.E.C.	$	5,000,000
8051	Skilled Nursing Care Facilities	$	5,000,000
8052	Intermediate Care Facilities	$	5,000,000
8059	Nursing and Personal Care Facilities, N.E.C.	$	5,000,000
8062	General Medical and Surgical Hospitals	$	5,000,000
8063	Psychiatric Hospitals	$	5,000,000
8069	Specialty Hospitals, Except Psychiatric	$	5,000,000
8071	Medical Laboratories	$	5,000,000
8072	Dental Laboratories	$	5,000,000
8082	Home Health Care Services	$	5,000,000
8092	Kidney Dialysis Centers	$	5,000,000

MAJOR GROUP 80 (CONT.)

8093*	Specialty Outpatient Facilities, N.E.C.	$	5,000,000
8099	Health and Allied Services, N.E.C.	$	5,000,000

MAJOR GROUP 81 - LEGAL SERVICES

8111	Legal Services	$	5,000,000

MAJOR GROUP 82 - EDUCATIONAL SERVICES

8211	Elementary and Secondary Schools	$	5,000,000
8221	Colleges, Universities, and Professional Schools	$	5,000,000
8222	Junior Colleges and Technical Institutes	$	5,000,000
8231	Libraries	$	5,000,000
8243	Data Processing Schools	$	5,000,000
8244	Business and Secretarial Schools	$	5,000,000
8249	Vocational Schools, N.E.C.	$	5,000,000
8299	Schools and Educational Services, N.E.C.	$	5,000,000
8299	Flight Training Services	$	18.50

MAJOR GROUP 83 - SOCIAL SERVICES

8322*	Individual and Family Social Services	$	5,000,000
8331	Job Training and Vocational Rehabilitation Services	$	5,000,000
8351	Child Day Card Services	$	5,000,000
8361	Residential Care	$	5,000,000
8399	Social Services, N.E.C.	$	5,000,000

MAJOR GROUP 84 - MUSEUMS, ART GALLERIES, BOTANICAL AND ZOOLOGICAL GARDENS

8412	Museums and Art Galleries	$	5,000,000
8422	Arboreta and Botanical or Zoological Gardens	$	5,000,000

MAJOR GROUP 86 - MEMBERSHIP ORGANIZATIONS

8611	Business Associations	$	5,000,000
8621	Professional Membership Organizations	$	5,000,000
8631	Labor Unions and Similar Labor Organizations	$	5,000,000
8641	Civic, Social, and Fraternal Associations	$	5,000,000
8651	Political Organizations	$	5,000,000
8661	Religious Organizations	$	5,000,000
8699	Membership Organizations, N.E.C.	$	5,000,000

MAJOR GROUP 87 - ENGINEERING, ACCOUNTING, RESEARCH, MANAGEMENT,
AND RELATED SERVICES

8711*	Engineering Services:		
	Military and Aerospace Equipment and Military Weapons	$	20,000,000
	Contracts and Subcontracts for Engineering Services Awarded Under the National Energy Policy Act of 1992	$	20,000,000
	Marine Engineering and Naval Architecture	$	13,500,000
	Other Engineering Services	$	25,000,000
8712*	Architectural Services (Other Than Naval)	$	25,000,000
8713*	Surveying Services	$	25,000,000
8721*	Accounting, Auditing, and Bookkeeping Services	$	6,000,000
8731*	Commercial Physical and Biological Research		
	Aircraft		1,500
	Aircraft Parts, and Auxiliary Equipment, and Aircraft Engines and Engine Parts		1,000
	Space Vehicles and Guided Missiles, their Propulsion Units, their Propulsion Units Parts, and their Auxiliary Equipment and Parts Parts, and their Auxiliary Equipment and Parts		1,000
	Other Commercial Physical and Biological Research		500
8732*	Commercial Economic, Sociological, and Educational Research	$	5,000,000
8733*	Noncommercial Research Organizations	$	5,000,000
8734*	Testing Laboratories	$	5,000,000
8741*	Management Services	$	5,000,000
8742*	Management Consulting Services	$	5,000,000
8743*	Public Relations Services	$	5,000,000
8744*	Facilities Support Management Services	$	5,000,000
....	Base Maintenance	$	20,000,000
8748*	Business consulting Services, N.E.C.	$	5,000,000

MAJOR GROUP 89 - SERVICES, NOT ELSEWHERE CLASSIFIED

8999	Services N.E.C.	$	5,000,000

SIC Footnotes

1. Size standards preceded by a dollar sign ($) refer to total dollars of annual receipts. All others are in number of employees unless specified otherwise.

2. **SIC code 1629-Dredging**: To be considered small, a firm must perform the dredging of at least 40 percent of the yardage with its own dredging equipment or equipment owned by another small dredging concern.

3. **SIC Division D – Manufacturing**: "Rebuilding on a factory basis or equivalent." For rebuilding machinery or equipment on a factory basis, use SIC code applicable for new manufactured product. The appropriate size standard is not limited to manufacturers. Ordinary repair services or preservation operations, however, are not considered rebuilding activities.

4. **SIC code 2033**: For purposes of Government procurement for food canning and preserving under SIC code 2033, the standard of 500 employees shall be exclusive of agricultural labor as defined in Section (k) of the federal Unemployment Tax Act, 68A Stat. 454, 26 U.S.C. (I.R.C. 1954) 3306.

5. **SIC code 2911**: For purposes of Government procurement, the firm may not have more than 1,500 employees, nor may it have more than 75,000 barrels per day capacity. This capacity may be measured in terms of either crude oil or bona fide feedstocks or both, but the sum total of the various petroleum-based inputs into the process may not exceed 75,000 barrels. In addition to the direct-owned capacity of the concern in question, counted capacity will include any leased facilities or any facilities made available to the concern under an arrangement such as (but not limited to) an exchange agreement or a throughput, or other form, or processing agreement (whereby another party processes the concern's own crude or feedstocks). Such an arrangement would have the same effect as though such facilities had been leased, and this would have to be included in the concern's own capacity. The total product to be delivered in the performance of the contract must be at least 90 percent refined by the successful bidder from either crude oil or bona fide feedstocks.

6. **SIC code 3011**: For purposes of Government procurement, a firm is small for bidding on a contract for pneu-matic tires within Census Classification codes 30111 and 30112, provided that:

(1) the value of tires within Census Classification codes 30111 and 30112 which it manufactured in the United States during the previous calendar year is more than 50 percent of the value or its total worldwide manufacture, (2) the value of pneumatic tires within Census Classification codes 30111 and 30112 which it manufactured worldwide during the preceding calendar year was less than 5 percent of the value of all such tires manufactured in the United States during said period, and (3) the value of the principal product which it manufactured or otherwise produced, or sold worldwide during the preceding calendar year is less than 10 percent of the total value of such products manufactured or otherwise produced or sold in the United States during said period.

7. **SIC code 4212**: The component "Garbage and Refuse, Collecting and Trasporting, Without Disposal" shall have a size standard of $6.0 million. This is the same size standard as SIC code 4953, Refuse Systems.

8. **Offshore Marine Services**: The applicable size standard shall be $20.5 million for firms furnishing specific transportation services to concerns engaged in offshore oil and/or natural gas exploration, drilling production, or marine research; such services encompass passenger and freight transportation, anchor handling, and relate logistical services to and from the work site or at sea.

9. **SIC codes 4512, 4513, and 4522**: Includes passenger of cargo transportation requiring the use of one or more helicopters of fixed-wing aircraft. This does not include offshore marine transportation services as defined in footnote 8.

10. **SIC codes 4724 and 6531**: As measured by total revenues, but excluding funds received in trust for an unaffiliated third party, such as bookings or sales subject to commissions. The commissions received would be included as revenue.

11. **SIC code 4953**: "Garbage and Refuse, Collecting and Transporting, Without Disposal," a component of SIC code 4212, Has the same size standard as SIC code 4953.

12. **SIC code 5599:** For retail firms whose principal line of business is the retail sale of aircraft, a $7.5 million size standard shall apply.

13. **Most in division H:** Finance, Insurance and Real Estate-are excluded from SBA assistance.

14. **Major Group 60:** As measured by total assets.

15. **Major group 65 – Leasing of building space to the Federal Government by Owners:** For the purpose of Government procurement, a size standard of $15.0 million in gross receipts is established for owners of building space that is leased to the Federal Government. The standard for these procurements shall apply to the owner of the property and not to those acting as an agent for the owner. There is no size standard concerning the agent in a leasing arrangement.

16. **Division J – Services:** For all industries not specifically listed in the division, the size standard is $5.0 million.

17. **SIC code 7699 and 3728:** Contracts for the rebuilding or overhaul of aircraft ground support equipment on a contract basis will be classified under SIC code 3728.

18. **SIC code 8731:** For research and development contracts requiring the delivery of a manufactured product, the appropriate size standard to use is that of the manufacturing industry in which the specific products is classified.

    Research and Development, as defined in the SIC Manual, means laboratory or other physical research and development on a contractor fee basis. Research and development for purposes of size determinations does not include the following: economic, educational, engineering, operations, systems, or other nonphysical research; or computer programming, data processing, commercial and/or medical laboratory testing.

    For purposes of the Small Business Innovation Research (SBIR) Program only, a different definition has been established by Law. See Section 121.7 of these regulations.

    Research and development for guided missiles and space vehicles includes evaluation and simulation, and other services requiring thorough knowledge of complete missiles and spacecraft.

19. **Facilities Management, a component of SIC code 8744, has the following definition:** Establishments, not elsewhere classified, which provide overall management and the personnel to perform a variety of related support services in operating a complete facility in or around a specific building, or within another business or Government establishment. Facilities management means furnishing three or more personnel supply services which may include, but are not limited to, secretarial services, typists, telephone answering, reproduction or mimeograph service, mailing service, financial or business management, public relations, conference planning, travel arrangements, word processing, maintaining files and/or libraries, switchboard operation, writers, bookkeeping, minor office equipment maintenance and repair, use of information systems (not programming), etc.

20. **SIC code 8744:** If one of the activities of base maintenance, as defined below, can be identified with a separate industry, and that activity (or industry) accounts for 50 percent or more of the value of an entire contract, then the proper size standard shall be that for the particular industry, and not the base maintenance size standard.

    "Base Maintenance" constitutes three or more separate activities. The activities may be either service or special trade construction related activities. As services, these activities must each be in a separate industry. These activities may include, but are not limited to, such separate maintenance activities as Janitorial and Custodial Service, Protective Guard Service, Commissary Service, Fire Prevention Service, Safety Engineering Service, Messenger Service, and Grounds Maintenance and Landscaping Service. If the contract involves the use of special trade contractors (plumbing, painting, plastering, carpentering, etc.), all such specialized special trade construction activities will be considered a single activity, which is Base Housing Maintenance. This is only one activity of base maintenance and two additional activities must be present for the contract to be considered base maintenance. The size standard for Base Housing Maintenance is $7 million, the same size standard as for Special Trade Contractors.

21. The size standard for map drafting services, mapmaking (including aerial), and photogrammetric mapping services, part of SIC code 7389, is $3.5 million.

Index